The Psychology of Interpersc

The Psychology of Interpersonal Violence

Clive R. Hollin

WILEY Blackwell

Library of Congress Cataloging-in-Publication Data

Names: Hollin, Clive R., author.
Title: The psychology of interpersonal violence / Clive R. Hollin.
Description: Chichester, West Sussex, UK : Hoboken, NJ : John Wiley & Sons, 2016. |
    Includes bibliographical references and index.
Identifiers: LCCN 2015031846 (print) | LCCN 2015042188 (ebook) | ISBN 9781118598498 (cloth) |
    ISBN 9781118598504 (pbk.) | ISBN 9781118598474 (pdf) | ISBN 9781118598481 (epub)
Subjects: LCSH: Violence. | Interpersonal conflict.
Classification: LCC HM1116.H65 2016 (print) | LCC HM1116 (ebook) | DDC 303.6–dc23
LC record available at http://lccn.loc.gov/2015031846

A catalogue record for this book is available from the British Library.

Cover image: © Terry Vine / Getty Images

Set in 10.5/13pt Minion by SPi Global, Pondicherry, India

1   2016

For the late Arnie Goldstein, much missed friend

violence (n.). late 13c., "physical force used to inflict injury or damage" from Anglo-French and Old French *violence*, from Latin *violentia* "vehemence, impetuosity", from *violentus* "vehement, forcible"

Online Entomology Dictionary

The Latin word *vis* (strength, force, power)

MyEntomology.com

Contents

Contents

Preface and Acknowledgements

This book has been in my head, as we psychologists say, for over two decades. I have a folder marked "Potential Ideas" which sits in a tray on my desk and into which I occasionally file my scribbled-down thoughts for books. The original jottings for a book on interpersonal violence are now looking rather yellowed. However, the outline in my folder is pretty well what has emerged at the end of writing, although there was one late addition which came in the form of Chapter 2. I included this chapter having been influenced by Arnie Goldstein's notion of "low-level violence". It is easy to be seduced by acts of extreme violence, which so readily capture one's attention, and skip by the low-level everyday violence in order to get to the serious stuff. The material in Chapter 2 reinforced my perception that some forms of violence have become so pervasive that we take them for granted as part of our everyday life. There was also a surprise in writing this chapter. In reading material, including green criminology texts, for the section of Chapter 2 given to cruelty to animals I thought deeply about my own feelings on this particular manifestation of violence. I have supported animal welfare charities for over 40 years, as it seems to me that animals, rather like young children, are the most elementary form of victim: they do not comprehend what is happening, they are often defenceless, and they are unable to respond effectively against we humans with our many personal and technological advantages. It's really not a fair fight. However, I would argue, as long as we are prepared to tolerate cruelty to animals, we are also able to tolerate the harm caused by other forms of low-level violence such as bullying and corporal punishment.

*

I should like to acknowledge some personal and academic debts. Although he does not know it, my old friend Kevin Howells taught me a great deal about the personal qualities inherent in the type of academic I have tried to be over my career. The vision of blending theory with research in order to inform practice is, when done well, a wonderful thing. I have been fortunate in knowing personally two academics who can do this better than most. The first is the late Don Andrews, who heavily influenced my own thinking and research. The second is the late Arnie Goldstein, to whom I have dedicated this book. Arnie was simply inspirational: he encouraged me in my efforts as a fledgling psychologist and later I knew him personally and worked with him. I defy anyone to find a better role model for an applied psychologist.

On a personal note, I have just retired from academic life. I had thought that my last book, the second edition of *Psychology and Crime* which was published in 2013, would be my swan song before I spent more time with my garden but this one came along. However, the trouble with writing is that as it goes along so it keeps suggesting new projects and I've just scribbled a note in my file. I'll have a word with the nice people at Wiley and then we'll see how we go.

Finally, to borrow from attachment theory, I know that I need a "safe base" to function effectively. My partner in life, Felicity Schofield, has provided me with that base for longer than we care to remember.

Clive R. Hollin
Leicester

1

Interpersonal Violence

Violence is a part of all our everyday lives. We read about violence in our morning newspaper, we hear about it in the daily news on the radio and television. We read murder mysteries for fun and play computer games that involve mayhem and death. Krug, Mercy, Dahlberg, and Zwi (2002) make the observation that "About 4400 people die every day because of intentional acts of self-directed, interpersonal, or collective violence. Many thousands more are injured or suffer other non-fatal health consequences as a result of being the victim or witness to acts of violence" (p. 1083). The accompanying costs are played out in the short-term costs of treating victims and helping families while the longer-term costs may be felt by victims whose lives are irrevocably changed and by the costs incurred in bringing the aggressor to justice.

We also know that violence comes in many shapes and forms. A report published by the World Health Organization (WHO; Krug et al., 2002) refers to three distinct classes of violence: first, *self-directed violence* as with suicide and self-harm; second, *interpersonal violence*, which is taken to be physical or sexual violence against a family member, a partner, or within the broader community; and third, *collective violence* in the sense of violent acts by large groups of people or by states such as so-called ethnic cleansing, terrorism, and war.

It is the second of the WHO classes of violence, *interpersonal violence*, which is of concern here.

What exactly is meant by the term *interpersonal violence*? "Interpersonal" can be understood in its literal sense to mean between people; however, "violence" is a little more problematic. The word "violence" is often used interchangeably with "aggression". However, aggression is not the same as violence and it is used differently according to context. In everyday use we use aggression as an adjective to help

The Psychology of Interpersonal Violence, First Edition. Clive R. Hollin.
© 2016 John Wiley & Sons, Ltd. Published 2016 by John Wiley & Sons, Ltd.

describe certain forms of behaviour: we may say that a football team has an aggressive style of play, which is very different to saying a team has a violent style of play. In ethology the term "aggression" may be used in the sense of an instinct which, given the right environmental stimuli, leads to fighting between members of the same species (Lorenz, 1966). Tinbergen's (1948) famous study of the three-spined stickleback provides an example of instinctive aggression. Tinbergen showed that when a male stickleback is faced with a strange male intruding into its territory, it is the perception of the intruder's red colouration which is the key stimulus that releases aggression in the territorial male. It seems that at some seaside resorts (I took the picture below near Filey in Yorkshire) the birdlife has become overly aggressive.

Source: Picture © Clive R. Hollin.

It is possible that, like sticklebacks, humans have evolved to possess an aggressive instinct that may help explain human conflict (LeBlanc & Register, 2003). However, unlike sticklebacks, for humans there are the complicating factors of the powerful influence of previous learning together with our cognitions in the form of appraisals of the situation and our personal intentions. Siann (1985) is helpful with the suggestion that with respect to interpersonal transactions the term "aggression" refers to the *intention* to hurt another person but without necessarily causing any physical injury. In a similar vein, Anderson and Bushman (2002) state that "All violence is aggression, but many instances of aggression are not violent. For example, one child pushing another off a tricycle is an act of aggression but is not an act of violence" (p. 29). This latter view suggests a continuum that stretches from aggression at one end to violence at the other: Anderson and Bushman suggest the tipping point from aggression to violence is reliant upon the associated level of harm: "*Violence* is aggression that has extreme harm as its goal (e.g., death)" (p. 29).

Yet further, an important distinction may be drawn between *reactive aggression* and *proactive aggression* (sometimes called *hostile aggression* and *instrumental aggression* respectively). The term "reactive aggression" refers to impulsive acts of violence in which the aggressor's psychological state is dominated by a negative affect such as anger. On the other hand, "proactive aggression" refers to premeditated acts of violence, typically carried out to achieve a personally satisfying goal such as financial gain or revenge (Polman, Orobio de Castro, Koops, van Boxtel, & Merk, 2007). As Babcock, Tharp, Sharp, Heppner, and Stanford (2014) point out, the terms "impulsive violence" and "premeditated violence" are also in use, with some overlap with reactive and proactive. The reactive/proactive distinction will be used here, acknowledging that other terms may carry similar if not identical meanings.

Thus, we can arrive at the understanding, as used in this text, that interpersonal violence is the direct, often face-to-face, actions of an individual, including acts of neglect, which inflict emotional, psychological, and physical harm on other people. These acts of violence may be carried out with premeditation or in the heat of the moment.

The complexity of violence has led to various theories from disciplines ranging from anthropology to zoology (Mider, 2013). However, an overview of contemporary *psychological* accounts of *interpersonal violence* provides the starting point here.

Psychological Accounts of Interpersonal Violence

There are several theoretical models with a psychological emphasis which have been formulated to provide an account of interpersonal violence. These various models seek to explain acts of interpersonal violence by drawing together in a cogent way a variety of psychological and social factors. In addition, there is a range of biological factors, although these are typically associated with aggression generally rather than interpersonal violence specifically (e.g., Farrington, 1997; Olivier & van Oorschot, 2005; Tiihonen et al., 2010; Umukoro, Aladeokin, & Eduviere, 2013).

In the first psychological model, shown in streamlined form in Figure 1.1, Bandura (1978) describes a tripartite system, based on social learning theory, that relates to the *origins*, *instigators*, and *regulators* of aggressive behaviour.

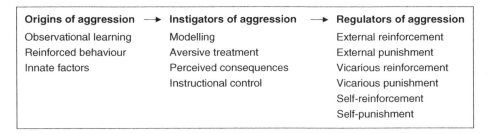

Origins of aggression	→	Instigators of aggression	→	Regulators of aggression
Observational learning		Modelling		External reinforcement
Reinforced behaviour		Aversive treatment		External punishment
Innate factors		Perceived consequences		Vicarious reinforcement
		Instructional control		Vicarious punishment
				Self-reinforcement
				Self-punishment

Figure 1.1 Bandura's Social Learning Model of Aggression. Source: After Bandura, 1978.

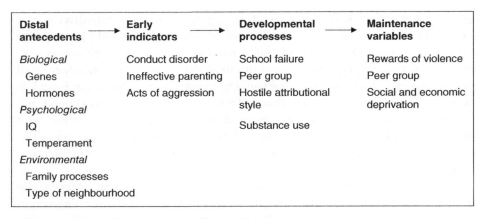

Distal antecedents →	**Early indicators** →	**Developmental processes** →	**Maintenance variables**
Biological	Conduct disorder	School failure	Rewards of violence
Genes	Ineffective parenting	Peer group	Peer group
Hormones	Acts of aggression	Hostile attributional style	Social and economic deprivation
Psychological			
IQ		Substance use	
Temperament			
Environmental			
Family processes			
Type of neighbourhood			

Figure 1.2 Developmental Model of Violence. Source: After Nietzel et al., 1999.

The model of the aetiology of violent behaviour presented by Nietzel, Hasemann, and Lynam (1999), also drawing on behavioural theory, describes four stages in the development and maintenance of violent behaviour. As illustrated in Figure 1.2, this model progresses through the lifespan identifying the various types of biological, psychological, and social risk factors which may be present at different times.

There is, not surprisingly, a reasonable degree of overlap between these two models: for example, Bandura's *innate factors* are congruous with Nietzel et al.'s *biological antecedents*, while the importance given by Bandura to reinforcement as a *regulator* of behaviour is mirrored in Nietzel et al.'s *maintenance variables*. As noted by Nietzel et al., the evidence base for the importance of the different variables is varied in strength, as is the evidence for the strength of relationships between the variables both within and across stages. Finally, there may be more than one pathway through the model so that individual differences in constitution and experience produce several combinations of variables which may be important in different circumstances.

The General Aggression Model (GAM), as formulated by Anderson and Busman (Anderson & Bushman, 2002; DeWall, Anderson, & Bushman, 2011), places an emphasis on the individual taking part in a social interaction that culminates in a violent act. The GAM views social interactions as a sequence of exchanges, each of which is termed an *episode*, involving verbal and nonverbal behaviour. The main components of the GAM, not unlike other models, consist of *inputs* from the person and the situation, the person's internal affective and cognitive state which is the *route* through which the input information is processed, and finally the *outcomes* of appraisal and the nature of the individual's decision on how to act.

These psychological models all highlight the importance of three, interconnected, areas: first, the formative factors in an individual's development which are associated with the likelihood of violent conduct; second, the environments in which violence occurs; and third the psychological and social processes which occur during the act of violence. However, before looking at these three areas in more detail, there is one more variable to consider, the gender of the violent person.

Gender

Inspection of the criminal statistics reveals that there is a gender divide as far as crime, including violent crime, is concerned (Ministry of Justice, 2010a). It is clear from the criminal statistics that men are significantly more involved in crime, including violent crime, than women. However, while a man or a woman may be convicted of the same violent crime, it does not follow that the factors associated with the development and maintenance of that violent act are identical for men and women (Collins, 2010; Putallaz & Bierman, 2004). It is likely that there are some background factors, such as poverty and harsh parenting, which are common to violent men and to violent women, and some gender-specific factors such as prosocial attitudes and emotional problems (Hollin & Palmer, 2006; Manchak, Skeem, Douglas, & Siranosian, 2009).

Crick and Grotpeter (1995) suggest that there is a relationship between gender and *type* of violence. They note that research typically finds that male children use physical aggression to a degree not seen in female children. However, they make the point that just because young girls do not hit, the assumption cannot be made that they are not aggressive; rather, the aggression may take forms other than hitting. Crick and Grotpeter note in support of their hypothesis that girls' aggression is often *relational* rather than *physical*: relational aggression is characterised by attempting to harm other children by damaging their friendships, excluding them from social activities and social groupings, and by spreading false stories so leading to the child's rejection by other children.

Cross and Campbell (2011) make a similar point about older age groups: men are more likely than women to use severe forms of violence such as kicking and punching which inflict physical injury. When the form of violence shifts to less physically aggressive acts, such as hurtful gossip and persistent teasing, so the gender difference is lost. An American study reported by Zheng and Cleveland (2013) compared the developmental trajectories of young men and women, aged between 15 and 22 years, with regard to acts of both violent and non-violent delinquency. They reported that at lower levels of delinquency there were only minimal variations in delinquency between the genders. However, at the higher levels of delinquency, which Zheng and Cleveland called *chronic*, the delinquent acts were violent in nature and perpetrated by males. It is highly likely that the higher number of men in the criminal justice system is a natural consequence of this gender variation although, parenthetically, it seems unlikely that prison has any effect on the recidivism of either men or women (Mears, Cochran, & Bales, 2012).

The role of gender will appear as appropriate in the following chapters. Attention now returns to the three areas—developmental factors, environment, and psychological and social processes related to the act of violence—highlighted by psychological models of interpersonal violence.

Development of Violent Behaviour

The most powerful way to study behavioural development is by employing a longitudinal research design. The essence of a longitudinal design is that a group of people, usually referred to as a *cohort*, is followed up over a long period of time, typically decades, with periodic measures of a range of variables associated with the behaviour of interest. There is a tradition of using longitudinal research to study the development of violent behaviour (Farrington, 1989).

McAuliffe, Hubbard, Rubin, Morrow, and Dearing (2006) found evidence for the temporal stability of both reactive and proactive aggression. Those individuals whose aggression was evident in childhood and continued into adulthood had poorer outcomes, in terms of both social functioning and criminal offences, than those whose aggression ceased during adolescence. A Canadian longitudinal study reported by Temcheff et al. (2008) covered a 30-year span, from school age into early adulthood, and investigated male and female violence within the family. The males who were aggressive as children showed stable levels of aggression as time passed: they moved from aggression towards peers at school to violence towards partners and children in adulthood. The level of childhood aggression evident for those females in the cohort who became mothers was predictive of their violent behaviour towards their own children. The strongest predictors of violent behaviour included low levels of educational attainment and a punitive parenting style.

Huesmann, Dubow, and Boxer (2009) conducted a longitudinal study investigating the continuity of physical aggression with a cohort of males and females. They monitored acts of aggression through peer report of mildly aggressive acts, such as pushing and shoving, alongside self-report of more serious acts such as punching, kicking, and weapon use. Huesmann et al. reported a moderate degree of continuity of aggression, more distinct for males than for females, from 8 years of age to adulthood. Kokko, Pulkkinen, Huesmann, Dubow, and Boxer (2009) compared data from longitudinal studies carried out in Finland and America: they reported that in both countries and for males and females the level of aggression displayed as a child was a significant predictor of physical aggression as an adult. Finally, the literature review carried out by Piquero, Carriaga, Diamond, Kazemian, and Farrington (2012) came to the conclusion that for some adult offenders aggression is a stable behaviour over the course of the lifespan as traced back to childhood.

The overall conclusion to be drawn from this body of research is clearly expressed by Huesmann et al. (2009): "One of the most consistent findings in aggression and criminology research is that aggression is a relatively 'stable,' self-perpetuating behavior that begins early in life" (p. 136). This point is reinforced still further by the findings of a meta-analytic study reported by Ttofi, Farrington, and Lösel (2012) which showed that involvement in acts of bullying at school was a strong predictor of perpetration of acts of violence in later life.

However, it is not the case that aggressive children are randomly distributed across society: it has long been understood that antisocial and criminal behaviour, including violent behaviour, runs in families. A body of research has looked at the characteristics of families that engender violent conduct. (The issue of family violence is also considered in Chapter 2 with respect to corporal punishment, throughout Chapter 3, and familial sexual violence is included in Chapter 4.)

Families

Farrington, Jolliffe, Loeber, Stouthamer-Loeber, and Kalb (2001) considered three generations—fathers, mothers, sons, daughters, uncles, aunts, grandfathers, and grandmothers—in a study of the concentration of offending by boys aged 8, 11, or 14 years, within a sample of 1,395 American families. In keeping with previous research conducted in the UK (Farrington, Barnes, & Lambert, 1996), Farrington et al. reported a high concentration of offending in families: indeed, less than 10% of the families in the study accounted for over 40% of all those who were arrested. While all relatives had some predictive power with respect to boys' offending, it was the father's offending which was the strongest predictor. This pattern of findings has been consistently replicated by studies using samples drawn from a range of populations (e.g., Bijleveld & Wijkman, 2009; Putkonen, Ryynänen, Eronen, & Tiihonen, 2007; Thornberry, Freeman-Gallant, & Lovegrove, 2009). It remains to be established whether the continuity of violence across generations is mainly a function of heredity and associated biological functioning, environment, or, as is more likely, a combination of these factors (Craig & Halton, 2009; Niv, Tuvblad, Raine, & Baker, 2013; Tzoumakis, Lussier, & Corrado, 2014).

Cycles of violence Widom (1989a) used the phrase "cycle of violence" to describe the continuity of violence through families and across generations. In particular, Widom's research (Kazemian, Widom, & Farrington, 2011; Maxfield & Widom, 1996; Widom, 1989a, 1989b; World Health Organization, 2007) has focused on the child's experience of neglect and violent abuse within their family and how such childhood experiences may act to increase the risk of their future antisocial and violent behaviour.

The focus on experiences across the lifespan is congruent with the second stage of the model proposed by Bandura (see Figure 1.2) where *aversive treatment* is nominated as one of the factors which instigates aggression. Yet further, also consistent with Bandura's model, it is likely that the abused child will witness violence both between their parents and between their parents and siblings (Holt, Buckley, & Whelan, 2008; Roberts, Gilman, Fitzmaurice, Deckerf, & Koenen, 2010). The child's observations of family violence serve both to model violence, with parents being particularly potent behavioural models, and to reinforce vicariously the potency of violence as an effective short-term means of dealing with interpersonal problems. One of the potential consequences for the child of this type of family background is an increased risk of developing problematic behaviours, including violence, as they grow through adolescence and adulthood (McCord, 1983). This issue is considered further in Chapter 3, as we now move to the environmental side of the equation.

Violent Places

Wherever people gather there is the potential for interpersonal violence. These potential settings for violence may be as intimate as the family home, as detached and impersonal as a crowd of commuters, or even a setting as seemingly unlikely as clinical medical practice (Hills & Joyce, 2013). There are several physical qualities of the immediate environment which are associated with an increased likelihood of violence.

Bystanders

The presence of a small number of other people, usually referred to as *bystanders*, at the scene may either inhibit or increase the likelihood of interpersonal violence (Levine, Taylor, & Best, 2011). This "bystander effect" is discussed below in the context of the transactions that lead to violence.

Crowds and crowding

The role of crowds in relation to violence can be thought of in two ways: first, there are crowds that assemble with the intention of committing acts of collective violence; second, there is the effect on the individual of the experience of being in a crowded space.

Violent crowds   As described by de la Roche (1996), violent crowds come in a variety of guises each seeking different goals through the use of collective violence. There are, de la Roche suggests, four common types of collective violence—*lynching*, *rioting*, *vigilantism*, and *terrorism*—which all serve the crowd's aim of seeking to right a perceived wrong.

Physical crowding and violence   It is known that humans have around them an area of *personal* or *defensible* space (Dosey & Meisels, 1969) which is a distance of approximately an arm's length, although the exact distance varies from culture to culture. If anyone intrudes into our personal space we find it stressful and we seek either to move away personally or to push the other person away. When we are in a crowd our personal space is invaded which, depending on the nature of the occasion, may make us anxious and hyper-alert for any signs of hostility which may threaten our wellbeing.

The relationship between crowding and violence is clearly seen in studies of closed environments such as institutions. The advantage of conducting a study in an institutional setting is that many institutions have an established capacity and so it is possible to measure overcrowding with a reasonable degree of precision. Thus, a study by Ng, Kumar, Ranclaud, and Robinson (2001) conducted in a psychiatric inpatient unit in New Zealand was able to calculate the degree of crowding in the unit according to the percentage of beds occupied. Ng et al. report a higher average occupancy when a violent incident, particularly an act of verbal aggression, took place than when there were no incidents. This crowding effect was independent of the ratio of staff to patients, although violence was significantly more likely to occur between 3 p.m. and 11 p.m.

A similar Finnish study by Virtanen et al. (2011) looked at violent incidents over a five-month period in 90 inpatient wards within 13 acute psychiatric hospitals across Finland. They found that almost one-half of the wards were overcrowded as measured by bed occupancy. In those wards that were overcrowded there was a significantly higher likelihood of a violent assault on hospital staff. Thus, explanations for aggression in institutions for psychiatric patients should not ignore situational and environmental factors (Peluola, Mela, & Adelugba, 2013; Welsh, Bader, & Evans, 2013).

Prisons are another type of institution where crowding may take place and is easily measurable according to the Certified Normal Accommodation (CNA) level. In England and Wales the CNA is the population level which the Prison Service accepts as commensurate with a decent standard of accommodation for prisoners. It follows that if its CNA is exceeded so a prison become officially overcrowded and, in turn, it may be predicted that the risk of violence increases accordingly.

However, establishing a definitive link between prison overcrowding and escalation of violent incidents is not straightforward. As Wooldredge and Steiner (2009) point out, there is a large range of variables—from type of prison, the nature of the prisoner cohort, and the research design—that may influence the degree of correspondence between prison crowding and numbers of violent incidents. In this light it is not surprising that an extensive literature contains a mixture of positive, negative, and null findings. For example, an American study by Gaes and McGuire (1985) looked at assault rates in 19 federal prisons and found that crowding had a marked effect on assault rates. In contrast, another large-scale study of 150 American prisons by Tartaro and Levy (2007) found that it was the racial composition of the prison population together with the level of prison officer supervision that best predicted violence.

Temperature

As humans we respond to the weather generally as seen, for example, in the impact of weather on daily mood (Denissen, Butalid, Penke, & van Aken, 2008). A relationship between hot weather and violence is implicit in everyday speech: we anticipate the likelihood of violence when we describe people as "hot under the collar" or "hot headed" or having a "fiery temper" and we are familiar with the notion of "hot spots" for crime. Indeed, such is the power of speech that even using words that we associate with violence can act to increase our aggressive thoughts and hostile perceptions of other people (DeWall & Bushman, 2009).

At one level the relationship between heat and aggression is very basic in nature: as it becomes hotter so the potential for violence increases accordingly. This principle extends across the animal kingdom: for example, a study of spiders by Pruitt, Demes, and Dittrich-Reed (2011) found that "At warmer temperatures *A. studiosus* exhibit diminished tolerance of conspecifics, increased activity levels, shorter latencies of attack, and increased tendencies to attack multiple prey items" (p. 318).

There is ample evidence of a similar relationship between heat and violent behaviour in humans as well as arachnids, although it is sometimes couched in terms of seasonality and crime rather than temperature and crime (e.g., Harries, Stadler, & Zdorkowski, 1984). In a typical study, carried out in Philadelphia, Song and Taylor (2011) found a significant association between temperature and number of robberies. However, as with the complexities that are evident for the link between crowds and violence, this association was attenuated by several variables, as Song and Taylor explain:

> Locations that were near major or moderate sized commercial venues, with moderate or upper income communities located there or nearby, and in some instances well served by subway lines (Center City, University City, South Street, Chestnut Hill, Roxborough), seemed to experience the strongest temperature-linked oscillation in robbery counts. Some of these communities contain or are near venues that are year-round tourist attractions more heavily visited in warmer months, or that are sites of special seasonal events such as runs, concerts, or festivals. (p. 468)

The relationship between physical violence and temperature is not restricted to street crime. A study by Larrick, Timmerman, Carton, and Abrevaya (2011) showed an interaction between temperature and sporting aggression. Larrick et al. analysed data from 57,293 Major League baseball games to look at the relationship between provocation and temperature in precipitating aggressive acts. They found that "Higher temperatures interacted with a greater number of teammates being hit by a pitch to increase the chances of a pitcher subsequently hitting an opposing batter" (p. 425). Thus, when temperatures are high the probability of a pitcher hitting an opponent rises, but this relationship is significantly dependent upon whether or not one of the pitcher's teammates has been hit previously by an opposition pitcher. Larrick et al. suggest that it is likely that set within the hot environment, the pitcher's retaliatory decision to hit an opponent is influenced by both their own anger and the promptings of their teammates.

Thus, the effects of temperature on behaviour are in part associated with social factors such as transient crowding, as when people gather for festivals and sporting events, or with the times when people leave work and begin to travel home and so congregate at stations for railway and underground services. Indeed, thinking more broadly, temperature itself is not independent of other influences: the weather is clearly reliant upon the season of the year while, as those of us who live in England know only too well, the summer temperature in one country may be very different from that in another country. There is corresponding evidence, from several countries, to suggest that factors such as weather and season are related to local crime rates generally and to violence specifically (Breetzke & Cohn, 2012; Ceccato, 2005; Hipp, Bauer, Curran, & Bollen, 2004). In this vein of thought, some commentators have extrapolated from our current understanding to speculate on the impact of climate change on crime (Gleditsch, 2012; Scheffran, Brzoska, Kominek, Link, & Schilling, 2012).

How does temperature influence violent behaviour?   There are several explanations for the relationship between heat and violence (Anderson, 1989), but the one which has attracted a great deal of attention is based on the GAM. This explanation holds that that rising levels of heat bring about physiological changes that increase the likelihood of violent behaviour in a linear fashion (Bushman, Wang, & Anderson, 2005). In other words, there is a one-to-one direct, linear relationship so that as heat rises so too does violence.

Does the potential for violence keep on increasing as the temperature rises further and further? It appears that the linear relationship between crime and temperature may hold only to a certain point. The *negative affect escape model* suggests that when it becomes very hot the individual's concern is with escaping from the unpleasantness and the discomfort brought about by the rising heat resulting in the net effect of *less* crime (Bell & Baron, 1976). Thus, the linear relationship between temperature and violence becomes curvilinear beyond a certain point.

Combinations of environmental variables

The effects of environmental variables on human behaviour generally and violence specifically are not straightforward. While there may on occasions be a relationship between both crowds and violence and crowding and violence it is evident that this relationship is attenuated by a wide range of factors. Thus, it cannot be assumed that crowds automatically equal violence, nor can the possibility of violence be discounted when crowds gather. Similarly, as shown by the study of baseball pitchers, previous events and teammates' comments act to fuel heat-driven acts of aggressive retaliation. The interactions between the various environmental influences that may prompt violence add to the complexities of understanding violence and predicting exactly where and when it is likely to occur.

Weapons

There is an inescapable association between weapons and interpersonal violence. Indeed, the mere presence of a weapon during a violent interaction is sufficient to prime aggressive thoughts among those involved, in turn heightening the chances of the weapon being used (Bartholow, Anderson, Carnagey, & Benjamin, 2005). As will be discussed in Chapter 4, it is axiomatic that the use of a weapon in a violent exchange, with some weapons decidedly more potent than others, increases the chances of a homicide. There is ample evidence that weapons are frequently used in violent exchanges: Brennan and Moore (2009) note that in the USA and in the UK weapons are used in about one-quarter of all violent altercations.

Why are weapons used in some violent incidents? An individual may carry a weapon for a variety of reasons. The weapon may serve an instrumental purpose, say to use for self-protection if attacked, or to threaten and intimidate in a robbery, or with the premeditated intention of harming another person. This instrumental use of weapons may extend to school bullying: an American study by Dukes, Stein, and Zane (2010) found that, for both male and female pupils, certain types of bullying perpetration and victimisation were associated with weapon-carrying. These findings are in accord with those of American studies which report that carrying weapons to school is associated, more so for males than females, with involvement in physical fights and other forms of delinquency as well links with a peer group where guns are carried and illegal drugs are used (Bailey, Flewelling, & Rosenbaum, 1997; Cao, Zhang, & He, 2008; Kulig, Valentine, Griffith, & Ruthazer, 1998).

It is also the case that weapons are perceived by some groups as a symbol of some desirable personal attribute, such as social status or membership of a certain peer group or sexual attractiveness (Barlas & Egan, 2006; McClusky, McClusky, & Bynum, 2006). Analysis of the beliefs about weapons given by a sample of 212 male and female school pupils in South Wales, aged between 16 and 18 years, led Penny, Walker, and Gudjonsson (2011) to suggest that the overarching belief, particularly for male pupils, is that weapons bring a sense of *potency*. Thus, the pupils believed that carrying and using weapons would bring heightened wellbeing and confidence. Further, weapons give feelings of increased personal power with regard to self-defence, making others comply with one's wishes, fitting in socially and feeling masculine and cool.

The complexity of the issues involved in weapon-carrying among some young people is also seen in a study by Bannister et al. (2010) of carrying knives and other weapons by youth groups and gangs in Scotland. Through interviews with a large sample of young people in several different locations in Scotland, Bannister et al. compiled a rich picture of young people's views about weapons.

The young people who carried knives said that this was for a variety of reasons including self-protection without any intention to use the weapon, to enhance their reputation, which may mean using the knife, and with the intention to use it if they thought it was necessary. The majority of the young people were aware of the risks, including imprisonment, associated with carrying and using knives, and many had been victims of a knife attack. A distinction was drawn between carrying and using a knife: simply carrying a knife was not respected, unlike being prepared to use or having used a knife, which gained respect and enhanced a reputation of being someone to be feared. The twin themes of self-protection and a sense of masculinity emerged in a study of knife-carrying by British males by Palasinski and Riggs (2012).

Some young people attempted to manage the risks of using a knife by targeting their victim's stomach or buttocks so as to reduce the chances of a serious or fatal injury.

However, this strategy is not a guaranteed success and some of the young people were serving prison sentences for seriously wounding or killing their victim. A variety of other types of weapon were used to avoid being caught carrying a knife and the potential prison sentence that would follow. These weapons included a screwdriver, a Stanley blade (a small but very sharp blade used in a tool called a Stanley knife), a hammer and a packet of nails, and a broken bottle.

Brennan, Moore, and Shepherd (2010) compared two groups of adult male prisoners convicted for a violent offence: one group had used weapons, the other had not. The weapon-using violent offenders had a more extensive delinquent history, scored higher on a measure of trait aggression, and were more risk-seeking than other offender types.

In summary, weapon-carrying and use may be associated with a history of involvement in delinquent acts and with delinquent peers, alongside the personal traits of a propensity to aggression and high levels of risk-taking.

The Violent Act: The Psychology of the Aggressor

If we move from the environmental variables that may influence violence behaviour to personal characteristics, there are three aspects of the individual's functioning to consider: social cognition, the role of emotion, and different forms of violent behaviour.

Social cognition

What is social cognition? The distinction may be drawn between *impersonal* cognition and *social* cognition. The former describes those facets of our cognitive functioning, such as mathematical ability and abstract thought, which are not directly related to social behaviour. The latter describes those aspects of cognition, such as empathy, perception and understanding of nonverbal behaviour, social values and morals, and social problem-solving, which have a direct influence on how we understand and behave towards other people. Several commentators have suggested that social cognition is an important element in understanding violent behaviour (e.g., Bowes & McMurran, 2013; Carlo, Mestre, Samper, Tur, & Armenta, 2010; Gannon, 2009; Gannon, Ward, Beech, & Fisher, 2007; Seidel et al., 2013). Indeed, it has been suggested that the lower rate of violence typically found with women is a function of their superior social cognitive skills when compared to men (Bennett, Farrington, & Huesmann, 2005).

In order to function effectively in social interactions we must process the continual flow of social information, both verbal and nonverbal, that originates from those around us, make sense of what we perceive, and finally decide how to act based on our understanding of the situation. An influential model of social information-processing was proposed by Dodge (1986), later revised by Crick and

Dodge (1994), and which continues to engage theorists (Orobio de Castro, 2004). While originally devised as a model of social information-processing to inform understanding of social competence in children, the model's principles apply to people of all ages. Crick and Dodge's revised model incorporates six discrete sequential stages.

- *Stage 1: Encoding of cues.* At this stage the individual must attend to their social environment in order to detect relevant social and situational cues. The ability to detect cues may be influenced by prior learning as well as by physical constraints such as hearing difficulties, poor eyesight, alcohol use, and so on.
- *Stage 2: Interpretation of cues.* Following cue selection, the individual next seeks to make sense of what they have perceived. The process of arriving at an understanding may involve forming a view as to what caused the current events, or making inferences and attributions of intent about the actions of the others in the situation.

    As with encoding, the interpretation of social cues may be influenced or guided by previous experience.

    Alongside interpretation of social cues, the individual may be aware of *internal* cues, such as their own emotional state, which occur in response to the situation. The importance of internal cues is discussed further below in considering the role of emotion.
- *Stage 3: Clarification of goals.* When the individual has arrived at their understanding of the situation they formulate a goal or desired outcome for the interaction: this goal may be to engage with the situation to gain an advantage, or to change the perceived course of events, or to disengage and seek to escape from what is unfolding. As social interactions may shift and change quickly, so the individual's goals may correspondingly shift as the situation develops.
- *Stage 4: Response access or construction.* In order to respond to the situation as they perceive it and so move towards their desired outcome, the individual may rely on previous experience in similar situations or, if faced with a situation they have not previously encountered, they may construct new behaviours.
- *Stage 5: Response decision.* At this stage the individual evaluates their potential responses, old or new, and selects a course of action. Their choice of response may be positively influenced by their expectations of the outcome of a specific course of action. These expectations are based on judgements of the appropriateness of their actions, the anticipated outcomes, and their self-belief in their ability to carry out the specific response they judge to be suitable for the situation.
- *Stage 6: Behavioural response.* Finally, having arrived at a decision the individual makes their response utilizing the appropriate repertoires of verbal and nonverbal skills.

There are two important points to note about Crick and Dodge's revised model. First, the individual's experience plays an important role in proceedings. The process of perceiving and processing social information is heavily influenced by previous social interactions. Thus, the individual's social information-processing is interwoven with the pre-existing information held, in Crick and Dodge's terminology, in their personal *data base*. This pre-existing information takes the form of stored memories alongside acquired rules, social schemas, and social knowledge gathered from previous social situations. Crick and Dodge suggest that as the child develops so over time its cognitive patterns become increasingly rigid. This rigidity in processing, which persists into adolescence and adulthood, influences future behaviour: thus, as Crick and Dodge state, "The result is that processing patterns and tendencies, as they are formed, come to act like personality characteristics that guide behavior. These increasingly stable characteristics account for consistency in behavior across time, self-fulfilling prophecy effects, and the failure of interventions in later life (relative to interventions in early life)" (1994, p. 81). This position is entirely consistent with the longitudinal studies which suggest that aggression is a stable characteristic across the lifespan.

The second point to note is that Crick and Dodge propose a dynamic, cyclical nature in social information-processing. An individual will perceive the effect of their behaviour on others, which then leads to a fresh round of cue perception, evaluation, and monitoring of progress towards goal attainment. This continued round of perception, interpretation, and generation and evaluation of potential responses is evident in social problem-solving approaches to understanding criminal behaviour, including violent crimes (e.g., McMurran & McGuire, 2005).

The social information-processing approach has led to research concerned with specific elements of the overall model. There are two elements of the model that have attracted particular attention: the first is the role of attributions, the second is the influence of emotion.

Attributions

At the second stage of the model, one of the cognitive processes involved in interpreting social cues lies in making attributions about the other person or people involved in the exchange. Of course, there is a long history to the study of attributions within social psychology in the context of many everyday types of social exchange (Kelley, 1967; Kelley & Michela, 1980). In the study of interpersonal aggression and violence particular attention has been given to the role of *hostile* attributions. A hostile attribution, as the name suggests, occurs when the individual explains another person's behaviour in antagonistic terms. If, for example, I am in the pub and someone pushes into me causing me to spill my drink what do I think? "Whoops, steady on that was a silly accident!" or "That was a deliberate push and it's made me look a right fool"? The former is a *benign* attribution, seeing the cause of the spillage as accidental, "I'm okay, no harm done"; the latter is *hostile* in that the act is seen as deliberate and a threat to my esteem and reputation. "Watch what you're doing mate or next time there'll be trouble." Moeller, Crocker, and Bushman (2009) showed that people with a high self-regard hold a sense of entitlement with regard to expecting admiration and respect from other people. When the expected respect from others is not forthcoming then the consequence may be interpersonal conflict.

Hostile attributions play a fundamental role in understanding both impulsive and premeditated interpersonal violence (Helfritz-Sinville & Stanford, 2014). Dodge (2006) goes so far as to state that "Individual differences in aggressive behavior occur as a function of characteristic styles of attributing hostile intent (or not) to others' provocative behavior" (p. 791). Dodge suggests that the stable trait of making hostile attributions about the actions of others has its roots in patterns of socialisation and childhood development. The important influences on this maturational process, as with so many other aspects of child development, lie in the nature of the child's attachment to a caregiver, the behaviours they see modelled in their everyday life, and their personal experiences of aggression and violence.

Orobio de Castro, Veerman, Koops, and Monshouwer (2002) reported a meta-analysis of 41 studies involving in total over 6,000 participants, the large majority of whom were males, concerned with the relationship between aggressive behaviour in children aged from 4 to 12 years and hostile attributions regarding the actions of peers. They found that, as anticipated, the levels of aggressive behaviours exhibited by children were strongly related to hostile attributions, which in turn were related to rejection by peers. However, this pattern was less marked with more intelligent children: indeed, higher IQ may have a protective quality in terms of commission of acts of violence (González, Kallis, Ullrich, Zhang, & Coid, 2014). Alongside the large literature on children, there are individual studies that illustrate the importance of hostile attributions in pathways to violence perpetrated by older age groups such as young adults (e.g., Guyll & Madon, 2004) and by violent criminals (e.g., Lim, Day, & Casey, 2011).

A study reported by Crowther, Goodson, McGuire, and Dickson (2013) looked at the accounts a group of boys aged 12 to 16 years, who were involved in aggressive incidents at a school for children with emotional and behavioural difficulties. The boys described how their aggressive behaviour was an essential part of the image of being tough which, in turn, functioned in an environment they perceived as hostile to prevent victimisation and establish friendships among peers. As they describe it, they had no other option than "having to fight".

The second of the fundamental points raised by Crick and Dodge (1994) concerns the role of emotion in the genesis of aggression and violence.

Emotion

How does emotion influence behaviour? Crick and Dodge (1994) suggest that the relationship between what we feel and what we do takes various forms. First, the qualities of a range of different situations can be emotionally arousing for different people: we may be emotionally aroused by, for example, a piece of art, another person's distress, or by the way that people act towards us. Such emotionally arousing situational cues would impact at stage 1 of the model in and additionally may lead to internal cues, such as feelings of anxiety, so that at stage 2 both external and internal emotionally arousing cues must be processed. At stage 3 high levels of emotional arousal may act to encourage, discourage, or modify the individual's motivation towards certain goals. Again, this is a dynamic system so that awareness of their emotions may bring the individual to change their goals. Thus, the person may decide to disengage from a social interaction in order to reduce uncomfortable levels of emotional arousal; alternatively, they may decide to hit out in response to the perceived provocation.

This sequence, in due turn, may influence what happens at stage 4 and stage 5 in terms of the individual deciding what response to use and then putting it into action. The net effects of the emotionally driven behaviour may be rewarding in that they help to achieve the goal, or less than rewarding in that they prompt retaliatory aggressive behaviour from others. The type of outcome will inform the individual's evaluation of the effects of their actions and so increase or decrease the likelihood of their repetition in similar situations. The degree to which a person is aware of and understands their emotions, their level of *emotional intelligence*, is associated with levels of aggression. García-Sancho, Salguero, and Fernández-Berrocal (2014) reviewed the evidence and found a negative relationship between the two: those with higher levels of emotional intelligence were less aggressive and vice versa.

There are two emotional states closely associated with violent behaviour: the first is excitement or thrill-seeking, the second is anger.

Thrill-seeking   Ching, Daffern, and Thomas (2012) highlight *thrill-seeking* or *appetitive violence* as a type of violence, mainly prevalent among young people, carried out simply for the enjoyment of being violent and inflicting suffering. This type of violence, typically carried out in groups, often accompanied by the drug and alcohol use alongside the use of weapons, is targeted against vulnerable groups such as the homeless. It comes in the guise of "bum hunting" in America or "happy slapping" when directed at unsuspecting victims.

If the fear of an increasing use of violence as a means of recreation, across several Western countries, can be substantiated this presents is a worrying trend. There are obvious knee-jerk reactions as to the best way to deal with this type of violence. However, as Ching et al. note, the development of effective preventative measures will rely on a more complete understanding of the psychological and social aspects of this type of violence.

Anger   The importance of anger in our understanding of interpersonal violence owes much to the work of the social psychologist Raymond Novaco. In a sustained and substantial body of work Novaco has developed an understanding of the role of anger in the commission of acts of violence (e.g., Novaco, 1975, 1994, 2007; Novaco & Welsh, 1989). For Novaco anger is conceived of as a subjectively experienced, adaptive, and complex emotion with both functional and dysfunctional effects for the individual. The state of anger is understood to entail interacting physiological

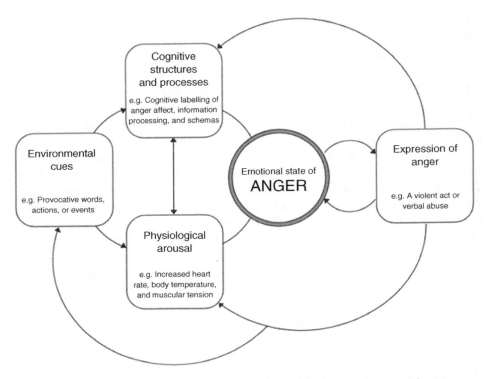

Figure 1.3   Schematic Representation of Novaco's Model of Anger. Source: After Novaco, 1994.

and cognitive elements, typically related to environmental cues. Thus, an individual becomes angry on those occasions when environmental cues provoke physiological and cognitive arousal and the person labels their subjective emotional experience as "anger". This emotional experience is then associated with a behavioural expression of anger, which may take the form of a violent act directed against another person. The expression of anger therefore depends upon a range of individual factors, including the perception of provocation, cognitive processing, and the ability to cope with the perceived provocation. Figure 1.3 illustrates Novaco's model schematically, showing the dynamic, interactive nature of the environmental, physiological, cognitive, affective, and behavioural elements.

There are several indices of the *physiological* arousal associated with anger: the angry person may, for example, experience increases in cardiovascular activity, muscular tension, and body temperature. Similarly, there are several features associated with increasing cognitive arousal which include cognitive *labelling* of anger and the activation of *schemas*. An individual's cognitive labelling of their emotional state as *angry* follows a subjective appraisal which settles on this term as a suitable descriptor for their internal state. The individual's appraisal of the situation may be affected by schemas which lead to their minimising or disregarding contextual factors and so impacts on their judgement of how best to proceed.

Schemas are described by Robins and Novaco (1999) as the psychological representations an individual holds of the relationship between a specific environment and associated behaviour. The content and functioning of schemas are typically based on one's own previous experience. The advantage of schemas is that rather than treating every recurrence of a situation as a novel encounter they enable fast and efficient processing of information and efficient responding. Schemas encompass procedural rules that allow us habitually to deal with a range of different types of interactions and situations. This is not to say, however, that schemas necessarily lead to accurate perception or to competent and appropriate responding to a situation.

In the context of Novaco's model, *anger schemas* predispose an individual, given the appropriate environmental cues, to perceive certain social cues in a negative manner so activating an angry schema and resulting in a behavioural expression of anger (Novaco, 2007; Novaco & Welsh, 1989). In some instances, the behavioural expression that follows activation of an anger schema is aggressive or violent in nature.

The emotion of anger may have beneficial as well as harmful consequences: the experience of anger may be positive in the sense that, for example, it may prompt the individual to act positively to protect themselves and others from an external threat (Novaco, 1994). Nonetheless, anger can have a negative effect both for the individual and others they encounter, in which case the emotion has become *dysfunctional*.

Dysfunctional anger   The emotion of anger can become dysfunctional when it is not appropriately *regulated*. The notion of anger regulation relates to an individual's ability to remain in a calm state when they perceive that they are being provoked. The level of control of anger of which an individual is capable may be dependent upon on several of the factors seen in Novaco's model. Thus, the appraisal of one's internal state, from mild irritation through to rage, may influence the degree of control; the same is true with regard to the individual's cognitive processing of social cues and information.

Novaco and Welsh (1989) described five types of information-processing which are characteristic of those who frequently show dysfunctional anger followed by violent behaviour. There are two *cognitive operations* (the term "cognitive operations" refers to the way information is encoded, stored, and retrieved from memory) associated with dysfunctional anger: these are attentional cueing and perceptual matching.

Attentional cueing refers to a preoccupation with some past provoking cue, such as another person's actions, which leads to rumination about the incident. The act of rumination may produce feelings of irritation about what happened so maintaining angry arousal for some time after the event has occurred. *Perceptual matching* is the process whereby emotions from a previous provoking incident are transferred to the current situation. The more provoking situations an individual has been exposed to in the past the more likely it becomes that they will perceive some degree of correspondence or matching between previous and current situations. This perception may lead to fast activation of a *violence schema* leading quickly to angry arousal in response to the perceived provocation.

In addition to the two cognitive operations described above, Novaco and Walsh also describe three *cognitive propositions* (the term "cognitive propositions" refers to the content of cognitive structures) associated with dysfunctional anger: these are fundamental attribution errors, false consensus, and anchoring effects.

A *fundamental attribution error* occurs when an individual consistently underestimates the importance of external situational pressures and overestimates the importance of internal factors such as motivation and personality when judging other people's behaviour. There is a clear link between attribution errors, dysfunctional anger, and aggressive and violent behaviour (Allred, 2000).

The phenomenon of a *false consensus* takes place when the individual overestimates the extent to which other people hold the same beliefs and opinions that they do. A false consensus may be associated with a lack of perspective-taking (seeing the other person's point of view) and it may lead to feelings of heightened tension, an increased sensitivity to provocation, and subsequent anger and aggression and violence (Russell & Arms, 1995).

Finally, *anchoring effects* refer to the propensity to adhere to one's first impressions of another person or a situation, despite later information which shows the initial impression was either only partially correct or absolutely wrong.

Consequences of dysfunctional anger   The interplay between patterns of anger and hostile behaviour towards others is evident from an early age (Lemerise & Dodge, 2008). When anger and its associated psychological states become an established part of an individual's functioning there are various consequences alongside an increased likelihood of interpersonal violence. Thus, the undesirable consequences of anger may be experienced directly by either the angry person alone or both the angry person and those on the receiving end of the "angry behaviour". Chronic levels of anger can result in serious psychological and health problems (Miller, Smith, Turner, Guijarro, & Hallet, 1996). Dysfunctional anger is associated with poor physical health as seen with hypertension, coronary heart disease, and carotid and coronary atherosclerosis (Kubzansky, Cole, Kawachi, Vokonas, & Sparrow, 2006), and with behavioural and mental disturbance. With regard to the latter, the Diagnostic and Statistical Manual of Mental Disorders (DSM-IV-TR; American Psychiatric Association, 2000) presents dysfunctional anger as a clinical symptom of several disorders including oppositional defiant disorder, conduct disorder, borderline personality disorder, major depressive disorder, antisocial personality disorder, and some types of schizophrenia. The closest association between dysfunctional anger and behavioural disturbance is evident in intermittent explosive disorder where anger is an integral component of acts of aggression and violence (Swaffer & Hollin, 2000).

As shown in Figure 1.3, and as is also seen in the Crick and Dodge model, Novaco suggests that environmental factors, in this case both the social and the physical characteristics of the setting, impact on the individual both psychologically and physiologically to bring about a state of anger. When the individual's expression of their anger takes the form of a violent act so, in common with other models, Novaco suggests that the social consequences of the behaviour function as feedback acting to intensify or relieve the individual's anger.

As well as social factors and the physical qualities of the environment there are two other factors related to violence through their effects on the individual's processing of social information. The first of these factors is the effect of substance use, particularly alcohol, the second lies in the quality of the individual's mental health.

Alcohol and violent crime

As with substance use generally (Boles & Miotto, 2003), the specific association between alcohol and violent crime has long been known across many cultures and societies (World Health Organization, 2008). This common knowledge is in evidence, for example, at some major events where large crowds gather where there are restrictions on access to alcohol. Thus, at football (soccer) matches where there is a fierce rivalry between opposing fans there may be an early noon kick-off (rather than the traditional mid-afternoon), public houses near to the ground remain closed, and alcohol is not sold inside the stadium. Parenthetically, there is an interesting contrast to be drawn here between crowd behaviour at different types of sporting event: while alcohol is controlled at football grounds it is sold (typically at exorbitant prices) before and during and after the game at cricket and rugby matches. Whether this variation in retail practice is due to the nature of the sport being watched or the composition of the crowd is a point to debate.

The no-alcohol policy at some sporting events raises the issue of the relationship between the availability of alcohol generally and the likelihood of violence. As noted by Heaton (2011), changes in the licensing laws governing the times at which alcohol may be sold have the potential to impact on rates of violence.

Box 1.1 shows the nature and extent of the alcohol–crime relationship, as taken from both official statistics and crime surveys, summarised from a factsheet published by the Institute of Alcohol Studies (2010).

Population studies show alcohol is associated with a significant number of acts of violence (Grann & Fazel, 2004) and so it is hardly surprising that violent incidents cluster around the immediate vicinity of bars and clubs (Ratcliffe, 2012). The alcohol–crime relationship is evident for male and female adolescents and young adults (Popovici, Homer, Fang, & French, 2012) and is apparent in many different types of crime including homicide (Miles, 2012; Rossow, 1996), intimate partner violence (Clements & Schumacher, 2010; Foran & O'Leary, 2008), sexual violence (Abbey, 2011), and property crime (Cordilia, 1985). It follows that that alcohol and other drug problems are endemic among convicted offenders (Fazel, Bains, & Doll, 2006; Greenfield & Henneberg, 2001; MacAskill et al., 2011) as well as among victims of crime (Branas et al., 2009).

It is known that many offenders who use alcohol to excess will use other drugs such as cannabis and amphetamines. Those offenders whose drug use does not include alcohol appear mostly to commit crimes of acquisition, presumably to fund buying

Box 1.1   Alcohol Crime Statistics

- A high proportion of both offenders and victims of violent crime were under the influence of alcohol when the assault took place.
- About over one-third of offenders have a drink problem which may be related to their violent behaviour; a similar proportion have a binge-drinking problem.
- Alcohol was particularly prevalent in domestic violence, with alcohol dependence evident in close to one-half of convicted domestic violence offenders.
- About 1 in 5 of people arrested by the police will test positive for alcohol.
- Alcohol is frequently found in many different types of violent crimes including homicide, wounding, affray and domestic violence.

Source: After Institute of Alcohol Studies, 2010.

drugs, while a pattern of polydrug drug use that includes alcohol is characterised by crimes of violence (Miller & Welte, 1986). Varano, McCluskey, Patchin, and Bynum (2004) focus specifically on the relationship between drugs and homicide. They suggest that there are two principal types of drug homicide: (1) *peripheral drug homicides* where drugs are present or being used by those involved but are not a causal factor; (2) *drug-motivated homicides* where the sale or use of drugs is central to the crime.

There is a variety of explanations for the association between alcohol and violent behaviour (Martin, 2001). The notion of *alcohol outcome expectancies* relates to the formation of "if-then" expectations based on previous experience (Goldman, Del Boca, & Darkes, 1999) as, for example, "If I drink, then I'll have a good time". McMurran (2007) conducted a study looking at alcohol expectancies among a sample of male prisoners, with a mean age of around 30 years, some serving sentences for violent offences. McMurran found that the violent offenders expected alcohol to act to increase their social confidence. As McMurran notes, increased social confidence may lead some men to be drawn to particular settings: "The increased likelihood of violence may be explained by intoxicated, confident (perhaps overconfident), young men meeting others who are drinking for the same reasons in noisy, crowded drinking venues, which may well lead to clashes where aggression and violence result" (p. 282).

Another explanation for the effect of alcohol on violent behaviour is the Alcohol Myopia Model (Steele & Josephs, 1990). There is some support for the proposition that alcohol acts to focus attention on interpersonal cues which are salient to aggression in threatening situations (Giancola, Duke, & Ritz, 2011). Once primed by their myopic processing of the social information, the intoxicated person then acts in an aggressive manner towards the other person. This aggressive behaviour towards others, given the right setting, may produce McMurran's "clashes where aggression and violence result".

McMurran, Hoyte, and Jinks (2011) have elaborated on the nature of the triggers for violence in young male offenders. McMurran et al. interviewed a sample of young offenders serving custodial sentences for violent crimes. They identified six themes relating to triggers for violence: (1) being offended or insulted by another person; (2) seeing the opportunity for a material gain; (3) seeing a friend, male or female, in need of help; (4) the perception of the threat of a personal attack; (5) distress brought about by arguing with others or by seeing an ex-girlfriend with someone else; (6) wanting to be involved in a fight.

A Canadian study reported by Graham et al. (2011) analysed Friday and Saturday night incidents in large bars and clubs. They discerned four types of motive for aggressive or coercive acts among those out for the night—(1) to gain compliance; (2) to express a grievance or to put right a perceived wrong; (3) to make a particular impression, such as being important or "tough"; (4) for fun and excitement—which are not a million miles away from types of offenders as described by McMurran, Hoyte, and Jinks (2012).

In a further large-scale study Graham et al. (2013) reported a gender difference in motivation to aggression in the context of a bar room. For women, who accounted for about one-quarter of the aggressive bar-room patrons, the prime instigation to aggression was an unwanted sexual advance. For men, the main motivator to aggression, towards both males and females, was a perceived risk to their identity in the sense of a personal affront or a threat to their social status within a group.

Not all acts of alcohol-related violence are committed with the same end in sight. McMurran, Jinks, Howells, and Howard (2011) describe three distinct goals evident in a sample of young offenders whose violent offence was alcohol-related. Analysis of the young offenders' description of their offence allowed three "ultimate goals" to emerge: (1) the violence was used for material gain; (2) the violence was intended to establish social dominance over others; (3) the violence was a defence against the perceived threat of violence from others. Those young offenders who fell into the first two classifications were, perhaps not surprisingly, higher in trait aggression and trait anger than those in the third group.

Mental health

The relationship between mental health and violence has been approached by researchers in several ways: some studies concentrate on a single type of mental disorder, such as the association between schizophrenia and violence, while other studies are concerned with the more generic *psychosis* or *mental illness*; studies may use different criteria, typically DSM or ICD (International Classification of Diseases), in reaching a specific diagnosis; there is a contrast between violence in the community and inpatient violence; and research may employ one of several research designs. A weight of evidence has accrued which allows some broad conclusions to be reached, particularly concerning the association between schizophrenia and violence and between personality disorder and violence.

Schizophrenia and violence   Opinion on the relationship between schizophrenia and violence has fluctuated over time between the position that there is no relationship at all to the view that in given circumstances a relationship may exist (Monahan, 1992). As Hodgins (2008) states, "There is now robust evidence demonstrating that both men and women with schizophrenia are at elevated risk when compared to the general population to be convicted of non-violent criminal offences, at higher risk to be convicted of violent criminal offences, and at even higher risk to be convicted of homicide" (p. 2505). The research evidence supporting the view expressed by Hodgins is to be found in several large-scale cohort studies, in systematic reviews, and in meta-analyses.

In a cohort study a sample formally diagnosed with a mental disorder is compared with a matched sample (e.g., Alden, Brennan, Hodgins, & Mednick, 2007; Soyka, Graz, Bottlender, Dirschedl, & Schoech, 2007). In a typical example, Wallace, Mullen, and Burgess (2004) compared with a matched sample the criminal records over a 25-year period of a cohort of 2,861 male and female schizophrenic patients. For both males and females, a criminal conviction for any offence was more prevalent in the schizophrenic group (21.6%) than in the comparison group (7.8%): when focusing specifically on violent crimes the same pattern was found (8.2% versus 1.8%), as was also the case for sexual crimes (1.8% and 0.7%). Wallace et al. note that the majority of violent and sexual offences were committed by men, while rates of offending were higher for patients with a comorbid diagnosis of substance use disorder.

A Swedish cohort study was reported by Fazel, Grann, Carlström, Lichtenstein, and Långström (2009): the cohort of 8,891 men and 4,951 women was composed of people with two or more periods of hospitalisation for schizophrenia. With an average 12-year follow-up following hospital discharge, Fazel et al. found that just over 17% of the men and 5.6% of the women had been convicted of a violent offence. The most common types of crime were physical assault and threats and harassment, with very few sexual offences: however, there were 125 homicides, 109 committed by men and 16 by women.

Several substantial contributions to the literature have come from systematic reviews and meta-analyses (e.g., Bonta, Blais, & Wilson, 2014; Douglas, Guy, & Hart, 2009; Fazel, Långström, Hjern, Grann, & Lichtenstein, 2009; Large, Smith, & Nielssen, 2009). In a typical study, Bonta, Law, and Hanson (1998) carried out a meta-analysis of 58 studies investigating predictors of recidivism for offenders in the criminal justice system and for mentally disordered offenders. Bonta et al. reported that that for both general offending and violent offending the strongest predictors of recidivism were the same for mentally disordered offenders as for mainstream offenders. These strong predictors were of three distinct types: (1) *criminal history* such as a juvenile delinquency and a history of serious offences, both violent and non-violent; (2) a *deviant lifestyle* as seen with high unemployment, family problems, and living in poor accommodation; (3) *personal characteristics* including age, being male, antisocial personality, and a history of substance misuse.

Bo, Abu-Akel, Kongerslev, Haahr, and Simonsen (2011) concluded their review of the literature with the conclusion that there are two pathways or trajectories that may explain the overlap between schizophrenia and violence. In the first trajectory the individual has no history of violence and their positive symptoms, such as persecutory delusions, appear to account for the violent behaviour. In the second it is personality factors, including psychopathy, which predict violence irrespective of any other symptomatology related to schizophrenia.

Schizophrenia and homicide   Given the association between schizophrenia and violence, is there any particular relationship between schizophrenia and homicide?

Meehan et al. (2006) reviewed 1,594 homicide cases in England and Wales from between 1996 and 1999: they reported that 85 (5%) of these 1,594 murderers had a formal diagnosis of schizophrenia. Meehan et al. also noted the contribution to the homicide made by the high frequency of delusions and the intensity of the person's emotional response to their delusions immediately before the offence. A Swedish study by Fazel, Buxrud, Ruchkin, and Grann (2010) compared patients with a diagnosis of schizophrenia, bipolar disorder, and other psychoses who committed homicide within six months of discharge from a psychiatric hospital with a similar group of patients who did not commit another violent offence after discharge. Fazel et al. found that poor levels of self-care, a failure to take prescribed medication, and high levels of substance misuse were closely associated with homicide.

Schizophrenia and alcohol abuse   It is known that a substantial number, perhaps one-half (Volkow, 2009), of people with schizophrenia have a comorbid substance use disorder. Given what is known about the relationship between alcohol and violence, the combination of schizophrenia and alcohol abuse may represent a heightened risk of violence. A Swedish longitudinal study reported by Fazel, Grann, Carlström, Lichtenstein, and Långström (2009) investigated the relationship between schizophrenia, substance abuse, and violent crime. Fazel et al. compared the level of convictions for a violent crime of over 8,000 people with a diagnosis of schizophrenia with a non-schizophrenic control group drawn from the general population. There was a higher prevalence of violent crime among those with schizophrenia (13.2%) than among the controls (5.3%). However, Fazel et al. noted that in those cases where the schizophrenia was comorbid with substance abuse the rate of violent offending increased threefold.

Another longitudinal study was conducted in America by Elbogen and Johnson (2009). This study gathered a wide range of clinical, criminological and personal data at first contact then again at a two-year follow-up with a cohort of 34,653 patients. The data analysis was directed at identifying predictors of any violence which had occurred in the interval between the two points at which data were collected. Elbogen and Johnson reported that on its own severe mental illness alone is *not* a strong predictor of violence. However, when severe mental illness is comorbid with substance abuse and dependence so the risk of violence increases. Thus, it appears that alcohol and other substance use disorders are the most powerful risk factors, with schizophrenia and other psychoses adding relatively little to the risk of violence associated with substance abuse alone (Fazel, Gulati, Linsell, Geddes, & Grann, 2009; Steadman et al., 1998). Elbogen and Johnson reach the view that it is not correct to accept the position that violence among those with a mental illness is directly caused by the mental illness. A more reasonable view is that mental illness may contribute to the risk of violence, but that a full understanding of the causes of violence among those with a mental illness must include complex interactions between a range of individual and situational factors. There may be, for example, factors such as social deprivation which are common to violence and schizophrenia and so play a similar aetiological role.

However, a finer-grained view of schizophrenia, rather than a blunt dichotomous categorisation of schizophrenic/non-schizophrenic, may show that there are certain symptoms of schizophrenia, not experienced by all those with schizophrenia, that have the potential to be considered as specific predictors of violence. The phenomenon of "control/threat override" symptoms, often manifest as delusions that others are trying to cause you harm or control your thinking and actions, may be a causal factors in violence (Braham, Trower, & Birchwood, 2004; Bucci et al., 2013). Similarly, an overtly hostile attribution bias may also play a role in violence by those with schizophrenia (Harris, Oakley, & Picchioni, 2014).

Another type of delusion is seen in *Capgras' syndrome*, which is a type of *delusional misidentification syndrome* (DMS; see Christodoulou, 1991) marked by the false belief that imposters have taken the place of familiar people. In Capgras' syndrome the individual believes that familiar people have been replaced by a double who is physically identical to the original person but quite different psychologically. While people with DMS are rare, those individuals who experience this delusion are at heightened risk for both verbal and physical violence (De Pauw & Szulecka, 1998) including murder (Carabellese, Rocca, Candelli, & Catanesi, 2014). Finally, as with other populations, aspects of emotional functioning such as anger (Reagu, Jones, Kumari, & Taylor, 2013) and emotional empathy (Bragado-Jimenez & Taylor, 2012) may play a role in explaining violence by people with schizophrenia.

Personality Disorder and violence   Another aspect of mental health which has attracted attention is the association between Personality Disorder (PD) and violence. Of the various types of PD, Antisocial Personality Disorder (APD) is particularly evident in offender populations, including mentally disordered offenders. The DSM-IV-TR diagnostic criteria for APD (American Psychiatric Association, 2000) highlight the defining features of APD for those over the age of 18 years as an indifference to the rights of other people, impulsive verbal and physical aggression, involvement in fights, no remorse for victims, and an inability to maintain employment.

APD is associated with a range of crimes, including violent crimes, and is a strong predictor of recidivism, especially when comorbid with substance use disorders (Roberts & Coid, 2010; Walter, Wiesbeck, Dittmann, & Graf, 2010). A variation on the theme of PD is to be found with psychopathic disorder.

Psychopathic disorder   The modern conception of psychopathy stems from work of the American psychiatrist Hervey Milton Cleckley. Cleckley (1941) describes the psychopath as a superficially sociable and charming individual who uses these attributes as a "mask" for their total disregard for other people's feelings. Hare (1980) reported a factor analysis of data derived from the Cleckley criteria. This analysis yielded the five factors at the heart of the construct of psychopathy: (1) an inability to develop warm, empathic relationships; (2) an unstable lifestyle; (3) an inability to accept responsibility for antisocial behaviour; (4) an absence of intellectual and psychiatric problems; (5) weak behavioural control.

Hare (1980) used this analysis to formulate a scale for the assessment of psychopathy. This scale, the items on which are summarised in Box 1.2, eventually became the 20-item Psychopathy Checklist (PCL; Hare, 1991), later revised (PCL-R; Hare, 2003).

Box 1.2   Characteristics of the Psychopath

1   Glibness/superficial charm
2   Previous diagnosis as a psychopath (or similar)
3   Egocentricity/grandiose sense of self-worth
4   Proneness to boredom/low frustration tolerance
5   Pathological lying and deception
6   Conning/lack of sincerity
7   Lack of remorse or guilt
8   Lack of affect and emotional depth
9   Callous/lack of empathy
10   Parasitic lifestyle
11   Short-tempered/poor behavioural controls
12   Promiscuous sexual behaviour
13   Early behaviour problems
14   Lack of realistic long-term plans
15   Impulsivity
16   Irresponsible behaviour as a parent
17   Frequent marital relationships
18   Juvenile delinquency
19   Poor probation or parole risk
20   Failure to accept responsibility for own actions
21   Many types of offence
22   Drug or alcohol abuse is not a direct cause of antisocial behaviour

Source: From Hare, 1980. Reproduced with permission of Elsevier.

The PCL-R is widely used in clinical forensic assessment, particularly to assess the likelihood of future violence (Lestico, Salekin, DeCoster, & Rogers, 2008). The PCL-R is used with women as well as men (Weizmann-Henelius et al., 2010), with children and adolescents (Stockdale, Olver, & Wong, 2010), and with mentally disordered offenders (Vitacco, Rogers, Neumann, Harrison, & Vincent, 2005).

In summary, there is clearly a great deal for theory and research to address in seeking to refine our understanding of the association between mental health and violence (Steinert & Whittington, 2013).

Interpersonal Violence

It is evident that the topic of violence is both complex and diverse. However, in seeking to understand the actions of the violent individual it is important not to lose sight of the fact that interpersonal violence has a social dimension. Acts of interpersonal violence involve one or more aggressors and victims, sometimes accompanied by bystanders, in a social exchange. One way to emphasise the social nature of the interpersonal violence is through the application of the notion of a *situated transaction*. Luckenbill (1977), using the example of homicide, explains that: "By definition, criminal homicide is a collective transaction. An offender, victim, and possibly an audience engage in an interchange which leaves the victim dead. Furthermore, these transactions are typically situated, for participants interact in a common physical territory" (p. 176).

Luckenbill's approach

To investigate the nature of transactions leading to homicide Luckenbill (1977) analysed the official documents in 70 cases of murder committed in a county of the state of California. Luckenbill explains that:

> All official documents pertaining to these cases were secured. The character of the larger occasion as well as the organization and development of the fateful transaction were reconstructed from the content analysis of police, probation, psychiatric, and witness reports, offender interviews, victim statements, and grand jury and court testimony. These materials included information on the major and minor participants; who said and did what to whom; the chronology of dialogue and action; and the physical comportment of the participants. (p. 177)

The use of multiple sources of information, via the various types of documentation, allowed any inconsistencies in the evidence to be controlled in the analysis. Luckenbill reports that most of the murders occurred during leisure time (i.e., between the hours of 6 p.m. and 2 a.m.), and at weekends. It follows that the murders most often took place in the settings where people spend their leisure time, that is at home, in a bar, or on the street with friends or cruising in a car. In over 60% of cases, the offender and victim were in some way related—married, family, partner, or friend; in the other cases the offender and victim were variously enemies, acquaintances, or strangers.

In an illustration of the *bystander effect*, Luckenbill notes that when the offender and victim were not closely acquainted, either one or both were accompanied by a family member, friends, or partners.

Against these background details of who, where, and when, Luckenbill was concerned with the transactions, the dynamic interplay, between the offender, the victim, and (when present) the bystanders. As outlined in Box 1.3, Luckenbill described six stages which culminated in murder.

Box 1.3   Stages in Transaction Leading to Murder

Stage 1. The eventual victim makes the first move, a word, an action or a refusal to comply with a request. This move may take place in front of other people, both acquaintances and strangers.

Stage 2. The eventual offender perceives the victim's words or actions as a personal insult.

Stage 3. The offender stands their ground, seeks affirmation of the perceived affront and, in most cases, retaliates with an insult and issues a verbal or physical challenge to the victim. In a small number of cases the offender has killed the victim at this point.

Stage 4. The surviving victims are now in a similarly problematic position to that previously experienced by the offender: they can either respond to the challenge, apologise, or leave the situation. The last choice comes at the cost of "losing face" and displaying weakness in front of those present. When the victim elects to stand firm the situation escalates so that victim and offender enter a manner of "working agreement" that violence is appropriate.

Stage 5. With the agreement made, the offender, and in some cases the victim, are committed to combat. In many cases weapons are available with which to reinforce verbal threats and defeat the victim. In just over one-third of cases the offenders have brought hand guns or knives with them which they put to use to inflict the fatal blow. In other instances the offender has either temporarily left the situation to return with a firearm or knife, or they have used an available object, such as a pillow, telephone cord, beer glass, or baseball bat, as a weapon. In just over one-half of cases the offender has killed the victim quickly, with a single shot or stab; in the remainder the fight has been two-sided, with one or both armed, and after an exchange of blows the victim has fallen.

Stage 6. With the victim dead, the offender ends the transaction in one of three ways: (1) in over one-half of the cases they flee the scene; (2) in about one-third of cases they voluntarily remain waiting for the police; (3) in the remaining cases they are restrained by bystanders pending the arrival of the police.

Source: After Luckenbill, 1977.

It is not difficult to flesh out the details of a typical scene exemplifying the six stages (expletives deleted): an insult is uttered in a crowded bar: the offender-to-be hears some remark and pointedly asks the victim-to-be "What did you just *******say?"; the victim disparagingly replies "What the **** is it to you?"; the offender steps up to the mark, "You ****, you think you can make something of it?"; "Any time you ******* like", replies the victim; a punch is thrown, a knife brandished, a shot fired; the victim lies dead.

The stages described by Luckenbill are not, of course, relevant to all murders. Savitz, Kumar, and Zahn (1991) estimated that about 60% of homicides in Philadelphia were a Luckenbill-type "character contest" or "contest of wills". In a similar study, Deibert and Miethe (2003) reported an analysis of 185 dispute-related assaults, finding that character contests were significantly more likely to be found in disputes involving men rather than women, although they are to be found among female offenders and also among older as well as younger people. Deibert and Miethe also found that such character-laden disputes are to be found more often in public rather than private settings. While such disputes are a fruitful source of aggressive behaviour, of course not all disputes end in homicide. As exemplified by a typical public dispute, when customers are aggressive towards service providers the aggression is mainly verbal, sometimes accompanied by physical aggression or sexual harassment (Yagil, 2008).

Luckenbill's analysis is a potentially rich ground for social psychology but there are several additional points to be made. The first lies the notion that the victim is complicit, indeed may actually have precipitated, their own injuries and death. It is not difficult to see how this view could be taken as "blaming the victim", particularly when the victim is much weaker than their assailant. Luckenbill is sensitive to this issue, as is seen in his analysis of cases where the victim refused to comply with the offender's demands. "The offender subsequently interpreted the victim's action as a denial of his ability or right to command obedience. This was illustrated in transactions where parents murdered their children. When the parent's request that the child eat dinner, stop screaming, or take a bath went unheeded, the parent subsequently interpreted the child's activity as a challenge to rightful authority" (1977, p. 180). Although the child plays a role in such transactions, the responsibility for what happens clearly rests with the offender.

However, a study reported by Muftić and Hunt (2013) of 895 homicides in Dallas, Texas, found a substantial number of the victims in victim-precipitated homicides were also known offenders with similar characteristics to their assailant. Muftić and Hunt suggest that: "It is more likely that within victim precipitated acts it is victim-offenders, and not nonoffending victims, who are inciting offenders, as found in this study. Within this context there may be a lessened perception of victim blaming" (p. 250).

It is evident that, for both offender and victim, the perception of the other person's actions and intent plays an important role in the transactions. As Luckenbill points out, these perceptions are not necessarily accurate and, given the context, it is not difficult to see how misperceptions may arise. If we refer to models of social information-processing (cf. Crick & Dodge, 1994; Dodge, 1986), there are several situational factors present that may sway perceptions in interactions of the type described by Luckenbill. First, there may well be the omnipresent bystanders who offer their version of what is happening and how one or both of the protagonists should respond. Second, as the transaction progresses through the stages so emotions are likely to be aroused: one or both of those involved may become angry, excited, or anxious as violence draws nearer, so narrowing the focus of their attention and impeding their cognitive functioning with regard to thinking of ways to resolve the situation (cf. Novaco & Welsh, 1989). Third, given the location of many of the incidents, it is highly likely that all of those involved, offender, victim, and bystanders, will have been drinking. One of the effects of alcohol is the attenuation of aspects of cognitive functioning such as person perception and social problem-solving (Giancola, Duke, & Ritz, 2011). This particular effect of alcohol acts to increase the likelihood of misperceptions of the words and actions of others, particularly in terms of imputing hostile intent, and restricting thinking with regard to resolving the conflict without resorting to violence.

After Luckenbill

Luckenbill and Doyle (1989) moved on to develop *grievance escalation theory*, proposing that there are three stages in the process whereby grievances are escalated. Stage 1 is termed "naming" and is seen when the victim of a harmful act blames the aggressor and holds them personally responsible for what's happened. At stage 2, called "claiming", the victim demands reparation from the aggressor, and if that is not forthcoming then there is escalation to the final stage in the use of force. Luckenbill and Doyle suggest that some grievances escalate into violence because of the contribution of the psychological characteristics of *disputatiousness*, a willingness to seek revenge and maintain the grievance, and *aggressiveness* in the sense of believing that violence is a means of solving problems and being willing to use violence.

An Australian study of violent prisoners reported by Kelty, Hall, and O'Brien-Malone (2012) found that the grievances which led to violence were frequently a consequence of psychological harm caused, for example, by broken promises and insults. Further, in another instance of the bystander effect, the men had been encouraged to use violence and even provided with weapons by friends and girlfriends. However, as suggested by Vandello, Ransom, Hettinger, and Askew (2009), men may be unreliable in their estimates of both the aggressiveness of their peers and in the attractiveness of violence to women.

The stance taken by Luckenbill in focusing on the situational aspects of the interaction sits comfortably within the established situational analysis approach to theory and research within criminology generally (Birkbeck & LaFree, 1993) and violence specifically (Felson & Steadman, 1983). Luckenbill's approach has been taken a stage further by Collins with the notion of *micro-sociological dynamics* in violent encounters (Collins, 2008, 2013). Collins suggests that at the tipping point between violence and non-violence those involved experience a state of confrontational tension or fear. In most instances this shared emotional tension acts as a barrier and the protagonists step back from violence. However, this tension may be bypassed so that an act of violence takes place. Collins (2013) suggests that there are four principal ways by which this bypass can take place: "(1) finding a weak victim, especially a victim who is emotionally dominated; (2) orienting to an audience that encourages a small number of performers of violence; (3) remaining at a distance to launch weapons without having to confront the enemy face-to-face; (4) a clandestine approach which pretends there is no conflict until the very last instant" (p. 136). The first two of the above are most closely associated with interpersonal violence; the latter two with "violence at a distance" as found in warfare or terrorism (see also Dutton, 2012).

Conclusion

From both a psychological and a social perspective it is clear that interpersonal violence is a complex social phenomenon. There are multi-faceted theories encompassing behaviour, cognition, and emotion, alongside the covarying influences of drugs, particularly alcohol, the state of the individual's mental health, and the role of bystanders. Interpersonal violence may occur in several different settings and it can take many forms, ranging from what we might think of as "everyday violence" to highly serious acts which inflict significant harm, even death. The next chapter moves on to examine what we may think of as the lower end of the seriousness scale considering the forms of violence we have learned to tolerate, even accept, as simply being part of our everyday lives.

2

"Everyday" Violence

Some types of interpersonal violence, including both verbal and psychological violence, are so pervasive that we have learned to tolerate, even accept, them to such a degree that we are almost habituated to their presence. Thus, some types of violence have in effect become part of our everyday lives. Sabo et al. (2014) use the term "everyday violence" in the context of acts of violence which have become normalised in the lives of those who are exposed to and experience such acts. This "everyday" violence, or *low-level aggression* to use Goldstein's (2002) terminology, may take the form of interpersonal violence and will be discussed here in the context of bullying, road rage, violence and sport, violence towards animals, and corporal punishment of children.

It should be stated emphatically at the outset that the terms "low-level" and "everyday" are not used here in a pejorative sense, as if seeking to minimise the harm which such behaviour can cause. Indeed, as Jay (2009) notes with reference to verbal aggression, "Harms experienced by victims of hateful speech . . . include psychological and physiological symptoms similar to post-traumatic stress disorder (PTSD): panic, fear, anxiety, nightmares, intrusive thoughts of intimidation and denigration" (p. 83).

We begin consideration of everyday violence by looking at bullying in its various forms and the settings in which it can take place.

Bullying

The behaviour of the group in preying on an individual is by no means exclusive to humans. In the wider animal kingdom there is the phenomenon of *mobbing*, as described by Lorenz (1966), which is a behaviour which occurs when large

The Psychology of Interpersonal Violence, First Edition. Clive R. Hollin.
© 2016 John Wiley & Sons, Ltd. Published 2016 by John Wiley & Sons, Ltd.

numbers of a species group together, or *mob*, to target an individual animal. For example, mobbing is seen when large numbers of birds incessantly harry a predator in order to protect their young. This behaviour may be highly specialised to the extent that some birds, such as gulls and crows which breed in colonies, have specific mobbing calls which carry over long distances to summon assistance when a predator has been observed. It is arguable from an evolutionary perspective that bullying is a human form of mobbing and, indeed, the term is sometimes used in this context within the bullying literature (e.g., Shallcross, Sheehan, & Ramsay, 2008). In keeping with this perspective, Salmivalli (2010) suggests that human bullying is a group activity, involving a group of people, such as a peer group or a school class, ill-treating an individual.

There is a substantial literature given to the topic of bullying in humans, ranging through issues of definition, theoretical understanding, psychological factors, and prevention (Hansen, Steenberg, Palic, & Elklit, 2012; Olweus, 2013; Smith & Jones, 2012). The types of behaviour that are generally classed as bullying fall into several broad categories. The distinction has been drawn between direct and indirect forms of bullying (Carbone-Lopez, Esbensen, & Brick, 2010; Card, Stucky, Sawalani, & Little, 2008). *Direct bullying* is characterised by physical and verbal violence, typically pushing and hitting, name-calling, and threats of physical violence. On the other hand, *indirect bullying* is psychological rather than physical in nature: the aim is often to set the victim apart from their peers, typically by spreading stories and starting rumours, so souring their social relationships. Indirect bullying is also referred to as *relational bullying*, a contemporary form of which has become known as *cyberbullying* (Campbell, 2005).

No matter what form it takes, there is a general consensus regarding the defining characteristics of bullying. First, there is intent, such that the aggressor means to inflict harm on another person through their actions. Second, the aggressive behaviour is not an isolated event but occurs repetitively over a period of weeks, months, or even longer. Third, the bullying is directed against a vulnerable individual who is unable to defend him or herself against the aggressor's actions.

The obvious place for bullying to take place is where substantial numbers of people consistently gather for reasonably long periods of time. In the case of children and adolescents this place is likely to be their school, while for adults it may be their workplace.

Bullying at School

Hopkins, Taylor, Bowen, and Wood (2013) have shown that the defining features of bullying as described above are clearly understood by children. Hopkins et al. asked a sample of male and female school pupils, aged from 11 to 17 years, about their understanding of terms such as aggression, bullying, and violence. They found that the pupils understood the terms in the same way as they are used in the research literature. This finding indicates a good level of correspondence between the research literature and pupils' experiences: this suggests, in turn, that the research has a reasonable level of validity. The diversity of the research into bullying very much suggests that it is an issue with no respect for international boundaries (e.g., Mlisa, Ward, Flisher, & Lombard, 2008; Olweus, 2011; Wang, Iannotti, Tonja, & Nansel, 2009; Wolke, Woods, Bloomfield, & Karstadt, 2000). This point is reinforced by the findings of Due et al. (2005), who conducted a large-scale survey of the prevalence of bullying, with a sample averaging over 4,000 11–15-year-old school pupils per country, across 28 Western industrialised countries. They found that 18% of the boys and 15% of the girls reported being bullied during their current school term.

It is evident that levels of bullying vary from school to school and over time within the same school and may occur in various contexts, including school sports (Steinfeldt, Vaughan, LaFollette, & Steinfeldt, 2012). This naturally occurring pattern may be a result of the changes in pupils, both individually and in terms of school entrants and leavers, that occur over time. Alternatively, it may be that there is something about the qualities of a school at a given time that make bullying more or less likely to occur. What are the qualities of the individual pupil and the school environment that are instrumental in bringing about bullying?

School bullies

It is tempting to think in terms of a dichotomy, categorising children as either bullies or victims. In fact there are three types of children with regard to bullying: (1) children who are bullies; (2) children who are victimised by bullies; (3) children who are both bullies and victims. This three-way divide is clearly seen in a study of bullying in a large sample of primary school children (aged 6–9 years) reported by Wolke et al. (2000). They reported that 4.3% of the children were bullies, 39.8% were victims of bullying, and 10.2% were frequently both bullied and victimised.

Wang et al. (2009) noted some gender variations in patterns of bullying. The boys in their study were more likely to be involved in direct physical or verbal bullying, while the girls were more likely to take part in relational bullying. This finding is in keeping with the general finding that boys are more involved in direct bullying, while girls are more likely to be involved in indirect bullying (Bjorkqvist, 1994; Crapanzano, Frick, & Terranova, 2010; Pepler, Craig, Yuile, & Connolly, 2004). Wang et al. also noted that the pupils' level of social behaviour was associated with bullying. Those pupils who had a high number of friends were more likely to be involved in bullying and correspondingly less likely to be victimised. A combination of individual characteristics, such as low levels of depression and high self-esteem, alongside engagement at school and an emotionally supportive family, may increase a child's resilience to bullying (Sapouna & Wolke, 2013; Ttofi, Bowes, Farrington, & Lösel, 2014).

The question of what rewards bullying has been addressed in several studies, leading to the identification of three main goals: (1) to be accepted by the wider social group; (2) as a means of gaining social status; (3) as a means of countering perceived provocation from the victims (Wilton & Campbell, 2011). It is apparent that these reasons for bullying all have a social dimension, in keeping with the view that school bullying is essentially a group activity (e.g., Goldstein, 2002). Further, bullies may seize on some characteristic of the victim, such as their race, sexuality, or a chronic health problem, which defines them as a member of a minority group within the school (Rivers, 2001; Scherr & Lawson, 2010; Sentenac et al., 2011; Swearer, Turner, Givens, & Pollock, 2008). The act of bullying may therefore be seen as a complex social act involving not only the bullies and their victims but also other members of the social group who may variously act as bystanders, facilitators, challengers of the bullying, or supporters of the victim.

The psychology of the bully

Farrington and Baldry (2010) have reviewed a range of risk factors for school bullying encompassing behavioural, individual, family, and socio-economic factors. They reported several risk factors, as variously noted by peers, teachers, the children's mothers, direct measurement, and archival records (in some cases these sources were combined to identify a risk factor), that distinguished bullies and non-bullies at ages 8–10 years. In terms of behavioural differences the bullies showed higher levels of troublesome and antisocial behaviour than their non-bullying peers. Farrington and Baldry note that alongside low empathy, hyperactivity, low verbal IQ, and low school attainment, some bullies also have low self-esteem. However, perhaps contrary to stereotype, the smaller boys were the more aggressive so that male bullies were physically shorter and weighed less than non-bullies. Farrington and Baldry also noted that a convicted parent was a family factor which distinguished bullies from non-bullies. Lereya, Samara, and Wolke (2013) found that for children involved in bullying, including children who bully, victims of bullying and bully/victims were more likely to be experience negative parenting including both abuse and neglect.

The evidence on the popularity of bullies is mixed, with some studies suggesting that bullies are popular with their peers (although not their victims) while other studies find that bullies are unpopular. This discrepancy may, in part at least, be explicable in terms of methodology: self-report studies tend to find that bullies perceive themselves as popular, while studies employing peer ratings of popularity tend to suggest that bullies are unpopular. However, not all bullies enjoy high levels of psychological adjustment, as seen by their adverse levels of self-esteem and enjoyment of life and heightened feelings of stress (Estévez, Murgui, & Musitu, 2009).

As with the aetiology of aggression and violence generally, there are interactions between individual and social factors that culminate specifically in bullying. It is not surprising therefore that there is considerable overlap between the factors that predict violence and bullying. While bullying is widespread it is not equally distributed across schools. There are some schools where there is a high frequency of bullying and other schools which are free from bullying. It is possible that this variation may be explained by variations in pupils across schools, but it may also be explicable by considering environmental variables. A body of research has therefore looked at whether there are any characteristics common to those schools where bullying takes place.

Bullying schools

In seeking to understand the role of the school environment with regard to the risk of bullying the notion of *school climate* has received attention (Stewart, 2003). However, as Steffgen, Recchia, and Viechtbauer (2013) point out, the term "school climate" is difficult to define and in practice may encompass a wide range of factors. Thus, school climate may relate among others to the level and type of interpersonal relationships between teachers and students, the degree of students' positive or negative attachment to the school and their perceptions of threat and feelings of fear, and to school security and management.

Steffgen, Recchia, and Viechtbauer (2013) conducted a meta-analysis of 36 studies investigating the relationship between perception of school climate and actual levels of school violence. They reported a moderate and negative effect size ($r = -.26$) indicating that as one variable changes so the other tends to shift in the opposite direction. The important question is: What moderates this effect? What are the characteristics of the pupils and the schools which are associated with the degree of bullying? Steffgen et al. found that their analyses were unable to provide an exact answer to this question: they suggest that the diversity of measures of both school climate and violence worked against their finding strong conclusions.

An American study reported by Zaykowski and Gunter (2012) utilised data from the Delaware School Survey to investigate the relationship between school climate and incidents involving serious violence such as those involving weapons, and minor acts of violence including verbal abuse, threats, and bullying. For the less serious incidents, the overall probability of victimisation varied across schools, with greater explanatory power accorded to the individual rather than the school variables. However, Zaykowski and Gunter reported that racial minorities were at a greater risk of victimisation compared to white non-Hispanic students and that rates of victimisation were higher overall in schools where the pupils were mainly white. School climate variables did not impact at the level of minor victimisation.

Atria, Strohmeier, and Spiel (2007) make the point that when looking at rates of school bullying the unit of analysis is typically at the level of the whole school. This approach, they suggest, neglects the possibility that bullying may vary significantly across classes *within* the same school. If bullying is seen in terms of group behaviour then it not unreasonable to assume that classroom dynamics will vary across the same school and so the prevalence of classroom bullying will vary accordingly. Atria et al. investigated this possibility by asking pupils of different ages attending a range of schools in Austria to report any instances of bullying which they had experienced.

When the data were considered at school level, Atria et al. found rates of bullying which ranged between 5.4% and 12.8% for physical bullying, from 4.4% to 26.4% for verbal bullying, and from 6.2% to 11.7% for bullying as globally defined. As Atria et al. note, these figures for the whole school are what would be anticipated when set against the extant literature. However, when the unit of analysis shifted to the classroom a high variability of bullying became apparent, ranging from no bullying in some classes to 54.5% in the highest instance.

It is not clear why this variability across classes occurs, although there is a variety of potential explanations. At the group level, taking the classroom as the group, there may be variations in group cohesion or competitiveness which, in turn, may depend upon the pupil mix within the classroom. The behaviour of the teachers with regard to bullying is also potentially important both with regard to classroom management and teachers' relationships with parents. Indeed, an American study reported by Brown, Aalsma, and Ott (2013) found that when parents approached schools with concerns about their child being bullied they were on occasions met with resistance from the school. Brown et al. make the comment that "Our data suggest that all but one parent believed their child's victimization would continue even though they followed through in reporting bullying to their youth's school officials" (p. 513).

Bullying in the Workplace

The same types of bullying as found in schools—i.e., direct bullying, indirect (including relational) bullying, and cyberbullying—are evident in the workplace. Similarly, workplace bullying is also characterised by *intent, repetition*, and a *power imbalance* between the aggressor and their vulnerable victim. As with bullying in the classroom, it is impossible to say with any degree of certainty just how frequently workplace bullying occurs. There is ample evidence from surveys, however, to suggest that this manifestation of bullying is common across a range of professions and types of organisation (e.g., Einarsen, Hoel, Zapf, & Cooper, 2003; Sanner-Stiehr & Ward-Smith, 2103; Zapf, Einarsen, Hoel, & Vartia, 2003).

Samnani and Singh (2012) offer a succinct summary of the behaviours that constitute workplace bullying:

> These behaviors range from subtle acts such as gossip, personal jokes, withholding critical information, and ostracism (i.e., giving the silent treatment) to overt acts, such as insults, being told to quit one's job, and violence. The behaviors also range from work-related acts such as excessive workloads, criticism of work, and excessive monitoring of work to person-related forms such as belittling, personal jokes, and aggression. (p. 582)

Lutgen-Sandvik and Tracy (2012) are in agreement with Samnani and Singh and suggest that bullying in this context has multiple victims: "Workplace bullying is a toxic combination of unrelenting emotional abuse, social ostracism, interactional

Box 2.1 Categories of Workplace Bullying

1 Open *"calling out"* of the target because they are in some way different to the majority, or not part of the in-group because of previous instances of bullying.

2 *"Scapegoating"* to draw attention to the target, and sometimes away from the bully, to account for a failure: this behaviour may pose a threat to the scapegoat's professional standing.

3 *Sexual harassment* by an individual with greater power or a higher position in the organisational hierarchy (this form of bullying may be either within or between genders).

4 *Increasing work pressure and workload* by imposing, for example, impossible deadlines for completion of tasks and overloading with work compared to others in the workplace with accompanying threats if the work is not completed on time.

5 *Isolating* the targeted by denying them access to opportunities for advancement, or withholding the information necessary for doing a good job, or physically moving them away from other workers.

6 *"Destabilisation"* by not giving credit when earned, setting the target up to fail at impossible tasks and then continually reminding them of their failures.

7 *Verbal and physical aggression* towards the target.

Source: After Harvey et al., 2006.

terrorizing, and other destructive communication that erodes organizational health and damages employee well-being" (p. 5). As shown in Box 2.1, Harvey, Heames, Richey, and Leonard (2006) add more detail in classifying the bullying acts found in the workplace into seven types.

The different bullying tactics shown in Box 2.1 may be carried out in combination so that the victim experiences two or more types of bullying. Harvey et al. (2006) address the issue of whether workplace bullies graduate from the schoolyard to the boardroom. They note that there are many similarities between bullying in these two different environments—in relation to the characteristics of the organisation, the bully, and the victim—all of which suggests a continuum of behaviour across settings. If aggression is a stable aspect of an individual's behaviour which is likely to emerge given appropriate environmental conditions this proposal makes perfect sense. As discussed below, there are several empirical longer-term investigations which provide support for the temporal continuity of the aggressive behaviours that constitute bullying.

Sexual harassment in the workplace is bullying which uses sex-related behaviours. This sexualised bullying is typically carried out by the victim's supervisor or a co-worker (although the bully may be an individual such as a customer) which is viewed by the victim as unwanted and threatening. Fitzgerald, Gelfand, and Drasgow (1995) suggest that sexual harassment may occur in one of three forms: (1) *gender harassment*, which encompasses behaviours, both verbal and nonverbal, such as sexual taunting, insults and gestures, and comments about appearance, alongside the overt display of pornography, which may be hostile as well as insulting and degrading; (2) *unwanted sexual attention*, which may be intended to initiate sexual co-operation and take the form of unwanted physical contact or persistent requests for a date; (3) *sexual coercion*, which occurs when the harassment and attention are combined with threats or bribes associated with workplace performance and rewards such as promotion.

In their review of the research literature on workplace bullying, Samnani and Singh (2012) distinguish four levels at which bullying may occur: these four are (1) individual level; (2) group level; (3) organisational level; and (4) societal level. This approach to organising the literature is helpful in considering what is known about both bullies and victims.

Individual

As with the majority of instances of aggressive and violent behaviour, most bullying, including workplace bullying, is carried out by men. Women may be more likely to be the victims of bullying (Salin, 2003) particularly sexual harassment (McLaughlin, Uggena, & Blackstone, 2012). Those members of the workforce who are in the minority, typically a racial minority, are also at an increased risk of victimisation: a state of affairs that appears to be as likely in locations as diverse as South Wales (Lewis & Gunn, 2007) and Illinois (Fox & Stallworth, 2005).

Are there any personality characteristics which are particularly related to bullying? A Canadian study reported by Linton and Power (2013) found an overlap between the personalities of bullies and victims, "The majority of bully-typifying traits (Machiavellianism, narcissism, psychoticism, and the aggression measures) were associated with being a victim" (p. 741). This finding reinforces the point that regardless of context it is often difficult to separate aggressors and victims into neat categories. Parenthetically, in hierarchical organisations bullying may pass up and down the managerial chain of command. Thus, individual employees may be bullied by those in higher positions of authority while they, in turn, bully individuals below them in the managerial pecking order. Yet further, those individuals who work at a high rate, so called *workaholics*, may be more likely to become involved in interpersonal conflicts that escalate into aggressive encounters with colleagues and with supervisees (Balducci, Cecchin, Fraccaroli, & Schaufeli, 2012).

An Australian study reported by Jenkins, Zapf, Winefield, and Sarris (2012) carried out interviews (telephone and face-to-face) with 24 managers from a range of types of organisation all of whom had been accused of bullying those they were responsible for managing. In keeping with the blurring of the division between bully and victim, Jenkins et al. note that two-thirds of the managers said that they were themselves being bullied. This managerial bullying came from either their own manager or, as "upward bullying", from the employees they managed. In accounting for the allegations against them, the managers described how the work environment contributed by placing them in positions for which they were not trained or by having to cope with staff shortages. The dynamic, interactive nature of bullying is seen in the managers' view that sometimes their own behaviour was labelled as bullying when, as they saw it, they were managing conflict in an acceptable manner as the situation demanded. Thus, the managers said that such times it was the staff who were acting as bullies towards them (upward bullying) rather than vice versa: although, doubtless, the staff would have expressed a contrary view.

Group

Samnani and Singh identify several factors associated with bullying at the level of the group: these factors are the *group norms* which govern the behaviour of members of the group; *status inconsistency*, where an employee differs on the basis of age, race, or gender from other members of the group; and *situational factors* that produce stress and insecurity such as disagreements over how to complete a particular task.

It is true of any group of people engaged in a common task that over time behavioural norms will develop. These norms may be explicit, as when they are written down in the form of a code of conduct, or implicit, as seen in a shared understanding among members of the group of what is and is not acceptable behaviour. It is possible for a group to have bullying as a norm so that its occurrence is accepted simply as the way life functions. It is also true that group norms may be broken by members of the group, leading to group disharmony, conflict, and bullying. The types of situation that can produce such a breakdown in group norms are when there is a complex task to complete, pressure to meet tight deadlines, or an organisational restructuring which threatens group members.

Organisation

As we move from the individual to the group and to the organisation, so the complexity of the factors involved in bullying increases accordingly. Thus, at an organisational level, as with "bullying schools", the factors associated with bullying are as diverse as the organisational culture, the management ethos, and how that translates into leadership and management practice functioning alongside policies which clearly delineate acceptable and unacceptable behaviour (Baillien, De Cuyper, & De Witte, 2011). A Swedish study reported by Oxenstierna, Elofsson, Gjerde, Hanson, and Theorell (2012) found that the risk of bullying increased during periods of organisational change and when conflicting demands were made on employees. Such difficult situations can be eased by good managerial decision-making or made worse by dictatorial leadership and an organisational attitude that staff are expendable.

Society

Does the individual's or the group's behaviour at work in some way mirror the national culture? This is a difficult question to answer and may invoke dubious national stereotypes, such as the highly industrious Germans and the super-efficient Japanese. However, different countries do have different employment laws which may impact upon the levels and types of bullying in the workplace.

As several prescient writers have noted, the speed of change in the world in which we live is so rapid that we are left dazzled and bemused by the continual need to reappraise our everyday lives (e.g., Kurzweil, 2005; Toffler, 1970). Sparks, Faragher, and Cooper (2001) reflect on the rapidly changing nature of the workplace in the twenty-first century. They point to the transforming power of information technology in the workplace, the force of globalisation in precipitating changes in work time, and the shifting nature of the workforce, with more women workers, dual-earner couples, and older workers (the latter particularly so as the age of retirement is no longer set in stone as in years gone by).

Whether at school or in the workplace, it is self-evident that bullying occurs when the environment is one that allows such behaviour to take place. However, not all bullying takes place in a physical environment: as technology advances so there are new arenas in which the bully can operate.

Cyberbullying

The phenomenon of cyberbullying, which may have both children and adults as victims, can take place in several ways as shown in Box 2.2. A related form of online activity, known as *trolling* or *cyber-trolling*, involves acting in a deceitful, negative, or troublesome way for no apparent purpose. Nonetheless, while not intended as bullying this type of activity has the potential to be perceived as bullying by those on the receiving end (Hardaker, 2010).

The cyberbully may make direct contact with their victim, typically through email or texting on a mobile phone, or make more publicly accessible contacts via social media, such as Facebook or MySpace, or through posts to blogs (Kowalski & Limber, 2007; Marsh, McGee, Nada-Raja, & Williams, 2010). The cyberbully has a range of strategies at their disposal to discomfort their victim: for example, they can pretend online to be another person to trick the victim into revealing personal information, either in text or photographs, which they then make public.

As with research into the interaction between technology, technological advances, and antisocial and criminal behaviour generally, the study of cyberbullying has passed through several stages to reach the point where it is now viewed as a significant form of bullying alongside the traditional types (Calvete, Orue, Estévez, Villardón, & Padilla, 2010; Patchin & Hinduja, 2006). As with most antisocial and criminal behaviour, it is impossible to state exactly the extent to which cyberbullying takes place. However, surveys conducted in several countries can give an estimate of the extent of the issue.

Box 2.2 Manifestations of Cyberbullying

Cyberstalking: continued online harassment and threatening messages.
Denigration: sending untrue or harmful statements.
Flaming: distributing offensive messages.
Online harassment: repeated distribution of offensive messages.
Outing: distributing sensitive or private information which the individual would prefer to keep private.
Impersonation: pretending to be someone else for malicious purposes.
Trickery: fooling someone into revealing personal information which is then distributed.

An American survey of 3,767 students reported by Kowalski, Limber, and Agatston (2008) noted that 1 in 4 girls and over 1 in 10 boys said they had been bullied via an electronic medium at least once over the past two months. In a study carried out in Canada with a sample of 264 school pupils aged 12 to 13 years, Li (2006) found that the rate of victimisation of cyberbullying was highly similar for males (25%) and females (25.6%).

Rivers and Noret (2010) carried out a survey of bullying among 11–13-year-old pupils in 13 secondary schools in the north of England. This survey, conducted annually between 2002 and 2006, was concerned specifically with bullying via text and email. Rivers and Noret found that over the five years spanned by the research, the use of text and email to send nasty or threatening messages was a real and increasing problem in the schools. This form of bullying particularly affected girls, twice as many of whom—20.8% compared to 10.3%—received bullying messages at least once a school term compared to the boys. Rivers and Noret also found gender differences in the patterns and content of bullying. The males who received the bullying texts and email messages were more likely than the females also to be a victim of direct physical bullying. However, although they were not directly bullied, girls who received the bullying messages were unpopular with their peers. Rivers and Noret state that the males were more likely to receive hate-related messages such as "I h 8 u" and "You fucking clown-faced bastard"; while the females experienced a great deal of name-calling, "I hate you, you fucking bitch" and "You're a slag".

The initial studies of cyberbullying, as may be expected, were focused on describing and understanding this new manifestation of aggressive behaviour. This exploratory research has been followed by more detailed investigations of the perpetrators of the cyberbullying and its effects on victims (Dooley, Pyzalski, & Cross, 2009; Hinduja & Patchin, 2008; Schenk, Fremouw, & Keelan, 2013). Thus, as with traditional forms of bullying, boys were more likely to be cyberbullies, while girls were more likely to be cyber-victims (Wang et al., 2009). An American study reported by Marcum, Higgins, Freiburger, and Ricketts (2012) looked at male and female patterns of cyberbullying. As with traditional forms of bullying in which females are more likely to engage in non-confrontational forms of bullying that aims to hurt emotionally and psychologically, so the female cyberbullies more frequently posted online messages containing both true and false hurtful gossip.

Predicting cyberbullying

A focus of more contemporary research has been to search for any specific risk factors or predictors of cyberbullying. A large-scale Finnish study of cyberbullying reported by Sourander et al. (2010) was carried out with 2,214 Finnish male (1,046) and female (1,078) adolescents aged from 13 to 16 years. The percentages falling into the traditional three bullying categories were reported as: 4.8% were cyber-victims (6.0% female and 3.5% male); 7.4% were cyberbullies (5.6% female and 9.3% male); and 5.4% were cyberbully-victims (4.6% female and 5.8% male).

The social and psychological factors associated with cyberbullying revealed a high degree of overlap across these three groupings. The adolescents in the cyber-victims grouping were more likely to live in a family that did not contain two biological parents, they reported high levels of emotional and peer problems, physical ailments such as headaches, recurrent abdominal pain and sleeping difficulties, and said that they did not feel safe while at school. The adolescents in the cyberbully grouping had a more antisocial profile, as indicated by conduct problems, low prosocial behaviour, and frequent smoking and drunkenness, alongside difficulties associated with hyperactivity and frequent headaches. These adolescents also said that they did not feel safe at school. The final grouping, cyberbully-victims, showed all of the risk factors evident in the other two groupings.

As research in this area has matured so some thinking has moved in the direction of seeing cyberbullying as simply a new form of an old behaviour (Campbell, 2005; Olweus, 2012). This is not to say that the consequences of cyberbullying are any the less serious, rather that, in the same way that the availability of pornography on the Internet does not change the issues surrounding the production and effects of pornographic material, cyberbullying is simply bullying in a new guise. This point extends to the theoretical understanding of cyberbullying: an American study by Barlett and Gentile (2012) suggested that the practice of cyberbullying stems from positive attitudes towards cyberbullying, in turn related to attitudes that support bullying and aggression generally. However, Barlett and Gentile point to two distinctive features of cyberbullying which merit further attention. The first feature lies in the anonymity afforded to the cyberbully by their technological cloak; the second lies in the removal of the variations in physical and psychological strength that mediate real-world bullying.

The issue of anonymity has several correlates. The bully may not see the victim's distress and so not appreciate the pain their actions cause. Further, as the message is devoid of any interpersonal nuances of tone, expression, and other nonverbal cues so the chances of misperception are increased. A message intended as a joke may be read by the victim and others as sarcastic or insulting, with painful consequences for the victim, particularly if others join in with the bullying.

There are physical and psychological differences between individuals that play a role in defining their place in the social order. Some individuals are perceived as strong, physically and socially, others are afforded social status on the basis of the personal strengths. However, given the skills and the right equipment, anyone can anonymously and safely cyberbully another person, so even physically weak or lower-status children can put aside the real-world strength imbalance and set out to harm their peers.

The Effects of Bullying

Children

The effects of childhood bullying are evident across the lifespan (Ttofi & Farrington, 2008). It is a fundamental feature of human behaviour that we will avoid environments which causes pain and distress. Thus, students bullied at school will opt to spend their time elsewhere. A survey of school absenteeism in England was conducted by Brown, Clery, and Ferguson (2011) in which the distinction was made between bullying as the *primary* reason for absenteeism and bullying as one of a constellation of reasons for absence. The report estimates that "16,493 young people aged 11–15 are absent from state school, where bullying is the main reason for absence . . . We estimate 77,950 young people aged 11–15 are absent from state school, where bullying is a reason given for absence" (p. 5). Thus, substantial numbers of young people are absent from school at least in part because of bullying. As school absenteeism is itself a risk factor for further psychological and social difficulties in later life, including educational failure, this is patently a serious state of affairs for those involved.

The immediate effects of childhood bullying are seen in several adverse consequences such as lowered self-esteem, emotional problems, feelings of insecurity and personal threat at school (Wolke et al., 2000). In some instances the problems experienced by both female and male victims of bullying become even more serious, as seen with depression and suicide ideation (Turner, Exum, Brame, & Holt, 2013), self-harm (Lereya et al., 2013), and post-traumatic stress disorder symptomatology (Idsoe, Dyregrov, & Idsoe, 2012).

The association between bullying and aggression was considered by Thomas et al. (2006). They found that the development of aggressive behaviour in children was related to the experience of aggression in the classroom. Thomas et al. further reported that the degree of developmental impact of the exposure to aggression was related to the length and severity of the exposure. In extremis, bullying has been held to be an explanatory factor in school shootings such as that at Columbine High School in Colorado, USA (Hong, Lee, Park, & Faller, 2011).

The immediate consequences of bullying play out over the medium term with effects that include lowered educational attainment and an increased likelihood of involvement in both delinquency and drug use in both childhood and adolescence

(Lösel & Bender, 2011). The increased likelihood of delinquency among bullies appears to be the case for both males and females (Barker, Arseneault, Brendgen, Fontaine, & Maughan, 2008). In the longer term, the effects of bullying may reach into adulthood as, for example, with adverse effects on mental health, particularly a heightened risk of anxiety and depression, and difficulties in forming and maintaining relationships. With regard to violence, bullying is strongly associated with an elevated risk of violent conduct in later life. Ttofi, Farrington, and Lösel (2012) carried out a systematic review and meta-analyses of the evidence concerning the role of school bullying, both perpetration and victimisation, in predicting later aggression and violence. They found that carrying out bullying at school significantly increased the risk of violence six years later by approximately two-thirds. The effect of being a victim of bullying on later perpetration of violence was less— increasing the risk of later violence by approximately one-third—than for being a bully although it was still highly significant. It is possible that these adverse effects of bullying could persist into adulthood, although the evidence for this possibility is limited (Piquero, Piquero, Craig, & Clipper, 2013).

Workplace

As with school bullying, the victim of workplace bullying may experience psychological and physical reactions. These adverse reactions typically include anxiety and depression, which may escalate into panic attacks and suicidal thoughts, stress-related symptomatology such as feelings of a loss of control and being powerless, disturbed sleep, fluctuations in appetite, and angry outbursts, alongside physical health problems such as high blood pressure, chronic headaches, and stomach ailments. There is also a social dimension to victimisation, as evident in withdrawal from social contact with colleagues and a growing mistrust of managers and supervisors. Social contact is a two-way process in which colleagues may become distant, weakening the victim's support network, or where the victim may find themselves out of favour in professional circles. The glare of the spotlight is bound to attract attention, so that those on the periphery of the bullying become aware of the situation and the victim becomes the object of increasing public scrutiny and gossip.

The effects of bullying may spill over into the victim's home life, affecting their relationships with family and friends, so producing another set of problems. If the bullying has a sexual dimension then this may exacerbate the victim's reaction (Dionisi, Barling, & Dupré, 2012). The psychological and physical reactions noted above may be accompanied by feelings of personal and social violation alongside shame, guilt, and humiliation. A loss of sexual appetite may also impact on intimate relationships, so affecting home, social, or family life.

The effects of bullying are not cost-free: an unhappy employee is unlikely to be a productive employee. The effects of victimisation on work performance will, obviously, depend on the type of organisation: the bullied nurse may make mistakes that impact on patients' well-being, the bullied accountant makes financial mistakes affecting profits, the teaching and research of the bullied academic (oh the stories I could tell!) suffer in quality (Oravec, 2012). The individual's level of absenteeism may rise, so affecting their chances of promotion, or even leading to disciplinary actions and loss of employment with all the attendant effects on finance, family, career, and so on.

It may be the case that colleagues see what is happening to the victim, even reporting it to managers, but do not wish to be drawn personally into the conflict. Thus, a sense of distrust may spread within the workplace where people fear that they could be the next victim and, should that happen, do not trust the organisation to act on their behalf. In such an unpalatable climate people may feel that it is time to move on and, of course, the most able individuals will find it easiest to leave, so reducing the strength of the workforce.

Aggressive Driving

There are few road-users who have not witnessed or been involved in incidents of aggressive driving or what has colloquially become known as *road rage*, particularly when highly aggressive driving results in collisions and injury. As Harris and Houston (2010) point out, aggressive driving can take several forms, ranging from offensive hand gestures, excessive use of the horn, flashing headlights, tailgating, to even deliberately causing a collision. The actions of aggressive drivers are a cause of concern in many countries, including Australia (Lennon & Watson, 2011), Israel (Shamoa-Nir & Koslowsky, 2010), Pakistan (Shaikh, Shaikh, & Siddiqui, 2012), Romania (Săucan, Micle, Popa, & Oancea, 2012), the UK (Lajunen, Parker, & Stradling, 1998), and the USA (Mann et al., 2007).

Aggressive driving can cause both minor and major accidents, sometimes involving cars not directly involved in the initial incident, leading Houston, Harris, and Norman (2003) to define aggressive driving as "A dysfunctional pattern of social behaviors that constitutes a serious threat to public safety" (p. 269). The use of the term *road rage* to describe aggressive driving stems from the perception that the aggressive driver is reacting angrily to some misdemeanour, real or imagined, by a another driver. While this view is correct in some cases, Shamoa-Nir and Koslowsky (2010) note that sometimes the driver's aggressive behaviour is better described as instrumental rather than hostile aggression. Aggressive driving for instrumental purposes may, for example, have the aim of reaching one's destination as fast as possible despite hazards and obstacles on the road: this style of driving includes hazardous overtaking, weaving and cutting across lanes at traffic queues, and jumping traffic lights.

The motivations of aggressive drivers were considered in an Australian study reported by Lennon and Watson (2011), who interviewed 30 drivers, aged 18–49 years, about their experiences with aggressive driving. Analysis revealed that a key theme underpinning aggressive driving was the intention to manage or to change the other driver's behaviour. Within this overall intention there were two subthemes: the first was where the interviewee said that their aggressive driving was to display their disapproval of the other driver's actions; the second was to teach the other driver a retaliatory lesson so that they (the other driver) could become a better driver. Needless to say, such actions can have a far from didactic effect and may escalate the exchanges as the other driver responds to the aggressive driver.

A study conducted in Israel by Ruvio and Shoham (2011) looked at a wide range of variables associated with aggressive driving (AD): they concluded that "General aggression, compulsivity, risk attraction, impulsivity, negative attitudes about AD, viewing the car as an extension of the self, hedonic perceptions about driving, time pressures, and materialism were related to AD tendencies" (p. 1105).

As Ruvio and Shoham suggest, while the behaviour is context-specific, the individual, cognitive, and emotional factors inherent in aggressive driving are the same as in any other form of aggression. Thus, as with aggression generally, age and gender are involved in aggressive driving, with younger males most likely to drive aggressively, overestimating their driving ability while underestimating the risks (Balkmar & Joelsson, 2012; Roberts & Indermaur, 2005; Shinar & Compton, 2004). In addition, aggressive driving may be associated with psychological and behavioural problems (Malta, Blanchard, & Freidenberg, 2005; Sansone & Sansone, 2010; Sansone, Lam, & Wiederman, 2010), including the use of drugs and alcohol (Butters, Mann, & Smart, 2006; Mann, Smart, Stoduto, Adlaf, & Ialomiteanu, 2004).

Lennon, Watson, Arlidge, and Fraine (2011) pointed to the role of attributions in aggressive driving and in particular the difference between attributions about our own and others driving. When we are on the receiving end of bad driving we tend to make negative attributions about the other driver—"What an idiot", "They need to learn to some manners"—while we attribute out own bad driving to momentary errors of judgement or transitory states—"Whoops missed that sign there", "Gosh, I'm feeling tired"—rather than to stable aspects of our personality. The cognitive processes of aggressive drivers, not surprisingly, may be character-ised by high levels of hostility towards other road-users (Deffenbacher, White, & Lynch, 2004).

As implied by the term "road rage", anger is readily associated with aggressive driving. There is evidence to suggest that aggressive drivers have a high propensity to anger (Galovski, Malta, & Blanchard, 2006), although not all instances of aggres-sive driving can be ascribed to anger given that situational factors or other aspects of driver cognition may be of the most importance in a given incident (Ellison-Potter, Bell, & Deffenbacher, 2001). Nonetheless, as discussed in Chapter 1, anger can play an important role in aggression so that for the angry driver it increases the likelihood of perceiving the driving of others as aggressive, biases decision-making towards responding in type, and affects performance.

As shown in Box 2.3, Harris and Houston (2010) draw together the evidence to suggest that a range of situational and individual factors may overlap and interact to produce aggressive driving.

Box 2.3   Classification of Factors in Aggressive Driving

Environmental Aspects
Type of road
Traffic density
Weather conditions
Psychological Factors
Hostility
Sensation-seeking
Competitiveness
Gender
Social Factors
Passengers in driver's vehicle
Target vehicle has passengers
Target age and gender
Target status (inexpensive or expensive vehicle)
Temporal Factors
Time pressure
Time of day

Source: After Harris & Houston, 2010.

Overall, as is the case with aggression generally, aggressive driving is likely to be the outcome of a range of factors.

While aggressive driving may be a relatively recent manifestation of aggressive and violent behaviour, the exact opposite is true of the next form of everyday violence.

Violence Towards Animals

A characteristic of bullying is that the bully selects a vulnerable target to intimidate and to harm. The same is often true of another type of target, the animals with which, in one way or another, we share our lives. We humans are not the kindest of creatures when it comes to our fellow animals. There are many ways in which we inflict harm on a range of types of animal: we conduct scientific experiments in which animals suffer, we hunt for pleasure, we exploit animals as a resource, and we destroy the natural habitat of many animals for our own gain. Closer to home, we are cruel to the many types of domesticated animals with which we share our everyday lives. In considering the issue of cruelty to animals there are two broad areas of concern: first, the nature of this specific form of violence; second, the strength of the association between animal cruelty and interpersonal violence.

Cruelty to animals

In many parts of the world humans depend on domestic animals—we farm cows, pigs, and sheep for various products and many of us have animals as household pets—and we have a positive relationship with those animals. There are many affirmative aspects to pet ownership for both children and adults. For the developing child, Robin and ten Bensel (1985) suggest, the companionship of a pet can play an important role in socialisation. Robin and ten Bensel note that a pet gives a child a constant companion providing unconditional affection with which to share growing up. The child, perhaps guided by their parents, must learn to take responsibility for the well-being of their pet, to understand their pet's likes and dislikes, and eventually to cope with and understand the death of a pet. I know this all to be true from personal experience: my family has had a range of pets— including lizards, geckos, mice, guinea pigs, freshwater and tropical fish, dogs, and horses (do horses qualify as pets?)—which have given us all a great deal of pleasure and some tears.

The benefits of pets extend beyond children, and many adults have a close relationship with their cat or dog, and horse-owners may well develop a very close affiliation with their steed. Animals also contribute to our well-being and safety: for example, there are guide dogs for the blind and partially sighted, sniffer dogs that search out contraband, bombs, people trapped in buildings after earthquakes, and climbers and skiers lost in avalanches. Yet further, dogs help farmers round up sheep and, together with horses, form part of Her Majesty's Constabulary; animals are used in therapy, as seen with equine psychotherapy (Bachi, 2012). The list could go on and on; given these benefits, it is understandable that there is both public and academic (e.g., Beirne, 2009; Nurse, 2013) concern about cruelty towards animals.

However, there is nothing at all contemporary regarding concern about the way animals are treated. The extract below is taken from a letter in *The British Medical Journal* published on 6 February 1875.

> In addition to the forcible instances of cruelty to animals which you give in your article in last week's JOURNAL, permit me to jot down the following.
>
> 1   There is the one of the bearing-rein, which has been so much condemned in the daily press of late.
> 2   The practice of nicking and docking horses' tails, which is continually done. These operations are done to the manifest improvement of the appearance and carriage of the horse; still they cause pain, and are done to please fashion.
> 3   The practice of rounding foxhounds' ears, which means cutting off a considerable amount of the ears, so as to made the pack look uniform and light; it is, I am told, done in most kennels.
> 4   The practice of dubbing gamecocks. This consists of removing the skin and wattles from the throat, cheeks, and face of the birds, and the large comb on the head. This leaves a large surface which has to cicatrise. I am informed that no gamecock is

exhibited without having been "dubbed". Now, as cock-fighting is not permitted, surely this must be a most unnecessary act of cruelty, and is simply done at the behests of fashion.

Yours obediently,
Fishguard, February 2nd, 1875. J. HANCOCKE NWATHEN
(p. 191)

This nineteenth-century description of animal cruelty is as accurate today as it was when written. A survey of animal abuse in the state of Massachusetts over the period 1975–1996 (Arluke & Luke, 1997) found that the abuse, mainly perpetrated by young men, took the form of shooting, beating, stabbing, or throwing animals at solid objects. Dogs were the most frequently abused animal and they, together with cats, accounted for the large majority of abusive incidents. In the UK, the Annual Report from the Prosecutions Department of the Royal Society for the Prevention of Cruelty to Animals (RSPCA) makes harrowing reading (RSPCA, 2012).

The report states that in 2012 there were over 1 million calls to the RSPCA 24-hour cruelty line and over 4,000 convictions for offences against animals, with dogs the most abused animals. The cruelty took many forms, including hitting and beating, neglect, hoarding, and organising animal fights. The phenomenon of *hoarding* refers to the practice of keeping large numbers of animals in highly unsuitable conditions. The RSPCA report describes a case of a couple living with five children in their four-bedroom house along with 56 large dogs and a collection of cats, birds, and chinchillas: following a successful prosecution, the animals were rehomed and the children taken into the care of social services. The juxtaposition of cruelty to animals and to children is discussed below.

The RSPCA report notes that practice of bringing animals together to fight as a sport is far from extinct and may in fact be increasing in prevalence:

> Many people believe the barbaric activities involved in animal fighting were consigned to the history books bearing in mind that the first piece of animal fighting legislation was passed in 1835. Unfortunately, many aspects of animal fighting still take place today and in recent years these activities appear to have grown in popularity. The core activities we are seeing include organised dog fighting, cockfighting and badger baiting. Dog fighting that is less organised also takes place with participants meeting in quiet parks and on rough land. (2012, p. 28)

The use of animals to provide entertainment and sport, legal and illegal, has a history as long as mankind. There are zoos and circuses where animals perform for the audience's amusement, there are waterparks where seals and dolphins and other aquatic mammals act out their incongruous and unnatural repertoires, and we watch television commercials in which chimpanzees dressed as humans advertise various products. There are moral arguments against this use of animals and, although animals still feature in many sporting activities, there have been some positive changes: for example, many circuses now no longer have performing animals.

Animals in sport

There are two broad types of sport involving animals. The first type is where the sport is regulated, of limited cruelty, and where the risk of harm to the animal is minimised. In the second type it is the harm to the animals that constitutes the "sport". Thus, in the first type there are sports such as horse racing and greyhound racing where the welfare of the animals is protected. This is not to say that animals do not suffer injuries and fatalities, of course they do, but that such harm is the exception rather than the rule. However, the fate of many animals once their sporting prowess has waned and they have no economic value is another matter altogether.

In the second type the "sport" involves two categories: in the first, the animals inflict harm on other animals; in the second it is people who hurt and kill the animals. In the first category there are activities such as cockfighting, dogfighting, and bearbaiting (where the bear is trapped in a pit and is attacked by dogs). Depending on where they take place, these animal fights, typically arranged for the purposes of betting as well as the pleasure of the onlookers, may be illegal. The second category involves a range of activities that may be subsumed under the generic heading of hunting.

Hunting

It is probably the case that the survival of mankind, as well as that of other species such as chimpanzees (Boesch & Boesch, 1989), has at times depended upon hunting animals for food and other resources. In the modern world there are very few people who must hunt to survive, yet the practice of hunting persists with a range of animals stalked and killed for recreation. There is some hunting (not always legal) for commercial reasons, as seen in the hunting of whales and elephants, but most meat for human consumption is produced through farming. The practice of commercial hunting for fur—where the traditional quarries include beaver, bobcat, coyote, lynx, mink, marten, muskrat, opossum, otter, raccoon, skunk, and weasel—continues in many countries, albeit on a diminishing scale as animals are bred in captivity for their pelts.

In many countries the practice of hunting for recreation involves killing smaller mammals, such as deer, foxes, hares, and rabbits, as well as birds including ducks, grouse, pheasants, and even songbirds. There is some debate as to whether fishing is hunting: it is easier to think of catching large fish, such as marlin, shark, and tuna, in terms of hunting, although morally there is no difference between catching and killing large and small fish. There are several familiar forms of hunting, some involving the use of other animals, such as dogs and birds of prey, while others rely on equipment such as guns, traps, and fishing rods. As technology progresses so the equipment used in hunting becomes increasingly sophisticated. A new form of hunting, variously known as *internet hunting*, *cyber-hunting*, and *remote control hunting*, exploits the Internet as a vehicle for hunting. Internet hunting involves logging on to a website (the first of which was called Live-Shot.com) which allows access to a site that facilitates access to online webcams showing penned animals and to remotely controlled firearms. Thus, from the comfort of their own home and with their own computer, the "hunter" uses their mouse or joystick to shoot at and maim and kill the captive animals. An argument in support of this type of hunting is that it enables disabled people to hunt. However, Internet hunting is opposed not only by anti-hunting groups but also by hunters, who argue that this form of killing is not hunting as there is no fair chase in which the animal has the chance to escape.

Understanding cruelty to animals

The study of cruelty to animals is a topic that historically has been rather neglected by social scientists, although the situation is changing (Ascione & Lockwood, 2001), as is the complexity of the explanatory models (Dadds, Turner & McAloon, 2002; Flynn, 2001; Gullone, 2011). Indeed, there is ample evidence that the study of hunting alone would be instructive from both psychological and sociological stand-points. There are social rituals associated with hunting, such as "blooding" in fox-hunting where the new hunter, sometimes a child, is initiated into the hunt by having blood from the kill smeared on their face. There is also the phenomenon of gathering hunting trophies where the hunter takes a part of the animal's body—usually the head, although antlers, tusks, or even elephant's feet hollowed out to make an umbrella stand—as evidence of their prowess.

Kalof and Fitzgerald (2003) conducted an analysis of visual representations of dead animals in popular American hunting magazines. They noted that the vast majority of hunters shown in the photographs were men: "The 803 humans featured with the trophy animals were overwhelmingly white men. Children were present in about 4% of the images, and most were young males of about 10 posed with an animal that they had presumably killed themselves. About 16% of these young hunters were girls" (p. 116). Kalof and Fitzgerald observe that the animals are arranged for the camera in life-like poses, wounds carefully concealed. There is juxtaposition, they suggest, between the dead animals and the hunter's "Taken-for-granted stories of love and affection for nature, wildlife and magnificent animals" and the trophies contrary portrayal of the "Extreme objectification of animal bodies, with severed deer heads and cut-off antlers representative examples of the contradiction in the love-of-nature hunting stereotype" (p. 119). Kalof and Fitzgerald reach the conclusion that rather than a fun family day out, hunting and the collection and showing of trophy animals are rooted in an ideology driven by domination, colonialism, and patriarchy (see also Kalof, Fitzgerald, & Baralt, 2004). Indeed, it is clear that hunting has a long history as an activity through which the hunter can make statements about their own social class. There is nothing new about any of this commentary: thus, Baker (1983) notes that fox-hunting became especially popular in eighteenth- and nineteenth-century England "As a badge of class distinction on the one hand, and a convivial mingling of the classes on the other" (p. 56).

Does the widespread incidence of cruelty to animals, both now and across centuries past, tell us anything about interpersonal violence?

From animals to people?

There are many different reasons, with varying levels of moral defensibility, why we harm animals. Kellert and Felthous (1985) interviewed a sample of imprisoned criminals and, as shown in Box 2.4, suggested that there are nine motivations that drive animal cruelty. They note, however, that multiple motivations may accompany any single act of cruelty.

Hensley and Tallichet (2005a) gave questionnaires asking about childhood cruelty to animals to a sample of 261 prisoners serving custodial sentences in three American prisons. The motivations for their cruelty which the prisoners most frequently expressed were: first, "out of anger"; second, "for fun"; and joint third, "dislike for the animal" and "to control the animal".

Box 2.4   Motivations for Animal Cruelty

1   To control an animal: e.g., kicking a dog when it does not obey a command.
2   Retaliation for "wrong behaviour": e.g., hitting a cat for scratching a chair.
3   Satisfaction of a prejudice against a species or breed: e.g., hurting a rodent because rodents are bad and deserve it.
4   The expression of aggression through an animal: e.g., training dogs to attack other animals or people.
5   Enhancement of one's own aggression: e.g., using cruelty to practice aggressive forms of behaviour or to impress others with a willingness to be violent.
6   To shock and amuse peers: e.g., setting fire to cats and watching them run in an enclosed space.
7   Retaliation against others by harming their pets.
8   Displacement of hostility from a person to an animal following child abuse: e.g., aggression against an animal in connection with a feared figure of authority as revenge for previous suffering.
9   Non-specific sadism refers to the wish to injure and cause suffering or death in the absence of provocation or feelings of hostility towards the animal. The motivation is to take pleasure derived from the animal's pain and suffering perhaps as an exercise of power and control or to compensate for feelings of weakness or vulnerability: e.g., breaking an animal's bones "for laughs".

Source: After Kellert & Felthous, 1985.

In their review of the literature Petersen and Farrington (2007) note that cruelty to animals is often mentioned as a feature of the childhood histories of violent offenders. Petersen and Farrington also note the possibility that cruelty to animals may be associated with interpersonal violence, including experience of child abuse. A body of work has looked at the development of attitudes towards animal cruelty and progression to interpersonal violence.

The development during childhood of cruel behaviour directed towards animals has been seen as a significant indicator of other childhood problems such as conduct disorder and acts of aggression (Dadds et al., 2002). Indeed, based on Freudian theory, cruelty to animals was once thought to be part of a triad of childhood behaviour problems, with the others being enuresis and firesetting, which was predictive of violence in later life (Hellman & Blackman, 1966). However, more recent research strongly suggests that childhood cruelty to animals is associated with antisocial personality disorder and poly-substance abuse (Gleyzer, Felthous, & Holzer, 2002).

As in many other aspects of life, childhood is an important period in the development of an individual's world-view. Why does some children's developing behaviour encompass cruelty to animals, particularly domestic pets? There are several practical issues to resolve before beginning to answer that question. In particular, as Dadds et al. (2002) note, in order to consider cruelty to animals researchers need an agreed definition and a means of measuring cruelty. Thus, Dadds et al. arrive at a suitable definition: "Cruelty to animals refers to repetitive and proactive behaviour (or pattern of behaviour) intended to cause harm to sentient creatures" (p. 365). This definition encompasses two important components, first that the cruelty is *repetitive* behaviour and second that it is *intentional* in nature.

The measurement of cruelty can be undertaken by direct observation, with the obvious attendant difficulties, or through the use of protocols such as the Cruelty to Animals Inventory (Dadds et al., 2004). The use of measures such as the Cruelty to Animals Inventory (see Box 2.5) allows researchers to estimate a range of variables including frequency and types of cruelty, animals targeted, and the social context in which the cruelty takes place. However, like any other self-report measure, the quality of the data such measures produce is dependent upon the truthfulness of the respondents. The Cruelty to Animals Inventory is a reasonably reliable measure: Dadds et al. reported a good level of agreement between parents' reports of their children's behaviour and the child's responses.

The process of learning through observation followed by behavioural imitation is a fundamental aspect of the human development. It follows that childhood observation of cruelty towards animals may play a role in an individual's similar behaviour, with the home as one of the most likely settings within which the child may witness violence towards animals. Thus, following the principles of social learning theory and social information-processing as discussed in Chapter 1, the child first observes violence to animals by role models, say, parents or siblings. The child then develops the view that violence to animals is permissible, while their aggressive acts against household pets and other animals may be socially reinforced. The individual learns that violence towards animals is an acceptable form of behaviour.

Box 2.5 Sample Items and Responses from the Cruelty
to Animals Inventory

Have you ever hurt an animal on purpose?
Never : Hardly ever : A few times : Several times : Frequently
How many times have you hurt an animal on purpose?
What types of animals have you hurt in the past? (tick as many as needed):
None : Wild animals : Stray animals : Farm animals : Pet animals

Do you treat animals cruelly in front of others or by yourself?
I have never hurt an animal : In front of others : Alone
If you purposely hurt an animal, do you feel very sorry for it and feel sad that
    you hurt it?
*I have never been cruel to an animal : Yes, I feel very sad for the animal :
    Sometimes I feel bad, not always : No, I do not feel bad for the animal*

Source: Dadds et al., 2004.

Flynn (1999a) conducted a survey about animal abuse and attitudes and experiences of family violence with a sample of 267 students attending an American university. Flynn report that over one-sixth of the sample said that as a child or an adolescent they had perpetrated some form of animal abuse, ranging from killing and inflicting pain to sexual activity, on domestic pets or on wild or stray animals. The attitudes towards other forms of violence of those students who admitted animal abuse were compared with those of their non-abusing peers. The multivariate analysis controlled four sets of variables—the frequency of physical punishment experienced at 13 years of age, the respondent's age and their race, and a belief that the Bible is literally true—and found that the students who committed animal abuse had more favourable attitudes towards spanking children and were more likely to approve of a husband slapping his wife. Thus, Flynn concludes that: "Committing animal abuse during childhood is related to later approval of interpersonal violence against children and women in families" (p. 169). A conclusion which, as Flynn notes, includes animals within the finding that early experience of aggression towards people is related to adult approval of interpersonal violence (e.g., Owens & Straus, 1975).

Given this pattern of findings, it is reasonable to suggest that within a household where the child can observe violence or perpetrate acts of violence towards animals it is unlikely that the animals are the only victims (Felthous & Kellert, 1986). Ascione (1998) asked a sample of women who had experienced high levels of domestic violence about violence to household pets. Almost three-quarters of the women said that their abusive partner had threatened, hurt, or killed their pet. Over one-half of the women had children, some of whom were reported also to have abused animals.

A great many acts of violence, including animal abuse, are perpetrated by men, although there is an overlap between the genders with regard to views about animals and animal welfare (Herzog, 2007). Baldry (2003) carried out a study with a sample of 1,392 Italian young people aged 9 to 17 years looking at the relationship between exposure to violence between parents and perpetration of animal abuse. Baldry found that approximately one-half of the sample, with males more prevalent than females, had committed some type of animal abuse at least once: of the young people admitting to abusing animals "Almost all reported a higher level of exposure to domestic and animal violence" (p. 270). Currie (2006) similarly found that children who witnessed domestic violence were significantly more likely to commit acts of animal cruelty than children who had not been exposed to violence.

The association between childhood experience of physical punishment and animal cruelty is evident in a study reported by Flynn (1999b). With a sample of 267 undergraduate students, Flynn looked at the relationship between corporal punishment administered by parents and animal abuse. It was found that those students who admitted committing acts of animal cruelty in their childhood or adolescence had been more frequently physically punished by their fathers than had those who did not abuse animals. McEwen, Moffitt, and Arseneault (2014) conducted a large-scale UK study with 2,232 children aged between 5 and 12 years. They found that based on mothers' reports those children who were known to be cruel to animals were twice as likely to have been physically maltreated as those children who were not cruel to animals. However, acts of cruelty were quite rare overall, reported in approximately 9% of the sample, mostly by younger children.

It is plain that animal abuse does not stand apart from the social developmental processes involved in the acquisition of aggressive and violent behaviour (Gullone, 2011). Further, if it is true that one type of behaviour predicts yet more similar behaviour, then a close relationship may be envisaged between cruelty to animals and other forms of delinquency, including interpersonal violence (Felthous & Kellert, 1986).

There is some evidence to support the hypothesis of an association between animal cruelty and minor acts of delinquency as demonstrated by studies with undergraduate students (e.g., Henry, 2004). A study reported by Lucia and Killias (2011) used data drawn from the Swiss National Self-Reported Delinquency Study involving over 3,600 school pupils to investigate the relationship between animal cruelty and delinquency. Lucia and Killias found that 12% of the sample admitted to hurting animals and that the occurrence of animal cruelty was correlated to offending: there was a greater chance of *serious* violence, not including minor property offences and shoplifting, amongst those who abused animals.

Where the association exists between animal cruelty and delinquency it is evident that other predictors of delinquency, such as conduct disorder and substance abuse, are likely also to be present (Miller, 2001; Vaughn et al., 2009).

If the experience of animal cruelty is associated with interpersonal violence then, it follows, this relationship should be evident in offender populations. There are several studies, conducted with a range of different types of offender, held in varying types of institution, which show a preponderance of witnessing cruelty to animals in the childhood of offender populations (e.g., Hensley, Tallichet, & Dutkiewicz, 2012; Merz-Perez & Heide, 2004; Ressler, Burgess, Hartman, Douglas, & McCormack, 1998). In a typical study, Hensley and Tallichet (2005b) gave questionnaires to a sample of 261 male prisoners serving custodial sentences for a range of violent and non-violent crimes. They reported several findings: (1) it was more likely that those prisoners who had personal experience of animal cruelty at a younger age had persistently perpetrated animal cruelty at a young age; (2) prisoners who had seen a friend abuse animals were more likely frequently to abuse animals.

While it is undoubtedly the case that many people abuse animals, it is less certain which of these individuals will graduate to interpersonal violence. The nature of the psychological and emotional features and processes that may link cruelty to animals and violence towards people also remain uncertain (McPhedran, 2009; Patterson-Kane & Piper, 2009; Tallichet & Hensley, 2009). A meta-analysis reported by Walters (2013) included 14 studies of cruelty to animals by violent and non-violent offenders. As may be predicted, the violent offenders were significantly more likely than the non-violent group to have a history of animal cruelty. However, a second meta-analysis based on five different studies showed that animal cruelty was associated equally well with both non-violent *and* violent offending. Walters concludes that for male offenders the relationship between animal cruelty and offending is broader than just violent offending. It is possible that the link between animal cruelty and violent offending is part of a wider pattern of antisocial behaviour.

The overall position, as Petersen and Farrington (2007) suggest, is that more sophisticated research is needed, using large samples and prospective experimental designs, in order to gain a full understanding of the exact nature of the association between cruelty to animals and interpersonal violence.

It is clear that the vulnerable and the powerless are high up the list of likely victims of violence. This situation is evident in both bullying and cruelty to animals and it is also the case with the next type of everyday violence, the corporal punishment of children.

Corporal Punishment of Children

There are three topics associated with crime on which everyone has a strong opinion and which are guaranteed to start an argument: the first is whether we should have the death penalty for criminals; the second is whether hunting is a defensible activity; and the third is whether it is right or wrong to hit children (see Benjet & Kazdin, 2003).

The topic of hitting children requires some clarification. Those in favour of hitting children are not in the main advocating the use of excessive and abusive physical force: although exactly what is and what is not acceptable in the corporal punishment of children is a moot point. There are various terms used to describe corporal punishment, such as *smacking* and *spanking*, while *paddling* and *whupping* are also in use in the United States (Knox, 2010). The act of hitting the child may take place through use of an open hand, i.e., smacking using the palm, or by use of an instrument. In the USA a spanking paddle may be used: a paddle looks rather like a small cricket bat, in that it has a handle and a wooden blade, and is held in one hand to strike the child's buttocks. At one time the cane, widely used in schools, was the British equivalent of the paddle. I know from personal experience that the cane (or a leather strap) was variously applied by schoolteachers to outstretched palms and to buttocks alike. (At my school one or two of the masters were not averse to the whole-hearted application of gym shoe to buttock or to administering a sharp rap on one's cranium with their knuckles.)

With regard to hitting children, Knox (2010) makes a telling observation:

> In contrast to the growing disapproval of violence against women, social sanctions for violence against children still remain strong in the United States. In the United States, it is against the law to hit prisoners, criminals, or other adults. Ironically, the only humans it is still legal to hit are the most vulnerable members of our society—those we are charged to protect—children. (p. 103)

Why is it thought acceptable to hit children?

There are various arguments put forward in favour of corporal punishment: from a cursory search of the term "smacking" on the Internet (a salutary experience and, hint for today, avoid the term "spanking"!) the following justifications could be gleaned: "It never did *me* any harm"; "It is down to parents not governments/social workers/the politically correct to discipline their children as they see fit and proper"; "Physical chastisement teaches children respect"; while as for the fine line between corporal punishment and abuse, "Any fit parent knows the difference between smacking and child abuse"; and finally with an appeal to historical precedent "It has been an accepted practice for hundreds of years".

There are many obvious problems with these justifications. For example, the view that "it never did me any harm" may not be strictly accurate: it is highly unlikely that many people are prepared to admit that the problems in their private life, interpersonal or otherwise, stem from their painful childhood experiences. Nonetheless, it is the case that those who experienced physical punishment as children are likely to endorse its use (Deater-Deckard, Lansford, Dodge, Pettit, & Bates, 2003; Dietz, 2000).

In the UK there is some support for the physical punishment of children, although perhaps not as pronounced as in the USA (Bunting, Webb, & Healy, 2010). With reference to the USA, Flynn (1999a) makes the comment that "The physical punishment of children enjoys strong normative support in this country. In 1986, 84% of Americans agreed that 'it is sometimes necessary to discipline a child with a good, hard spanking'" (p. 162).

As Flynn suggests, while the number of people in favour of the corporal punishment of children may have fallen slightly in more recent times, nonetheless there are

specific individual characteristics associated with favouring the physical chastisement of children: "Race, religion, and region have been important variables related
to spanking attitudes" (p. 162). Thus, the American groups Flynn cites as most likely
to support hitting children are African Americans, conservative Protestants and
other religious groups who take the Bible to be the literal word of God, and those
from the Southern states. Indeed, Gershoff (2010) makes a similar point: "Corporal
punishment also persists because it is a practice with strong ties to religion, particularly to Christianity" (p. 32). Gershoff suggests that the close association between
religion and the corporal punishment of children is a function of the view that the
child's spiritual well-being is dependent upon strong discipline.

This list of demographic variables points to the importance of culture and associated economic and social conditions in the formulation and maintenance of attitudes
towards the corporal punishment of children (Dietz, 2000; Gershoff et al., 2010;
Lansford, 2010; Maldonado, 2004). Litzow and Silverstein (2008) have made the
point that as corporal punishment is widely used as a means of discipline in many
countries and cultures, it follows that the varying levels of acceptance are related to
local cultural values. Litzow and Silverstein give examples such as south-west
Ethiopia, Jamaica, and, specifically, Hong Kong Chinese families as settings where
the corporal punishment of children is commonplace. In agreement with Flynn,
Litzow and Silverstein also note that variations in the acceptability of corporal
punishment may be positively associated with the role and prominence accorded to
religion within a given culture. Thus, research is increasingly looking outside North
America and the UK in order to take a wider perspective on the issue (e.g., Ma, Han,
Grogan-Kaylorb, Delvab, & Castillo 2012).

Another aspect of corporal punishment lies in the parents' understanding of their
child's behaviour and the nature of their interactions. An American study by Combs-
Orme and Cain (2008) looked at mothers who spanked their children during the
first 13 months after birth. They found that spanking was at its most prevalent
among those young mothers who reported high levels of life stress, who saw fewer
alternatives to corporal punishment, and who saw their infant as problematic.

The child's view

Not surprisingly, children have their own views about smacking. A UK study asked
children a range of questions about their understanding of and views on smacking
(Crowley & Vulliamy, 2002). The children said that they feared the emotional distress and humiliation of being smacked more than the physical pain. The children
perceived the situations in which they were smacked as sometimes those where the
adult, usually but not always a parent, had become angry. With a display of wisdom
beyond their years, the children said that there were disciplinary methods, such as
doing chores like "cleaning the bathroom" or restricting their access to television and
toys, which would be more effective than smacking because they were longer-lasting

and more aversive. A similar American study also reported that children had clear views on the utility of physical chastisement (Vittrup & Holden, 2010).

There are two core issues at the heart of the debate about the use of corporal punishment with children. First, is corporal punishment an effective method of facilitating the child's development? Second, is the use of corporal punishment with children morally defensible?

Developmental help or hindrance?

The question of the effectiveness of corporal punishment and its effect on child development lends itself to empirical investigation and, indeed, there is a large body of work given to this issue (Fuller, 2011; Gershoff, 2010; Knox, 2010).

In typical study Aucoin, Frick, and Bodin (2006) compared the emotional and behavioural functioning of a sample of 12-year-old American schoolchildren. Over a two-week period some of the children had received no corporal punishment, some had received mild levels of corporal punishment (defined as one or two punishments), and some had received high levels (three or more). It was found that corporal punishment was associated with problems in both emotional and behavioural adjustment, with the strongest relationship evident in children who had experienced high levels of punishment. In addition, the deleterious effect of punishment was most marked for impulsive children and for those children without a supportive family.

Gershoff (2002) reported a meta-analysis of 88 studies which investigated the positive and negative effects of corporal punishment on children. A positive effect was evident in that corporal punishment acted to increase the child's immediate compliance with parental commands. On the negative side Gershoff reported both short- and long-term detrimental effects of corporal punishment. The short-term effects during childhood were evident in a lowering of the child's moral internalisation, an increase in aggression, antisocial and delinquent behaviour, a decrease in the quality of the parent–child relationship, lower levels of mental health, and an increase in the risk of being a victim of physical abuse. The long-term effects seen in adulthood included increased aggression, antisocial and criminal behaviour, decreased mental health, and an increase in the risk of perpetrating abuse of one's own child or spouse. These negative effects of corporal punishment were also found by Ferguson (2013) in a tightly controlled meta-analysis of 45 studies.

Research has continued to highlight the damaging effects of corporal punishment on the child's development—as seen, for example, in studies of later aggression (Lee, Taylor, Altschu, & Rice, 2013), attitudes to hitting other children (Simons & Wurtele, 2010) and externalising behaviours (Lansford, Wager, Bates, Pettit, & Dodge, 2012; MacKenzie, Nicklas, Waldfogel, & Brooks-Gunn, 2012)—as well as emphasising the sometimes fine line between corporal punishment and child abuse (Lee, Grogan-Kaylora, & Berger, 2014; Straus, 2000; Zolotor, Theodore, Chang, Berkoff, & Runyan, 2008).

Moral defensibility?

The question of whether corporal punishment is morally defensible—i.e., regardless of intention, is it right that parents, caregivers, or teachers may inflict physical pain upon a child?—has been debated at length in many countries and jurisdictions (Gershoff & Bitensky, 2007). In 1989 this moral issue was addressed by Article 19 of the United Nations Convention on the Rights of the Child, which gave children throughout the world the right to be raised without violence. As can be seen from Box 2.6, several European countries followed Sweden's lead in 1979 by bringing into force legal bans of all corporal punishment of children before publication of the UN Convention. Since 1989, as may also be seen from Box 2.6, a number of other European countries have similarly introduced bans on all corporal punishment of children.

In some countries, including the UK, the ban on corporal punishment does not cover all settings, so that it is permissible for parents to hit their children but it is illegal for children to be hit in state schools.

The global statistics for countries with varying degrees of prohibition of the corporal punishment of children continually shift and change: the websites of organisations such as the Center for Effective Discipline and the Global Initiative to End All Corporal Punishment monitor the international picture.

The global movement towards prohibition has allowed studies to be conducted that compare the national effects of banning corporal punishment of children. Bussmann, Erthal, and Schroth (2011) compared five European countries—Austria, France, Germany, Spain, and Sweden—which have introduced legislation banning the corporal punishment of children. This type of research faces a myriad of practical problems, despite which Bussmann et al. were able to compile an extensive report. They reached the conclusion that prohibition does lead to a decline in violence

---

Box 2.6   European Countries Banning Corporal Punishment

1979	Sweden	2004	Ukraine
1983	Finland	2005	Rumania
1987	Norway		Hungary
1989	Austria		Greece
1994	Cyprus	2007	Netherlands
1997	Denmark		Portugal
1998	Latvia		Spain
1999	Croatia	2008	Luxembourg
2000	Germany		Lichtenstein
2003	Iceland	2010	Poland
	Bulgaria		Albania
		2011	Estonia

against children. Bussmann et al. also considered the long-term effects of experiencing corporal punishment during childhood. Those parents who as children had experienced severe corporal punishment used higher levels of punishment with their own children.

Much ado about not very much?

We have arrived at the position where statements regarding the adverse effects of hitting children are assertively made in professional journals: for example, Durrant (2012) states: "The growing weight of evidence and the recognition of children's rights have brought us to a historical point. Physicians familiar with the research can now confidently encourage parents to adopt constructive approaches to discipline and can comfortably use their unique influence to guide other aspects of children's health development" (p. 1373). Lee, Grogan-Kaylor, and Berger (2014) make a similar point: "It is important to educate professionals who come into contact with new parents regarding research showing that spanking is harmful to children and to encourage communication of this information to parents" (p. 288).

However, contrary to the positive messages that flow from the moral debate, research, and legislation, there are voices asking whether banning the corporal punishment of children is taking the issue far too far. The side of the debate in favour of corporal punishment has two broad concerns: (1) the validity of the empirical research pointing to the adverse effects of hitting; (2) the robustness of the moral case against corporal punishment of children.

It is true that in research into child development it can be very difficult to make exact predictions about specific events. There are so many influences over the course of a child's development—cultural stimuli, social and economic conditions, parental style, family functioning, school—that it seems improbable that any one event has the profound and consistent adverse effects claimed by opponents of corporal punishment. Thus, there have been challenges to the validity of the research showing a detrimental effect of corporal punishment (Fuller, 2009; Larzelere & Baumrind, 2010). Larzelere and Baumrind build their case on four conditions which they claim must be fulfilled before the evidence is convincing: (1) to defend removing from parents the option of hitting their children, spanking prohibitionists first must provide causal evidence that spanking is harmful when "It is considered most appropriate by parents, children, and psychologists" (p. 58); (2) the effects of spanking must be compared with the effects of alternative disciplinary strategies which parents may use in the same instances where disciple is required; (3) there must be evidence that parenting improves when parents are prevented from hitting; (4) it must be established that the detrimental effects of hitting are independent of potentially confounding variables including child temperament and socioeconomic status.

This particular challenge asks for an exceptionally high, perhaps impossibly high, standard of empirical evidence: for example, how would a consensus be reached on when hitting is "most appropriate", or that "parenting improves", and how can *all* potentially confounding variables be controlled? The solution would necessitate a large-scale longitudinal study lasting decades and conducted across a range of cultures, socioeconomic groups, and so on. Such a study may produce overwhelming evidence one way or the other, but it would not answer the moral question of whether it is right to hit children. In conclusion, it is sobering to reflect on the words of Knox (2010) as quoted above: "Ironically, the only humans it is still legal to hit are the most vulnerable members of our society—those we are charged to protect—children" (p. 103).

Violence as Entertainment

It is a feature of the twenty-first century that we are surrounded by a barrage of information and images from a range of media: there is radio, television, videos and DVDs, and the cinema; there are several forms of printed media; and there are the Internet-based social media such as Twitter and YouTube. It is inevitable that some of the media content will be, to varying degrees, violent in nature. This violence may on occasion come with a sprinkling of sexual content in the form of a television programme, a computer game, or even advertising (Ferguson, Cruz, Martinez, Rueda, & Ferguson, 2010).

The question of the effects of the media on violent behaviour has generated a large body of empirical research literature, not all American (e.g., Möller & Krahé, 2009), in turn generating several meta-analyses (e.g., Anderson et al., 2010; Ferguson & Kilburn, 2009; Savage & Yancey, 2008). The primary studies together with the meta-analyses strongly suggest that persistent viewing of violence, particularly violent video and computer games, in childhood and adolescence is significantly associated with committing acts of physical and sexual violence in adulthood. In keeping with this view, a longitudinal study of the effects of playing violent video games reported by Willoughby, Adachi, and Good (2012) offered support for the position that playing violent video games may be associated with later levels of increased aggression. However, another longitudinal study by Ferguson, Garza, Jerabeck, Ramos, and Galindo (2012) found no association between playing violent video games and several indices of aggression.

Thus, as with the debate about the effects on children of corporal punishment, there are reservations about the methodological robustness of the evidence claiming harmful effects (Adachi & Willoughby, 2011; Ferguson & Kilburn, 2009, 2010). Ferguson and Kilburn (2010) have also called into question the ecological validity of the research, much of which is laboratory-based. They note that while violent video games have become increasingly popular over time, recent years have actually seen a large drop in violent crime rates among youths and adults in the United States, Canada, United Kingdom, Japan, and many other industrialised countries.

It is possible to address the issue of validity by changing research strategy. Thus, many young people play violent video games but only a small proportion commit violent acts, so rather than study samples drawn from the general population more may be learned by looking at known violent offenders. An American study by DeLisi,

Vaughn, Gentile, Anderson, and Shook (2013) looked at the histories of a sample of 227 male and female young delinquents held in secure facilities. They found that for this particular group of adolescents playing violent video games correlated significantly with levels of delinquency and violent behaviour: this correlation remained when controlling for factors such as age, sex, race, criminal record, and psychopathic personality traits. The step of moving from a *correlational* relationship to establishing whether or not a *causal* relationship exists is the next step. Further, given that not all young people who play violent video games become aggressive, precision in identifying the individual risk factors is also needed. As DeLisi et al. note, until they are on very certain ground it is as well for researchers to be very cautious in their recommendations to policy-makers. Ferguson, Garza, Jerabeck, Ramos, and Galindo (2012) reinforce this point in quoting from a US Supreme Court decision:

> The majority decision of the US Supreme Court considered the existing research unconvincing noting that "[t]hese studies have been rejected by every court to consider them, and with good reason: They do not prove that violent video games cause minors to act aggressively (which would at least be a beginning). Instead, '[n]early all of the research is based on correlation, not evidence of causation, and most of the studies suffer from significant, admitted flaws in methodology'". (p. 1)

A notable aspect of the literature on both corporal punishment and the effects of video games is the way in which researchers are drawn into opposing camps. Of course, there are always issues to resolve such as the best research design, preferred measures, and the nature of the critical outcome variables, but disagreements can run deeper than technical matters.

Nonetheless, it may appear at times almost as if each camp has its own preferred position, formed on whatever basis, and so seeks evidence to support its preference while at the same time finding fault with contradictory evidence. Ferguson and Kilburn (2009) say as much in commenting that "The concern remains that media violence effects research may continue to be driven primarily by ideological or political beliefs rather than objectivity. Media violence has a long history of being driven by ideology. Why the belief of media violence effects persists despite the inherent weaknesses of the research is somewhat of an open question" (p. 762).

It's as well perhaps to remember that researchers are people too!

Sporting Violence

The relationship between sport and interpersonal violence functions at three discrete levels: (1) the violence is the sport; (2) violence within sport; (3) violence surrounding sport. There are variations within these three levels (Kimble, Russo, Bergman, & Galindo, 2010; Sekot, 2009) but they serve to give a structure by which to consider the issue.

The violence is the sport

There are several forms of sport which are dependent upon a physical fight between two people, typically males but increasingly less so. The obvious example in Western culture is boxing, but on a worldwide basis there are many types of sport that involve direct, face-to-face combat: there is wrestling, of which there are numerous varieties such as Greco-Roman and freestyle; some martial arts including judo and karate, as well as martial arts such as kendo that involve weapons; yet further, there is kickboxing and mixed martial arts (Buse, 2006), and the list goes on and on. Many of the issues that surround the issue of violence as sport have been rehearsed at length in the context of boxing and so this sport will be considered in some detail.

Boxing

Sporting contests recognisable as boxing have been traced back to antiquity so that we know that both Greek and Roman spectators would have been familiar with sports not too dissimilar from today's boxing. It is evident that both the Greeks and the Romans were aware of the potential for harm this sport held for the contestants. The Greeks sought to make boxing safer through the introduction of hand wrappings and protective headgear. On the other hand, the more combative and ferocious Romans (see Fagan, 2011) made the contests even more bloody by introducing a heavy metal weight with sharp spikes into the boxer's hand-wrappings. As may be anticipated, this step led to many deaths. (The Romans also introduced a ring within which the fight took place.) Indeed, boxing became so violent that around AD 500 the Roman emperor Theodoric acted to abolish boxing.

Boxing, of the bare-knuckle variety was known in Britain the 1600s, where it was a popular if somewhat bloody spectacle. It was not until 1867, when the Marquis of Queensberry published rules for the conduct of the sport, that boxing moved closer to the form with which we are familiar today. There was similar interest in the United States, and by the 1800s boxing was widespread across many states, drawing large crowds to premier venues, such as Madison Square Garden in New York City, some of which are still popular today.

The bare-knuckle prize fights eventually gave way to amateur boxing, which was introduced into the modern Olympic Games in 1904, held in St Louis, USA. The elevation of boxing to an Olympic sport gave it a worldwide impetus. The Soviet Union, which did not permit professional boxing, became a world force in amateur boxing, along with several other communist countries such as East Germany, Hungary, Poland, and particularly Cuba which dominated amateur boxing for many years. In the 1950s and 1960s African countries such as Egypt, Nigeria, and Tanzania came to the fore in the amateur form of boxing.

As with the Greeks and Romans centuries earlier, modern-day concerns have been expressed about the effects of boxing on the contestants. In the contemporary literature several commentators, such as the American physician George D. Lundberg, have expressed grave misgivings about boxing. The concerns of medical and other commentators are based on the likelihood of boxers suffering physical harm such as severe brain injury, blindness resulting from detached retinas, and other chronic physical injuries (Lundberg 1983, 1984, 1985, 1986). Concerns with the risk of head trauma to boxers remain to the current day and, indeed, have spread to other sports such as American football (Shurley & Todd, 2012).

Lundberg (1985) moves beyond the physical damage to include the following in his list of objections to boxing: "An affront to morality and ethics because it is the only major so-called sport which has as its principal purpose the intentional harm of the opponent . . . Boxing currently exploits minority youth for the benefit of the more affluent" (p. 197).

The debate about boxing continues on several fronts, encompassing the morality and acceptability of violence as a public spectacle (Annas, 1983). These concerns have resulted in bans on boxing in several countries, including Iceland, Iran, Norway, and Sweden; although some countries such as Sweden have subsequently rescinded the ban.

Violence within sport

As shown in Box 2.7, Kerr (2005) suggests that the purpose of aggression in sport, where it is allowed, is fourfold. Three of these four types of aggression, i.e., *anger*, *power*, and *thrill*, typically lie outside the written and unwritten rules of certain sports and will therefore be penalised by officials enforcing the rules of the sport.

Box 2.7   Kerr's Classification of Aggression in Sport

Anger aggression: The aim is retribution in response to the words and actions of an opponent (although members of the same side have been known to fight on the field of play).

Play aggression: This type of aggression is allowed within the written rules of the sport, there may be "unwritten rules" to which the majority of players adhere.

Power aggression: The aim is to subdue or intimidate a rival player or opposing team. The acts are serious, often premeditated and "off the ball" so as to avoid detection, and frequently justified by the end result.

Thrill aggression: The aggressive act is perpetrated against an opponent for the sake of it, giving the immediate feelings of pleasure to the aggressor. These acts typically take place when the perpetrator perceives that they will not be caught and punished.

Source: After Kerr, 2005.

These various forms of aggression are not mutually exclusive while on the field of play: in the manner of Luckenbill's transactions (1977; see Chapter 1), one type of act may develop into or precipitate another type of aggressive act with various intended consequences.

The occurrence of these various types of aggressive acts depends to some degree on the level of contact allowed with the rules of a given sport. This variation will interact with the aggressiveness and drive to win of the individual competitors (Donahue, Rip, & Vallerand, 2009) to produce both anticipated and unexpected violent encounters in different sports.

Contact sports   With boxing and similar sports there is no debate about the integral nature of interpersonal violence to the contest. However, there are other contact sports where interpersonal violence is not a fundamental aspect of the sporting contest but where, nonetheless, it occurs with varying degrees of frequency, severity, and permissibility (Kordi, Maffulli, Wroble, & Wallace, 2009). These sports may be classified, with varying degrees of agreement, as follows: (1) *full contact*, such as Australian rules football (Grange & Kerr, 2010) and ice hockey (Amin, 2011); (2) *semi-contact*, such as karate or kendo, which are characterised by limitations on the use of force, explicit rules against rendering an opponent unconscious, and the use of protective clothing to shield against injury; (3) *limited contact* such as basketball where the rules prevent most intentional or unintentional contact between players, with penalties often used to deter and punish illegal contact between players; and (4) *non-contact* sports such as athletics and tennis, where the contestants are not allowed physical contact and if this rule is broken disqualification is highly likely: contestants are typically separated by the use of lanes, as in athletics and swimming, or by a physical barrier, as in badminton and tennis, or by strict rules, as in cricket or golf.

While there are sports where contact is either forbidden or strictly regulated, there are nonetheless instances of violence. Association Football, aka "soccer", falls into the category of a limited contact sport in which aggressive acts are typically ignored by the players (Traclet et al., 2009) but which is occasionally marked by violent acts on the field of play. Kerr (2009) describes one such violent act that took place during a football match in The Netherlands. A player (called Ridderkerker) was dismissed from the field of play for head-butting an opponent (van der Gaag). Kerr describes what happened next: "Ridderkerker began to walk off the pitch, but turned around, ran toward the prostrate opponent, van der Gaag, and kicked him in the head. Van der Gaag's skull was heard to crack when he was kicked . . . Later, in hospital, it was found that van der Gaag had a fractured skull and bone splinters in his brain" (p. 41). This incident is clearly beyond the pale in terms of the mutual consent players implicitly give for physical contact within the rules (written and unwritten) of the sport. Ridderkerker appeared in court where his actions were judged as intending to kill his opponent and he received a three-year prison sentence.

Why did this uncommon—but not unique, as seen in a similar incident in ice hockey (Kerr, 2006)—violent act take place? Kerr (2009) notes that "Ridderkerker, an unemployed man without much education who was supported by his girlfriend, derived his feelings of self-esteem to a great extent from his prowess as a footballer. When he felt he was being belittled on the field, he could not deal with it" (p. 42). His dismissal from the field of play invoked uncontrollable anger and in this highly emotional state Ridderkerker exacted retribution on the cause of his fall from grace.

Within Kerr's account of the incident there are several of the familiar ingredients associated with violence: some previous level of transaction between attacker and victim, an appraisal of the situation by the aggressor in terms of a hurtful personal injustice, and anger precipitating a loss of control and the attack on the victim. It is possible that this violent act also contained an element of retaliation, a motivation not unknown in sport. Indeed, illustrating the similar functions that violence may hold in different contexts, there is evidence that violence and associated sports injuries in youth sport may sometimes serve the purpose of bullying (Fields, Collins, & Comstock, 2010).

Dixon (2010) notes that different sports have varying levels of tolerance for acts of retaliation and gives two examples: first, the "goon" in ice hockey whose role is to target opponents who have fouled teammates; second, the pitcher in baseball, who may aim to hit opponents when the opposition pitcher has hit a teammate. There are two types of justification for such retaliatory violence: (1) the opponent "had it coming" as a result of their team's previous actions; (2) the retaliation serves as notice that there will be reprisals and so deters future attacks. As Dixon notes, retaliatory violence may also be good for team morale and unity, a sense of being together in adversity and knowing that your teammates will take care of you, as you will of them. An infamous and somewhat extreme example of organised team retaliation is described in Box 2.8.

The appeal of sport reaches beyond playing and extends to watching as a spectator. There is a great deal of enjoyment and anguish to be taken from playing and watching sport (I support Newcastle United so know all about anguish and watching sport), whether it be on a grand scale such as competing in the Olympics or as prosaic as watching one's children play for the school team. However, as discussed in Chapter 1, wherever people gather in groups or in crowds there is potential for violence, and sport is no exception.

Violence surrounding sport

Preparing to compete   As anyone who has played sport seriously will know, a great deal of time is spent training and preparing to compete. This preparation time has been the subject of concerns about violence involving coaches and sportsmen and women. In particular, there are serious concerns regarding the sexual abuse of young athletes by their coaches (Brackenridge, Bishopp, Moussali, & Tapp, 2008; Brackenridge, Bringer, & Bishopp, 2005). Fasting, Brackenridge, and Kjølberg (2013)

Box 2.8   Team Retaliation: The Lions' "99" Call

The British & Irish Lions are a Rugby Union team formed once every four years from the best players in England, Ireland, Scotland, and Wales to tour, in turn, Australia, New Zealand, or South Africa. The 1974 Lions' tour of South Africa was marked by fierce physical exchanges on the field of play: in order to counter what was seen an attempt at physical intimidation the Lions adopted what they called the "99" call. Once a Lions player on the pitch made the call "99" then it was a "one in, all in" call to arms: all the Lions players immediately either joined a brawl or hit the nearest available opponent. The purpose of the "99" call was threefold: (1) it showed that the Lions would not be intimidated; (2) it engendered team unity; (3) it protected the individual from official sanctions as if all the Lions were involved it was highly unlikely that the referee would dismiss every player from the field.

The call was used several times and there is footage available that shows it in action. The most famous example occurred in the third test in Port Elizabeth, when the spirit of the call was taken to heart by Lions full-back, J. P. R. Williams, who sprinted half the length of the pitch to land a blow on a South African forward. Incidentally, the Lions won the series 3-0 with one match drawn.

analysed 15 Norwegian court cases in which a male coach was convicted of sexually assaulting one or more young male and female competitors aged from 6 to 16 years. A range of sports were involved including athletics, basketball, cross-country skiing, gymnastics, handball, karate, shooting, soccer, and swimming. Fasting et al. make the point that the offences took place mainly in the context of individual rather than team sports, allowing the coach the opportunity to groom the child over a period of time before committing the assault.

Spectators   When people gather to watch sport all the ingredients for interpersonal violence are to be found in one place: for example, depending on numbers of spectators and the type of sport, there may be crowding and loss of personal space, rivalry or even hatred between opposing sets of fans, and high emotions fuelled by alcohol (e.g., Ostrowsky, 2014; Priks, 2010; Slabbert & Ukpere, 2010; Spaaij, 2014). The most obvious example of crowd violence associated with sport is to be found in football (soccer). The rivalries between opposing supporters, for both club and country, sometimes lead to outbreaks of violence both inside and outside the stadium where the game takes place. The violent clashes between rival groups of supporters, as well as between supporters and the police, can lead to injury and death in public places such as bars and cafes. The consequences of such clashes can be serious

Box 2.9   The Heysel Stadium Disaster

In May 1985 the European Cup Final between Liverpool and the Italian club Juventus was scheduled to take place at the Heysel Stadium in Brussels. The trouble began before kick-off when sections of the rival supporters, standing only yards apart and separated by just a temporary chain-link fence and a thin line of police, began to throw missiles at each other. As kick-off grew closer the missile-throwing increased and a group of Liverpool fans moved towards a perimeter wall, causing the Juventus fans to try to climb over the wall to safety. The wall collapsed, causing 39 deaths—32 Italians, four Belgians, two French, and one fan from Northern Ireland—with a further 600 fans injured. In retaliation, Juventus fans in another part of the stadium began to riot and they moved down the ground towards the Liverpool supporters. The police intervened, and for the next two hours, even as the match was being played, the Juventus fans fought the police using rocks and bottles as missiles.

As a consequence, English clubs were banned from European club competitions: the indefinite ban lasted for five years. An investigation by the British police, using still photographs and films of the events, led in 1989 to 14 fans receiving three-year sentences from Belgian courts for involuntary manslaughter.

with grave injuries and even fatalities as seen, for example, in the thoroughly documented disasters at Heysel Stadium, Brussels in 1985 (see Box 2.9) and at Hillsborough Stadium, Sheffield, in 1989.

However, it would be wrong to attribute the blame for violence at soccer matches to the game itself as a cause of violence. Piquero, Jennings, and Farrington (2015) used longitudinal data to investigate involvement in football hooliganism and criminality. They concluded that football hooliganism is likely to be one aspect of the hooligan's wider criminal lifestyle rather than an isolated behaviour specific to attending a game of football.

Some sports reach such large audiences that their progress can affect a nation. Sheikh, Ali, Saleem, Ali, and Salman (2013) suggest that in South Asia the intensity associated with the national sport of cricket works at several levels: "Although severe health concerns exist for major cricketing events, their cultural significance cannot be undermined. Health and harmony prevail as a result of such events, and their organization brings economic stability to a country" (p. 6). On a personal note, as a cricketer lover, once a player—opening bowler, quite quick, as you ask—but now a spectator, I cannot but agree wholeheartedly that cricket is beyond doubt the most harmonious of sports. (As a former rugby full-back in my rich sporting career I would dearly like to say the same of Rugby Union but that, alas, would rather be stretching a point, as illustrated in Box 2.8!)

Conclusion

The point was made at the very beginning of this book that violence is endemic across many societies and cultures. While we are rightly shocked by the extreme acts of violence we read about in newspapers and see on the television, we have come to accept or, as with the corporal punishment of children, sometimes actively argue for certain forms of violence. In the next chapter the focus moves to an arena where, unlike activities such as hunting animals, the violent conduct is hidden from public view. We may like to think of the home as a haven where we are safe from life's perils, but for some people the reality is very different.

3

Violence at Home

The three categories of interpersonal violence within the family as described by Tolan, Gorman-Smith, and Henry (2006) form the basis of this chapter. These three categories are physical violence directed towards children, violence between intimate partners, and the physical abuse of older adults (familial sexual violence is discussed in Chapter 5).

It is impossible to be exact about the prevalence of any of these three acts of familial violence. There are several reasons why a family may seem calm and untroubled to the outside world while in reality it is a place of fear and hurt. The British Crime Survey (BCS) reports that the reasons most frequently given for not reporting partner abuse to the police were that the act was "too trivial or not worth reporting to the police", or that it was a "private matter or family matter", or it was "not police business" (Smith et al., 2010). Thus, the official statistics are highly unlikely to be an accurate estimate of the true prevalence of violence within the family home.

Physical Child Abuse

The physical abuse of children within the family may take two forms: (1) the direct use of physical force, sometimes including the use of objects, that injures the child; (2) the neglect of the child's welfare and safety. (The sexual abuse of children is covered in Chapter 5.) In some cases of physical abuse the child suffers extreme physical damage, sometimes over a prolonged period of time, which may result in death (child homicide is discussed in Chapter 4). Stith et al. (2009) provide helpful definitions of both child physical abuse— "Non-accidental injury (including bruises, welts, cuts, burns, broken bones or other tissue damage) to the child inflicted by the

The Psychology of Interpersonal Violence, First Edition. Clive R. Hollin.
© 2016 John Wiley & Sons, Ltd. Published 2016 by John Wiley & Sons, Ltd.

parent or a caregiver in a parenting role" (p. 14)—and neglect—"A failure of a parent or a caregiver in a parenting role to provide adequate supervision, safety, medical care, education, or other necessities to the child" (p. 14).

The abuse of children has been evident, most probably for centuries, in many parts of the world as reinforced by studies in countries as diverse as Brazil (Alexandre, Nadanovsky, Moraes, & Reichenheim, 2010), Canada (Trocmé et al., 2005), Chile (Benítez-Borrego, Guàrdia-Olmos, & Aliaga-Moore, 2013), and South Korea (Hong, Lee, Park, & Faller, 2011). It is impossible to say precisely just how many children are physically or otherwise abused (Fallon et al., 2010): as with crime generally, the official figures, such as recorded in the UK on the Child Protection Register, will significantly under-represent the scale of the issue (Gilbert et al., 2012). The issues of definition, methodology, and data-gathering—all of which pose difficulties when attempting to conduct research into the prevalence of child maltreatment—are discussed in two UK studies (May-Chahal & Cawson, 2005; Radford, Corral, Bradley, & Fisher, 2013). It is evident from these and other studies that an individual child may suffer several forms of abuse, resulting in children who may be said to be "poly-victims" (Finkelhor, Ormrod, & Turner, 2009). Iwaniec (2006) identified no fewer than six forms of child abuse: (1) *spurning* the child either through belittling or ridicule, or by rejection and abandonment; (2) *terrorising* the child through the use of threats; (3) *isolating* the child both socially and from other family members; (4) *exploitation/corruption* by encouraging the child to develop antisocial attitudes and behaviours which may lead to criminal acts; (5) *denying emotional responsiveness* by ignoring the child and so eliminating opportunities for closeness and affection; (6) *mental health, medical, and educational, neglect* by not monitoring, and so failing to provide for, the child's health and their physical and psychological development.

The phenomenon of a "battered child syndrome" began seriously to engage significant numbers of researchers in the 1960s (e.g., Galdston, 1965; Kempe, Silverman, Steele, Droegemuller, & Silver, 1962). Since that time a great deal of attention has been given to understanding the causes and consequences of child abuse.

Antecedents to physical child abuse

When looking at such an emotive topic as child abuse of any type it is tempting to focus exclusively on the perpetrators of the abuse. However, the behaviour of the abusers does not occur in a vacuum, and as well as their individual characteristics there are broader social and economic contextual factors to consider. There is evidence at a national level to show a complex association between economic conditions and low income, contingent parental stress, and an increase in the use of smacking and the frequency of physical abuse of children (Brooks-Gunn, Schneider, & Waldfogel, 2013; MacKenzie, Nicklas, Brooks-Gunn., & Waldfogel, 2011).

Box 3.1 Risk Domains in Physical Child Abuse

Adolescent stressors: Low self-esteem, negative life events
Antisocial behaviors: Aggression, substance misuse
Area characteristics: Percent in poverty, neighbourhood drug use
Education: Low commitment to school, low school grades
Family background/structure: Low parent education, teenage mother
Exposure to family violence: Parental partner conflict
Parent stressors: Parent depressive symptoms, parent drug and alcohol use
Parent–child relationships: Inconsistent discipline, poor supervision
Peer relationships: Delinquent peers, unsupervised time with friends
Precocious transitions to adulthood: Precocious sexual activity, school dropout

Source: After Thornberry et al., 2014.

The range of factors involved in the physical abuse of children has been drawn together by Thornberry et al. (2014). The main factors, together with examples of each factor, are shown in Box 3.1.

Bartlett, Raskin, Kotake, Nearing, and Easterbrooks (2014) reported an analysis of cases of neglect by young mothers. They found that the predictive factors for neglect had some overlap with those for physical abuse, including economic disadvantage, observing the violent behaviour of their own parents, and personally experiencing partner violence. The overlap in risk factors for physical abuse and neglect is further clarified by Stith et al. (2009), who carried out a series of meta-analyses of the relevant literature to identify risk factors for both types of abuse. They reported that the three principal risk factors for *physical abuse* were parent anger/hyperactivity, family conflict, and level of family cohesion; for *neglect* the main risk factors were quality of the parent–child relationship, parental perception of the child as a problem, parental stress, parent anger/hyperactivity, and parent self-esteem. As might be anticipated, a mixture of parental characteristics and social disharmony is involved in both types of abuse.

Those parents who physically abuse their children may use a combination of verbal aggression, such as screaming at the child, name-calling, and making threats, and direct use of physical force that may include slapping and punching (LeRoy, Mahoney, Boxer, Gullan, & Fang, 2014). The physical abuse of the child may be carried out by the mother or father alone or by both parents in combination. A large-scale study of family violence across 15 nations, reported by Straus and Michel-Smith (2014), found that about one-half of abusive incidents were perpetrated by both parents, with the other half almost equally divided between mothers and fathers. When the abuse was carried out by the father alone it was more severe in nature than abuse by the mother alone.

The diversity of forms which physical abuse can take, in conjunction with the characteristics and resilience of the individual child, suggest that the consequences of this form of violence are likely to be many and varied.

Consequences of physical child abuse

The potential long-term consequences of physical child abuse have been investigated in a wave of studies, identifying a range of individual and social problems for the abused child (e.g., Aber & Cicchetti, 1984; Kurtz, Gaudin, Howing, & Wodarski, 1993; Norman et al., 2012). The understanding of the effects of physical abuse has grown with the application of sophisticated research designs and methods of data analysis (e.g., Godinet, Li, & Berg, 2014; Mills et al., 2013). It is now evident that experience of childhood abuse is associated in later life with mental health and behavioural problems (Miller-Perrin, Perrin, & Kocur, 2009; Mills et al., 2013; Polcari, Rabi, Bolger, & Teicher, 2014; Turner, Finkelhor, & Ormrod, 2006), with developmental problems in terms of social adjustment and educational attainment and progression (Pratt & Greydanus, 2003), neurological development (Heim, Shugart, Craighead, & Nemeroff, 2010; Twardosz & Lutzker, 2010), and with the likelihood of suicide (Swogger, You, Cashman-Brown, & Conner, 2011).

In the same way as violence begets violence, so abused children are at an increased risk of physical and sexual criminal victimisation in later life. Widom's work shows how, particularly for females, childhood experiences of abuse and neglect are associated with later victimisation and perpetration with respect to intimate partner violence (McIntyre & Widom, 2011; Widom, Czaja, & Dutton, 2014).

It is also possible that physical child abuse has different short- and long-term effects on young boys and girls. Godinet, Li, and Berg (2014) found that the effects of childhood maltreatment on boys were strongest close to the abuse and then decreased gradually over time. The effect on girls was quite different: the psychological effects of the abuse were less marked close to the abuse but then became more pronounced as time passed. This finding is consistent with Griffin and Amodeo (2010), who examined the long-term effects of physical abuse as children on a sample of women. They noted that the long-term effects of childhood abuse were compounded by growing up in an adverse family environment with, for example, high levels of conflict and parental alcoholism. With specific regard to offending, physically abused children are at greater risk than their non-abused peers of committing delinquent acts in later life (Smith & Thornberry, 1995). In keeping with the notion of cycles of violence (Widom, 1989a, 1989b), these delinquent acts are likely to include a range of violent offences (Lansford et al., 2007), encompassing intimate partner violence (Renner & Slack, 2006). It is this latter form of violence, intimate partner abuse, to which I will turn my attention in due course. However, there is a form of family violence which has come to the fore rather more recently and which takes the form of children physically abusing their parents. (Child-to-parent violence is taken to exclude the abuse of older adults, which is discussed below.)

Child-to-Parent Violence

Harbin and Madden (1979) described child-to-parent violence as "battered parent syndrome", where parents are subjected by their child or children, typically aged between 14 and 17 years, to various forms of aggressive behaviour ranging from verbal abuse to physical assault. There is evidence that both male and female children will abuse their parents: however, males are more likely to commit acts of physical violence, while females are more likely to take part in emotionally and verbally abusive behaviour (Nock & Kazdin, 2002). As with other forms of violence, child-to-parent violence may be reactive, say in the context of an argument, or instrumental in that violence is used either to avoid a task or to persuade a parent to fund some activity.

A study by Calvete, Orue, and Gámez-Guadix (2013) noted a rising incidence of child-to-parent violence in Spain. They surveyed over 1,000 male and female adolescents and found that verbal abuse (yelling, name-calling, and threats) was by far the most common form of violence, followed by physical assault, and then the rare event of hitting with an object. Calvete et al. found that there were more proactive than reactive incidents of abuse, with no sex differences in the prevalence of physical abuse but a greater likelihood of girls carrying out verbal abuse. The best predictors of the continuation of abuse over time were the child's depression and substance abuse.

An Australian study by Purcell, Baksheev, and Mullen (2014) looked at data from 438 family court cases where juvenile family violence was involved. They found that a substantial number of these cases were concerned with child-to-parent violence. They were characteristically of the type where an adolescent, most often a male, typically with behavioural problems, subjected their parents (less so their siblings) to threats, property damage, and physical assault.

Intimate Partner Violence

Over time numerous terms have been used in the literature to refer to what is now called intimate partner violence. Thus, Robinson (2010) lists "Wife abuse, battered women, domestic violence, domestic abuse, spousal abuse, spousal assault, family violence, violence against women, intimate partner violence, gender-based violence" (p. 245) as all having been in use at various times. The terminology continues to evolve in its usage: unlike, for example, "wife abuse", the term "intimate partner violence" may equally well be applied to violence between partners who are not married and to partners of the same sex as well as to heterosexual partners.

Further, the use of terminology such as "wife beating" supports the perception that intimate partner violence is solely perpetrated by men against women. While it is undoubtedly the case than men do assault their partners, with all the attendant issues for any children in the family (Guille, 2004), there may be more gender symmetry in assaultive behaviour in heterosexual couples than was perhaps previously thought to be the case. Chan (2011a) reviews the evidence on self-reports of intimate partner violence, suggesting that overall there may be little in the way of a gender difference in rates of partner assault. There is a caveat to this point, as Chan notes, when all else is considered men are more likely to carry out serious acts of IPV often resulting in injury.

Intimate partner violence is a global problem (Garcia-Moreno, Jansen, Ellsberg, Heise, & Watts, 2006), as is seen by studies from countries as diverse as Australia (Bartels, 2010), Germany (Schlack, Rüdel, Karger, & Hölling, 2013), Italy (Romitoa & Gerin, 2002), Iran (Pournaghash-Tehrani, 2011), Mexico (Valdez-Santiago, Híjar, Martínez, Burgos, & Arenas Monreal, 2013), Paraguay (Ishida, Stupp, Melian, Serbanescu, & Goodwin, 2010), and Turkey (Balci & Ayranci, 2005). However, as with a great deal of family violence, it is difficult to be precise about the prevalence of intimate partner violence. The British Crime Survey conducted in England and Wales has considered intimate partner abuse (Roe, 2010). It gathered self-report data on intimate partner abuse from a sample of adults aged from 16 to 59 years, specifically including the participants' experiences of emotional, financial, or physical abuse, sexual assault, and stalking. The survey allows an estimate of prevalence to be made: thus, the data suggest that starting from the age of 16 years about one in four women and one in six men have experienced some form of partner violence. If this estimate is applied to the population of England and Wales then, as Roe suggests, this form of violence affects 4.5 million females and 2.6 million males. This finding is in keeping with research showing that women as well as men commit acts of intimate partner violence (Carmo, Grams, & Magalhães, 2011; Drijber, Udo, & Reijnders, 2013). The BCS reported that about one-third of those experiencing partner violence had been abused by more than one partner. Women were more likely to have suffered longer periods of abuse and to have experienced repeat victimisation, physical injury, and emotional harm.

The problems involved in accurately estimating the prevalence of partner violence are highlighted by the BCS finding that in the year preceding the interview only 16% of those experiencing abuse had reported it to the police. Of course, these estimates will vary by country, by the type of relationship, and over time (e.g., Berger, Wildsmith, Manlove, & Steward-Streng, 2012).

Violent behaviour between partners typically consists of punching and kicking resulting in injuries such as black eyes, bruising, teeth knocked out, and even broken bones (Falcão de Oliveira, Ribeiro de Lima Cardoso, Possante de Almeida, Cardoso, & Gutfilen, 2014). In extremis, the violence may lead to death, which may be legally determined to be homicide (Elisha, Idisis, Timor, & Addad, 2010). It should be noted that, as with other forms of violence, intimate partner violence can be of different types, such as psychological (name-calling, degrading personal comments) or physical assault (Williams, Richardson, Hammock, & Janit, 2012).

Following interviews with over 100 women and informed by data from official records, Dobash and Dobash (1984) describe a typical occurrence of intimate partner violence. The setting for the violent confrontation is most often the family home. In keeping with the pattern of situated transactions, the confrontation begins, sometimes with the added ingredient of drink or drugs, with a verbal exchange between partners. The confrontation may centre on, say, some aspect of the woman's behaviour such as not carrying out some task or her seeming to challenge the man's authority. Falcão de Oliveira et al. (2014) note that over two-thirds of the 1,000 women in their Brazilian study said that the man had been drinking or using drugs prior to hitting them. Falcão de Oliveira et al. also note that the women said that the most common motives for the violence were the aggressor's jealousy, anger over separation, and seeking revenge after discovering infidelity.

As the confrontation develops so the woman, who may be well aware from previous experience of the likely course of events, may try to withdraw physically or attempt to defuse the situation by trying to talk and calm down the situation. When the violence starts the woman may continue to try to negotiate a way out; in a minority of instances, however, she may hit back which, in turn, can provoke further and more serious violence. Once the violence is over, Dobash and Dobash describe how some men act as if nothing has happened, while the injured women sought contact with friends for comfort and sometimes for medical help. Falcão de Oliveira et al. (2014) note that the assaulted women described their partners as "jealous", "possessive", and, not surprisingly, "aggressive" and "violent"; yet, at the same time, they paradoxically described the man as a "good father" and "dedicated to the family".

Dobash and Dobash note that in some assaults there are bystanders to the partner violence. Some bystanders may be children for whom witnessing the assault within their family can have profound effects (see below). The bystanders may try to intervene to prevent the violence or leave to find assistance.

Finally, it is unlikely that the act of violence towards a partner will be a single, one-off, event. McLean (2005) suggests that repeat victimisation is to be anticipated the cases of intimate partner violence.

Antecedents to intimate partner violence

Some perpetrators of intimate partner violence are violent only towards their partners, while others are more generally violent and may commit a range of violent crimes (Klein & Tobin, 2008; Robertson & Murachver, 2007). To advance under-standing of the causes of intimate partner violence a group of studies has looked at the predictors, or risk factors, for intimate partner violence.

As with interpersonal violence generally, there are strong indications that intimate partner violence has its roots in childhood and adolescent experiences of violence such as familial physical child abuse (e.g., Renner & Slack, 2006), bullying (e.g., Corvo & deLara, 2010), or in the context of adolescent dating (O'Leary & Slep, 2003). These early experiences may become manifest in later life in the form of violence towards others, including family members, with the net effect that violence is trans-mitted across the generations (Askeland, Evang, & Heir, 2011; Franklin & Kercher, 2012; Temcheff et al., 2008). This generational transmission of violence is illustrated by Theobald and Farrington (2012), who used longitudinal data, covering a 40-year time span, to explore the association between factors present during childhood and adolescence and intimate partner violence in later life. The strongest predictive factors, assessed when the male cohort were 8–10 years of age, were associated with the characteristics of both the family and the child. Theobald and Farrington state that "The family factors were, a criminal father, a disrupted family, a low income family, large family size and experiencing poor supervision and (at age 18) not getting on well with parents. The individual factors were high impulsivity, daring, low verbal IQ and unpopularity at age 8–10, aggressive temperament at age 14 and drug use at age 18" (p. 1248).

An American study by O'Leary, Tintle, and Bromet (2014) reported variations according to gender in the risk factors for physical violence against partners. The unique risk factors for the men (mean age 27.6 years) were experience of parental violence, dating before the age 14 years, along with dating violence and experiencing violence from their partner. O'Leary et al. also pointed to the role of the psychiatric condition *intermittent explosive disorder* (IED) as a risk factor for partner violence. IED is characterised by extreme outbursts of anger which are sometimes out of all proportion to the situation and to any provocation, real or perceived, that may have occurred. For the women (mean age 38.0 years) the main risk factors for partner violence were age, such that younger women were more likely to behave aggressively towards their partner, experience of dating aggression, IED, cohabitation rather than marriage, experience of partner violence, and current tensions in their marriage or relationship.

Studies concerned with the risk factors for continued partner abuse have highlighted a variety of variables—ranging from number of children in the family, the quality of the relationship, previous violence, substance use, and poverty—associated with prolonged partner abuse, even after a prison sentence (Hilton, Harris, Popham, & Lang, 2010; Hilton, Harris, Rice, Houghton, & Eke, 2008).

The growth in understanding of the generational transmission of intimate partner violence and associated predictive variables informs the development of theory to produce a reasoned account of the development and continuation of intimate partner violence. As is often the case in social and human science there is a range of theoretical models—including sociocultural, intrapersonal, and interpersonal approaches—to explaining violence between intimate partners (Ali & Naylor, 2013a, 2013b; Corvo & Johnson, 2013; Finkel & Eckhardt, 2013; Hyde-Nolan & Julio, 2012). A fundamental issue across these various theories lies in the putative roles of nature and nurture in the continuity of intimate partner violence across the generations.

Biological factors   Pinto et al. (2010) note a range of biological influences, including genetics, brain functioning and head injury, neuropsychological factors, psychophysiology, neurochemistry, metabolism, and endocrinology, as biological correlates of intimate partner violence. There are two central areas of concern with respect to the role of biological factors in intimate partner violence: the first centres on *behavioural genetics*, the second on *neuropsychological factors*.

Saudino and Hines (2007) reported a behavioural genetics study, involving 134 monozygotic (MZ) and 41 dizygotic (DZ) twin pairs, investigating the genetic and environmental covariance between both physically violent intimate partner violence and psychological aggression. The analysis estimated the degree to which intimate partner aggression could be accounted for by shared genes. Saudino and Hines state that genetic influence explained about 15% of the variance for physical aggression, with a higher figure of about 22% for psychological aggression.

A similar study by Barnes, TenEyck, Boutwell, and Beaver (2013) looked at intimate partner violence, defined as hitting a partner, injuring a partner, or forcing sexual activity, in an American sample of 462 MZ twins and 721 DZ twins. The analysis revealed that a substantial percentage of the variance could be explained by genetic factors: specifically, for hitting one's partner, genetic influences accounted for 24% of the variance; for injuring one's partner 54% of the variance; and 51% for forcing sexual activity. Barnes et al. conclude that "Taken together, the current findings indicate that much of the intergenerational transmission of IPV may be due to the transmission of genetic risk factors as opposed to the transmission of certain values or because of the learning of these behaviors. This is not to say that IPV is completely under genetic control and that the environment holds no sway over these behaviors" (p. 376).

Neuropsychological factors are those biological processes which play a role in the relationship between functional and structural biological processes and cognitive and behavioural functioning. In studies of the neuropsychology of violence the focus typically is on frontal lobe functioning with respect to cognitive process and impulse control. However, other aspects of brain functioning may be involved in the aetiology of violence: for example, DeLisi, Umphress, and Vaughn (2009) suggest that the amygdala, part of the limbic system associated with emotion and with learning, may be involved in antisocial behaviour. A meta-analysis reported by Farrer, Frost, and Hedges (2012) found that 53% of perpetrators of intimate partner violence had a history of traumatic brain injury. This level of injury is far in excess of estimates of similar injury in the general population. Howard (2012) suggests that a possible explanation for this high rate of head injury may lie in the protagonists' own history of abuse: "Conservative estimates indicate that at least 40% of male perpetrators have been victims of childhood physical abuse with concomitant increases in the likelihood of perpetrating intimate partner violence as adults" (p. 330).

The weight of evidence shows that a complete theoretical account of intimate partner violence should include biological factors. There are, however, two points to note in this respect. First, are the biological factors discussed above unique to intimate partner violence? In other words, are there biological factors which have a *specific* contribution to make in intimate partner violence; alternatively, are these biological factors *general* correlates of violence? The latter may be the case: given the substantial overlap at the level of the individual male offender between risk factors for criminal violence and for intimate partner violence, Piquero, Theobald, and Farrington (2014) conclude that there is "Little need for a violence- or IPV-specific theory"; they suggest that "focus should be placed on general theories that combine all forms of violence and offending under a common explanation" (p. 297).

If we move to the nurture aspect of the equation so the focus shifts to the psychology of the perpetrator. In the context of the likelihood that their developmental history has been overshadowed by violence, what is known of the psychological functioning of the perpetrator?

Psychological factors   As may be anticipated, a wide range of psychological theories have been applied to intimate partner violence: Ali and Naylor (2013b) note that these theories include "Various psychological and psychiatric difficulties and disorders such as psychopathology, personality disorders, attachment needs, anger/hostility, substance and alcohol abuse, low self-esteem, and individual abilities such as excessive or weak assertiveness, communication difficulties, and poor problem solving skills" (p. 376).

If an individual's current psychological functioning is, in part at least, related to their developmental experiences as well as their biological functioning then it is likely that these twin influences will shape adult psychological functioning. If intimate partner violence is seen in a social context, in the sense of a disruption in the ability to form sound, stable relationships, then it follows that it makes sense to consider the psychological functioning of the aggressor from the standpoint of social cognition and social information-processing.

The model of social information-processing, as discussed in Chapter 1, formulated by Crick and Dodge (1994) has six sequential stages—(1) encoding of social cues, (2) interpretation of social cues, (3) goal clarification, (4) response access or construction, (5) response decision, and (6) behavioural response—can be used to build an understanding of the perpetrator's psychological functioning in intimate partner violence (Murphy, 2013).

The ability to recognise and accurately interpret facial expressions and other nonverbal cues is a fundamental aspect of understanding another person's emotional state. An impairment or deficit in recognising a partner's expressions has been studied in the context of intimate partner violence. There is evidence to show that some abusive men are poor at recognising at least some of their partner's emotional cues (e.g., Babcock, Green, & Webb, 2008; Marshall & Holtzworth-Munroe, 2010): in particular, abusive men may be insensitive to emotional expressions of fear. The misidentification of basic emotional cues, such as perceiving expressions of happiness as disgust (Marshall & Holtzworth-Munroe, 2010), must set any interaction off on the wrong track unless quickly corrected. If one partner misperceives the other's emotional state, perhaps particularly during a period of heightened discord in the relationship (Stith, Green, Smith, & Ward, 2008), then any ensuing interaction is in trouble from the onset. It is not difficult to see how an initial misreading of social cues, potentially exacerbated by the use of alcohol (Fals-Stewart, 2003; Simmons, Lehmann, & Cobb, 2008) or by mental disorder (Winstok & Straus, 2014), can set in train a set of situated transactions that culminate in a violent act. This pattern of behaviour may over time come to characterise the relationship, with the consequence that both parties come to see violence as inevitable in certain situations.

Substance use   The association between alcohol and interpersonal violence generally is firmly established. A body of research has considered the strength of any specific link between alcohol and intimate partner violence. Foran and O'Leary (2008) conducted a meta-analysis of 50 studies of the role of alcohol consumption in intimate violence. In keeping with the general finding of an association between alcohol and violence, they reported a significant relationship between alcohol and intimate partner violence for both males and females. This relationship proved to be particularly strong for alcoholic men. Foran and O'Leary describe three models of the association between alcohol use and intimate partner violence: these are (1) the spurious effects model; (2) the indirect effects model; and (3) the proximal effects model. The first model suggests that the relationship is correlational rather than causal and holds that both the excessive alcohol use and violent behaviour are the product of some other factor such as age or mental health problems. The second model states that there is a causal relationship but that it is mediated by other variables such as marital conflict. Thus, the excessive use of alcohol may lead to marital disharmony about the effects of drinking which, in turn, leads to arguments and so to violence. However, those studies which have controlled for marital dissatisfaction suggest that the association between alcohol and intimate partner violence nevertheless remains substantial (Fals-Stewart, 2003). The third model holds that alcohol intoxication is directly related to violence through its effects on cognitive functioning, as for example in distorted and inaccurate understanding of verbal and nonverbal interpersonal cues, and also in lowering social inhibitions.

The evidence suggests that the relationship is real rather than spurious, although it may be mediated by other variables, such as marital conflict. It must, however, be as true in the context of partner violence as it is in other settings that excess alcohol intake vitiates psychological functioning. Thus, the third model above will apply to partner violence, perhaps alongside other considerations relevant to that particular setting.

Alcohol use may be accompanied by the use of other substances. With a sample of men, Moore and Stuart (2004) found that a combination of alcohol and drug use significantly predicted partner violence.

With regard to substances other than alcohol, Moore et al. (2008) reported a meta-analysis of 96 studies of the relationship between drug use and intimate partner violence. They found that cocaine had the strongest relationship to violence, with marijuana also having a noteworthy association. Kraanen, Vedel, Scholing, and Emmelkamp (2014) looked at the rates of perpetration of intimate partner violence in a sample of males and females admitted for substance abuse treatment. They found that over the previous year approximately one-third of the sample had been involved, as either perpetrator or victim, in partner violence. The men's involvement in partner violence was best predicted by an alcohol use disorder together with a habit of cannabis and/or cocaine use; for the women, alcohol and cocaine abuse were strong predictors of perpetration and/or victimisation.

Consequences of intimate partner violence

The consequences of intimate partner violence are to be felt in several different ways throughout the family in which the violence takes place. However, it cannot be assumed that everyone in the family is agreed on the seriousness of the violence and its consequences. Williams et al. (2012) pointed to differences in the perception of the harm done by psychological and by physical forms of intimate partner violence. While outside observers, including mental health professionals, saw the physical abuse as the more serious, the victims of the violence said that both types of abuse were equally harmful. However, both observers and victims saw violence perpetrated by males as more harmful than that perpetrated by females.

Caldwell, Swan, and Woodbrown (2012) note that there are gender differences to be seen in the consequences of intimate partner violence. Given that the average male is more physically powerful than the average female, women may experience a greater degree of fear of violence and likelihood of physical injury. Women are also at greater risk of depression and anxiety disorders following intimate partner violence, but the evidence is less clear for substance use, including problem drinking. Caldwell et al. conclude that "In sum, both women and men experience negative effects of IPV, but many of these effects do appear to be more likely for women" (p. 50).

Physical harm   The degree of physical injury will depend on the force of the violent act. Thus, injuries such as bruising, hair torn out, broken noses, and displaced and broken teeth are a likely consequence of slaps and punches. The use of greater force, as with kicking, biting, burning or the use of a weapon, may result in greater harm such as broken limbs and internal injuries as well as psychological distress (Reijnders & Ceelen, 2014). The victim may be raped, with the attendant physical injuries associated with that form of violence.

If a woman is physically harmed while pregnant there are dangers to both her and the unborn child (Bhattacharjya & Deb, 2014; Taillieu & Brownridge, 2010). Devries et al. (2010) reported an analysis of data from several international surveys, spanning 19 countries, of intimate partner violence during pregnancy. The analysis revealed that this particular form of violence is not uncommon, with women aged under 35 at the highest risk of partner violence during pregnancy: "Over half of the surveys had a prevalence estimate between 3.8 and 8.8%. Prevalence appeared to be higher in the African and Latin American countries relative to the European and Asian countries surveyed, although estimates within regions (and countries) were highly variable" (p. 162). The figures can be much higher than those noted by Devries et al.: a survey of 313 pregnant women carried out in Iran reported that 175 (55.9%) reported intimate partner violence during pregnancy (Farrokh-Eslamlou & Oshnouei, 2014).

Psychological harm   Jordan, Campbell, and Follingstad (2010) reviewed the evidence on the effects of violence on women's mental health; Randle and Graham (2011) carried out a similar review for intimate partner violence in same-sex male couples. The reviews show that specific effects of intimate partner violence are to be found in elevated rates of various mental health problems, particularly depression and anxiety, and problem drinking. These problems may be enduring, as the woman sees herself as vulnerable which reduces the possibilities for her future success and happiness (Örmon, Torstensson-Levander, Sunnqvist, & Bahtsevani, 2014), and they may persist after a breakup of the abusive partnership (Adkins & Dush, 2010). In some cases the violence produces the extreme reaction of post-traumatic stress disorder (PTSD) with flashbacks to the violent event, social withdrawal, and so on (Golding, 1999). However, as Winstok and Straus (2014) show for depression (although the point is generic), given the individual differences among partners it cannot be assumed that all instances of intimate partner violence will necessarily have the same effects.

Social harm   It is highly likely that the psychological and physical consequences of partner violence will result in social change. If the relationship remains intact then there is the risk of increasing social isolation leading to lost friendships and wider family tensions. Further, there may be economic difficulties within the household if work and employment are adversely affected. Economic problems may mean that food becomes scarce, or that the rent is not paid, or the mortgage goes into arrears, so leading to threats of eviction. This family deterioration may trigger the involvement of social services if children are involved which, while potentially helpful, may in the short-term place greater strains upon the family. Yet further, as the family becomes increasingly unstable to the point of complete breakdown so the risk of homelessness increases. Baker, Billhardt, Warren, Rollins, and Glass (2010) note that in America "Evidence suggests that domestic violence is among the leading causes of homelessness nationally for women" (p. 431).

Long-term harm   The psychological, social, and economic sequelae of intimate partner violence may extend into the longer term in several different ways if the relationship ends and the family home breaks down. At a personal level, there may be long-term difficulties with enduring mental health problems. The costs of the breakdown may have been felt in loss of employment, loss of housing, financial debt, and even acquiring a criminal record. Thus, a gap in employment may make it difficult to find another job, so exacerbating and prolonging economic difficulties. A history of rent or mortgage arrears may make it hard to find new accommodation, particularly if coupled with a poor credit history. In light of these personal, social, and economic consequences, it is not surprising that, for women, previous exposure to intimate partner violence is associated with a high risk of future unemployment and ensuing poverty (Byrne, Resnick, Kilpatrick, Best, & Saunders, 1999).

Yet further, after a break in an abusive relationship it cannot be assumed that the violence is at an end. The perpetrator may continue to harass, stalk, and even physically assault their ex-intimate partner, so leading to concerns about managing risk after leaving a violent relationship (González-Méndez & Santana-Hernández, 2014).

As well as the short- and long-term issues for the adults, there may also be repercussions for children living in a household where violence between adults, typically one or both of the child's parents, is prevalent. Hamby, Finkelhor, Turner, and Ormrod (2011) analysed data drawn from the American National Survey of Children's Exposure to Violence. They found that for the nationally representative sample of over 4,549 children, aged up to 17 years, exposure to violence within the family was not uncommon, with 11% of the children reporting exposure in the past year and 6.6% reporting any exposure to parental physical violence. Hamby et al. (2011) suggest that if these figures are extrapolated to the youth population of the USA, then approximately 8.2 million young people were exposed to family violence in the past year, with a lifetime estimate of 18.8 million children.

Straus and Michel-Smith (2014) reported a survey across 15 nations, drawn from Asia, Europe, the Middle East, and North America, of 11,408 university students' experience of parental violence. They found that 14% of the students, with similar proportions of males and females, said they had witnessed one or more occurrences of physical violence between their parents. The most frequently observed violence was between both parents rather than one parent against the other parent.

Effects of intimate partner violence on children

The manner in which children observe violence within their family may vary considerably. As shown in Box 3.2, Holden (2003) has compiled a list of 10 ways in which a child may directly and indirectly become a part of the violence within their family.

What effects does the observation of family violence have on children? There is a large body of research given to this question, as discussed below, and summarised in several reviews (Chan & Yeung, 2009; Hamby et al., 2011; Holt, Buckley, & Whelan, 2008; Kitzmann, Gaylord, Holt, & Kenny, 2003; Van Horn & Lieberman, 2011). The

---

Box 3.2   Variations in Children's Exposure to Family Violence

1 Prenatal exposure.
2 Intervening to stop the assault.
3 Assaulted during an incident.
4 Joining the assault.
5 Witnessing the assault.
6 Hearing but not observing the assault.
7 Seeing the immediate consequences of the assault.
8 Experiencing life change as a result of the assault.
9 Hearing or being told about the assault.
10 Not knowing about the assault.

Source: After Holden, 2003.

broad conclusion from these reviews is that children and adolescents living with domestic violence are at an increased risk of a range of problems. These adverse effects include the development of psychological, social, and behavioural problems alongside an increased risk of emotional, physical, and sexual abuse. These risks may vary across the child's lifespan as they move through childhood and into adolescence and adulthood. However, as with research concerned with other forms of violence, the findings of an individual study are dependent upon the sample, the nature of the violence, the measures used, the research design, and the types of outcome measured. It follows that attempts to synthesise a large body of research will find variations according to these parameters (Chan & Yeung, 2009). Nonetheless, as discussed below, there are a number of consistencies in the research base which strongly suggest that there is every need to be concerned about the well-being of children living in the context of intimate partner violence (MacMillan, Wathen, & Varcoed, 2013).

Effects in childhood   The effects of physical and emotional violence during pregnancy are felt by the child as well as the mother. McMahon, Huang, Boxer, and Postmus (2011) looked at the effects of intimate partner violence during pregnancy on both maternal and child health one year after birth. They found that physical violence was strongly related to both maternal depression and the child's physical health. When the physical violence was accompanied by emotional abuse, defined as insults and personal criticism, there were significantly poorer outcomes in the mother's health and depression and in the child's health and temperament. The problems for the developing child caused by intimate partner violence during pregnancy are exacerbated if the child grows up in a household where they are exposed to and witness this form of violence.

An American study by Ybarra, Wilkens, and Lieberman (2007) compared the cognitive and behavioural functioning of two groups of preschool children, males and females, aged 3 to 5 years: one group of children had been exposed to family violence, the other not. As may be predicted, the mothers of the children exposed to intimate partner violence showed a higher level of psychological distress than did the mothers of the non-exposed children. A comparison of the children exposed to the family violence with those not exposed showed two main differences: first, the exposed children scored significantly lower on a test of IQ; second the exposed children showed a higher incidence of internalising behaviours, such as feelings of anxiety and depression, than the non-exposed children. The 11-point difference in IQ scores, evident for both boys and girls, was entirely explained by a difference in verbal, as opposed to performance, IQ. This level of verbal weakness places the child at a significant disadvantage compared to their peers functioning at an age-appropriate level. Given that the children are of preschool age, they will begin formal schooling well behind their peer group's level of cognitive functioning, with all the associated implications this holds for their readiness to start learning and their future educational achievement. The verbal disadvantage is likely to have an effect in other areas of the child's life, including their social development. The child may struggle with social interactions with peers and adults: indeed, a mother experiencing the effects of intimate partner violence may experience difficulties and frustrations in attempting to comprehend her child's communication regarding their unhappiness and distress.

A longitudinal study by Jouriles, Rosenfield, McDonald, and Mueller (2013) looked at child adjustment problems in children, males and females, between 7 and 10 years of age. They found that when children were involved in their parents' conflict they showed a range of difficulties, including both internalising and externalising problems. The externalising problems included disobedience and displays of aggression. Alongside problems in their psychological and social development and adjustment, the child exposed to intimate partner violence may also be at risk of impaired nutrition and hence delays in physical growth (Yount, DiGirolamo, & Ramakrishnan, 2011).

The effects of intimate partner violence on the child may be moderated by several factors (Howell, 2011). The socioeconomic status of the family, as assessed by level of poverty and the parents' marital status, may play a moderating role (Yoo & Huang, 2012). The child's place by age in a sibling group and the degree of closeness between siblings may also temper the effects of intimate partner violence (Piotrowski, Tailor, & Cormier, 2014).

Effects in adolescence   As the child grows older and reaches adolescence so the effects of intimate partner violence may become evident in several ways. First, the adolescent's own romantic relationships may be marked by violent behaviour. An American survey by Holt and Espelage (2005) reported that 32% of females and 43% of males said that they had been physically assaulted by a dating partner. This form of violence is also highly prevalent in dating by adolescent males and females belonging to sexual minorities (Martin-Storey, 2015). The likelihood of dating violence is further exacerbated if the adolescent, particularly a female adolescent, has both witnessed violence between parents and has also been subjected to harsh parenting (Jouriles, Mueller, Rosenfield, McDonald, & Dodson, 2012).

The pathways to dating violence may be different for adolescent males and females. Temple, Shorey, Tortolero, Wolfe, and Stuart (2013) found that for adolescent girls it was exposure to both father-to-mother and mother-to-father violence which was associated with perpetration of dating violence. For adolescent boys the link with dating violence was experience of mother-to-father violence. However, for both girls and boys, the perpetration of dating violence strongly related to an attitude which was accepting of violence. In light of all of the above, it is not surprising that Temple et al. (2013) have described dating violence as a "major public health problem" (p. 343).

Bartlett et al. (2014) found that intimate partner violence was one of a cluster of factors that predicted adolescent mothers' neglect of their children. The other factors, illustrating the complexity of the issues involved, were receipt of mental health services after becoming pregnant, a history of poor care during childhood, and living in a low-income neighbourhood. Similarly, Menard, Weiss, Franzese, and Covey (2014) found that a complex admixture of types of exposure to adolescent violence was related, differentially for males and females, to intimate partner violence.

Effects in adulthood   The pervasive effects of witnessing intimate partner violence as a child extend beyond adolescence and into adulthood. Dube, Anda, Felitti, Edwards, and Williamson (2002) found that witnessing intimate partner violence in childhood significantly increased the risks of a cluster of adult problems, including both depression and alcohol and drug use. In keeping with the notion of cycles of violence there is strong evidence to suggest that witnessing intimate partner violence as a child is related both to perpetration and being the victim of of the same form of violence in adulthood (Ehrensaft et al., 2003; Renner & Slack, 2006; Roberts, Gilman, Fitzmaurice, Deckerf, & Koenen, 2010). Cannon, Bonomi, Anderson, and Rivara (2009) took the scope of the notion of the intergenerational transmission of violence a stage further in showing that the children of women who had witnessed intimate partner violence during their own childhood were at heightened risk of similarly witnessing intimate partner violence.

Violence Against Elder Adults

As we live longer, the likelihood of which increases with advances in medical science and procedures, so we become increasingly physically frail and depend on others to care for our needs. The magnitude of the issue is seen in an estimate by the United Nations (2007) that between 2005 and 2050 one-half of the growth in the world population will be accounted for by a rise in the population aged 60 years or over; during the same period the UN estimates that the number of children under the age of 15 years will fall slightly. The daily care of this ageing population may lie in the hands of family members, or workers in care homes for the elderly, or members of the medical and allied professions. With frailty comes vulnerability so that some elder adults are at risk of experiencing violence as a direct consequence of their physical condition and personal situation. The types of abuse experienced by elder adults may be categorised, as shown in Box 3.3 as neglect and financial, physical, psychological, and sexual abuse (World Health Organization, 2002).

As with most forms of violence, elder abuse does not respect international boundaries. Notwithstanding the ubiquitous complexities of definition and measurement (for an example of which see Dixon et al., 2010), there is evidence of elder abuse from countries as geographically and culturally diverse as Australia (Kurrle & Naughtin, 2008), Canada (Podnieks, 2008), China (Dong, Chen, Chang & Simon, 2013), India (Chokkanathan & Lee, 2005), and Israel (Lowenstein, Eisikovits, Band-Winterstein, & Enosh, 2009). In Europe there is evidence for elder abuse from surveys in Austria, Belgium, Finland, Lithuania, and Portugal (De Donder et al., 2011) and in Germany, Greece, Italy, Lithuania, Portugal, Spain, and Sweden (Lindert et al., 2013), as well as in the UK (Biggs, Manthorpe, Tinker, Doyle, & Erens, 2009). There can be no doubt that elder abuse is a worldwide issue (Podnieks, Anetzberger, Wilson, Teaster, & Wangmo, 2010) and that it effects lesbian, gay male, bisexual, and transgendered elders as well as heterosexual elder adults (Cook-Daniels, 1998; Ristock, 2005).

Box 3.3   Categories of Elder Abuse

Financial Abuse
Theft of money, possessions, or property
Forced to give away money, possessions, or property
Fraudulent taking of money, possessions, or property
Misuse of power of attorney

Neglect
Ignoring repeated requests for help with day-to-day activities including:
    Shopping for groceries or clothes, preparing meals, and routine housework
    Personal care in washing dressing, eating and using the toilet
    Taking the correct dose of medication at the right time

Psychological Abuse
Insults, name-calling and being sworn at
Threats to self and others and belittling
Exclusion from family and friends

Physical Abuse
Physical restraint including tying and locking in room
Pushing, slapping, kicking, biting, punching
Burns and scalding
Threats with and use of weapons
Given drugs to control or make docile

Sexual Abuse
Sexualised comments and touching
Made to watch pornography
Attempted and actual sexual acts

Surveys provide information on a wide range of factors associated with the abuse, as illustrated by UK survey reported by Biggs et al. (2009). This UK survey was conducted using face-to-face interviews with a sample of 2,111 adults aged 66 years or older living in England, Northern Ireland, Scotland, and Wales. The survey found that 2.6% of the sample had been abused over the previous year: the most frequent form of abuse was neglect (1.1%), followed by financial (0.7%), psychological (0.4%), physical (0.4%), and sexual (0.2%) abuse. The women (3.8%) were more likely to have experienced abuse than the men (1.1%); the oldest members of the sample, aged 85 years and over, had the highest prevalence, due to particularly high rates of neglect. The perpetrators of the abuse were mainly family members: Biggs et al. note that "51% of mistreatment in the past year was carried out by a partner or spouse, 49% by another family member, 13% by a care worker, and 5% by a close friend" (p. 11).

As the volume of research has grown so reviews have offered an overview of the field (e.g., Daly, Merchant, & Jogerst, 2011; Lachs & Pillemer, 2004) highlighting the main parameters of this form of violence. In particular, there is now heightened knowledge of elder abuse within the family, elder abuse within institutions, and the risk factors for elder abuse.

Elder abuse within the family

The abuse of an elderly adult within a family can be seen as a form of domestic violence (Penhale, 2003) with, for example, some overlap in the characteristics of the perpetrators and victims. The typical scenario for elder abuse within the family is when an aging parent is being cared for either by one of their children or by one of their children and their spouse. As summarised below, Schiamberg and Gans (1999) offer an overview of the factors most closely associated with vulnerability to abuse by children.

Chronological age   Advancing age is accompanied by increasing risk of abuse. The older a person becomes the more likely they are to be physically frail, psychologically fragile, and have health problems.

Gender   The literature is divided on this point: Schiamberg and Gans (1999) note that some studies suggest that women are at greater risk, including risk of sexual abuse, while others suggest that men at are greatest risk. This contradiction may indicate that other factors either interact with or override gender when abuse occurs.

Health   It is a fact that ill health, both physical and psychological, places an extra demand on those caring for elderly adults. It is not surprising therefore that elder abuse is associated with the degree and severity of the individual's physical or mental impairment. Further, frailty due to poor health or physical disability may reduce the older person's ability either to find help or to defend themselves against an aggressor. These health-related factors are evident in the vulnerability to abuse brought about by the highly prevalent condition of dementia, sometimes due to Alzheimer's disease, with the associated impairments in cognitive and social functioning (Downes, Fealy, Phelan, Donnelly, & Lafferty, 2013). The loss of function reduces the individual's ability both to communicate with others and to understand and recall what has taken place. Further, dementia may bring about verbal and physical aggression which, in turn, provokes similar behaviour from others.

Marital status   A married person is more likely to be living with a relative, a spouse, or a child, hence marriage increases the chances of abuse.

Social isolation   If the elderly person lives alone and has few visitors then there is limited opportunity for the person to report their abuse or for it to be detected.

Davies et al. (2011) build on the reactive-proactive dichotomy in defining two types of abuser: (1) *the reactive abuser* is a "De-motivated, de-valued, stressed employee (or family member) who lacks adequate supervision and/or management support and commits acts of abuse out of desperation in impossible conditions (p. 5); (2) *the proactive abuser* is a "Serial abuser (or 'bad apple') who either has sought out contact with the vulnerable adult (e.g. through developing a friendship or working in the care sector) in order to commit acts of abuse, or has been opportunist" (p. 5).

In summary, there is a range of risk factors for elder abuse: these include *individual* characteristics such as cognitive impairment, functional dependency, and poor physical health or frailty; *perpetrator* characteristics such as being a paid carer or family member, type of relationship with the abused, or family conflict; and *setting*, such as community or an unsupervised care home (Johannesen & LoGiudice, 2013). Jackson and Hafemeister (2011) indicated that *financially* exploited older adults were likely to live alone, not to have children or a history of childhood family violence, and to perceive that they have a positive relationship with their abuser. Further, victims of financial exploitation were marked by an absence of physical and psychological deficits. In addition, Choi, Kulick, and Mayer (1999) reported that financially exploited elderly adults were, on average, in their late seventies with some level of cognitive impairment and likely to be living in their own home. The perpetrators of the financial abuse were likely to be relatives, typically children, of the elderly victims.

Jackson and Hafemeister (2011) also found that victims of *physical abuse* were likely to be living with the perpetrator and to have a history of violence both in terms of their own childhood and towards their abuser. Finally, *neglect* victims were younger, more impaired in terms of medical problems including dementia, and had communication deficits. It follows that they were likely to be dependent on other people on a day-to-day basis.

Conclusion

It is evident that for some people their home is far from being a safe haven from the outside world. There are various types of violence within the home involving all generations, from the most elderly to the very youngest. While many of the acts of violence perpetrated within the family home are against the law, they remain hidden from public view and hence remain free from prosecution. Nonetheless, there is a section of criminal law given to interpersonal violence, and it is to this topic that attention is now turned.

4

Criminal Violence

This chapter is concerned with the acts of interpersonal violence (excluding sexual violence) most often dealt with by the criminal justice system. Specifically, two broad types of violent crime which involve interpersonal exchanges will be considered: (1) non-lethal violent assault against the person; (2) violence which takes the life of another person.

Non-Lethal Violent Assault

A violent assault typically involves acts such as punching and kicking, sometimes with the use of a weapon, in order to inflict physical harm on a person. As with most behaviour, context is critically important, so in seeking to understand violent assault we begin by looking at the situations in which this type of violence occurs.

Violence in a public place

There is a variety of public places in which a violent assault may occur: reflecting the discussions in previous chapters, these settings include places where people interact such as schools, the workplace, public transport, sporting events, and public houses. There may be two people involved or groups of people, they may of the same sex or different sexes, and they may be acquainted or strangers. Of course, the country in which the assault takes place lends another dimension to the nature of the violence.

The importance of country is evident in considering school bullying. In Britain school bullying may take several forms, ranging from name-calling through to

The Psychology of Interpersonal Violence, First Edition. Clive R. Hollin.
© 2016 John Wiley & Sons, Ltd. Published 2016 by John Wiley & Sons, Ltd.

hitting and kicking. This British school violence contrasts sharply with that described in an American report looking at crimes in schools and colleges (Noonan & Vavra, 2007). Thus, Noonan and Vavra note the presence of handguns, shotguns, and explosives in schools with an annual number of around 400 recorded (who knows how many go unrecorded?) incidents of the use of a handgun. However, where America treads it seems the British invariably follow: while firearms are rarely seen in UK schools—Smith et al. (2010) noted just 13 occasions when firearms appeared in schools in England and Wales—who knows what the future may bring?

Violence in the workplace

There are professions, such as police and prison officers, where the nature of the job entails a heightened risk of personal violence. Thus, violence in prisons may involve both prison staff and prisoners and can range from bullying and assault to grievous injury and death (Schenk & Fremouw, 2012; Sorenson, Cunningham, Vigen, & Woods, 2011). Prison violence may be spontaneous, arising from exchanges between individuals, or it may be premeditated and the execution planned in advance. However, homicide in prisons is uncommon in England and Wales: the *Safety in Custody Statistics 2008/2009* (Ministry of Justice, 2010b) noted that in 2009 there were no homicides in prison custody. Given the association between some types of mental disorder and violent behaviour (see Chapter 1) it may be anticipated that, as is indeed the case, there are high levels of mental disorder to be found among prison populations (Fazel & Danesh, 2002).

Those people employed in settings which entail interactions with members of the public—shops, public houses, public transport—may also be at a higher risk of involvement in a violent altercation. In other professions the working environment in and of itself increases the risk of violence, as seen, for example, in Accident and Emergency hospital departments (Ferns, 2007).

There are some vulnerable people at risk of violence because of their living accommodation or lack of it. These people include children living away from home, vulnerable groups such as people with learning difficulties, and elderly adults living in institutions. The latter group exemplifies the issues associated with abuse in institutions.

Elder abuse in institutions   An elderly adult may leave their home and reside in an institution for one of several reasons: first, their age may mean that some personal frailty needs specialist care; second, they may have a physical or psychological condition which makes them particularly vulnerable; third, they may be serving a prison sentence.

An American study by Schiamberg et al. (2012) looked at the prevalence of abuse by staff by questioning a sample of 452 adults with elderly relatives living in nursing homes. They found that just under one-quarter of the respondents said they were aware of at least one incident of physical abuse. The abuse variously took the form of physical abuse such as hitting or slapping, maltreatment when administering care as with inappropriate use of physical restraints or forced feeding, and sexual abuse.

The issue of sexual abuse of elderly residents in nursing homes is addressed by Rosen, Lachs, and Pillemer (2010), who make the point that "Contrary to popular perception, most sexual abuse of this type commonly involves nursing home residents assaulting other residents rather than staff assaulting residents" (p. 1971). While pointing to the difficulties in obtaining reliable estimates, Rosen et al. suggest that men who are cognitively impaired are more likely to behave sexually towards other residents. However, it is also possible that some residents, including elderly sex offenders, may actively prey on other vulnerable residents (Zorza, 2005). Overall, the typical elderly victim of sexual violence is female and cognitively impaired, typically with some form of dementia and a physical impairment. While fewer in number, elderly male victims of sexual assault have similar characteristics to female victims.

There are several groups of people who require institutional care, such as people with a learning disability, those with a mental disorder, and those with a profound brain injury. It is certainly the case that some of these people will be elderly adults. As Cooke and Sinason (1998) note, these particular populations are at an increased risk of physical, sexual, psychological, and financial abuse because of their very high levels of dependence on others for their personal care. The purpose of the physical abuse may be to exert control over the resident or as an expression of power over another person.

The vulnerability of older adults in institutions is highlighted by the circumstances of those elderly people who are serving a prison sentence.

Elderly prisoners   We live at a time when prison populations are expanding, partly as a result of more people being sentenced to custody and partly because of the use of longer sentences. Thus, the implementation of policies in parts of the United States such as "three strikes and out", where three felony offences result in custodial sentences of 25 years or more, sometimes without the possibility of parole, has meant a significant growth in the numbers of elderly prisoners within an expanding population. In California, for example, the prison population reached 140,000 at one point, a figure so large that, as Bichler and Nitzan (2014) observed, "In May 2011, the U.S. Supreme Court ordered the State of California to release 30,000 to 40,000 of its 140,000 inmates" (p. 251).

In England and Wales, the prison population is set at around 80,000, with projections that it may rise over time (Ministry of Justice, 2013). The number of elderly prisoners has correspondingly continued to rise since the early 1990s, with a small number of prisoners aged over 80 years (Crawley, 2007). Ginn (2012) makes the point that prisons were originally intended for fit young men and so as institutions they are not designed nor equipped to meet the health and social needs of elderly male and female prisoners. Thus, the day-to-day problems faced by the elderly prisoner stem in part from the physical design of the building, with many stairways, difficulties for wheelchair access, and the lack of suitable facilities for exercise and hygiene.

The elderly prisoner is also likely to have increasing health needs. A survey of a sample of 15 English prisons reported by Fazel, Hope, O'Donnell, and Jacoby (2004) found that medication, mainly for cardiovascular, respiratory, and endocrine health problems, was being prescribed to three-quarters of the 203 older prisoners included in the survey. However, Fazel et al. reported that many elderly prisoners with psychiatric problems, particularly depression, were not being appropriately medically treated, nor was there any psychiatric and psychological treatment. While accepting that many elderly prisoners will have committed serious crimes for which they are serving long sentences, there is an argument to be made for some compassion towards this group, as with other physically deteriorating prisoners (Williams, Sudore, Greifinger, & Morrison, 2011), so that they do not have to die in prison.

Hate Crimes

The labelling of certain types of violence as hate crimes is a relatively recent phenomenon. The general context for the use of the term is one where acts of violence are perpetrated against another person on the basis of some aspect of their identity. Thus, a person may be subject to verbal and physical violence because of, for example, their race, religion, sexual orientation, or disability. The specific context, given that all victims of crime will belong to a race, have a sexual orientation, and so on, is that the crime is one where the offender's prejudice against the victim's characteristics is a motivating or aggravating feature of the attack. This is a broad explanation but what legally constitutes a hate crime? A legal definition is important because without an agreed definition it is impossible to draft the legislation that will enable the police and courts to function in arresting and prosecuting this type of offender.

In discussing the definitional issue, Garland (2012) joins with other commentators such as Gerstenfeld (2011) and Hall (2013) in pointing to several of the difficulties inherent in producing a satisfactory definition of hate crime. First, who are the victims of a hate crime? There are those groups, as above, who are readily identified as potential victims of hate crime but, as Garland points out, there are other groups, such as homeless people, who are not widely thought of in this context. Second, what is meant by the term *hate*? This term essentially refers to some psychological aspect of the offender's functioning in terms of their prejudice and hostility towards another group whose members are distinctive on the basis of their race, sexual orientation, and so on. Thus, a hate crime is an act against a particular individual or individuals which is motivated by the offender's prejudice towards that group. There are several forms of hate crime, evident on an international scale, such as attacks against Muslims (Chakraborti & Zempi, 2012; González, Verkuyten, Weesie, & Poppe, 2008) and against Indian minority groups (Mason, 2011).

As Hall (2013) notes, "The criminalisation of hate motivation arguably represents a shift in the criminal law from *deed* to *thought*. As a result the courts are now required to establish the offender's motives" (p. 127). Thus, in the normal course of events a violent act may result in a criminal prosecution as, say, grievous bodily harm or wounding depending on the details of what took place. However, to be prosecuted as a *hate* crime the traditional focus on the offender's actions has to be extended such that the violent act is demonstrably motivated by their prejudice against the victim. To accommodate this shift in emphasis there has been a world-wide change in legislation, with the same purpose differing in style and content from jurisdiction to jurisdiction, to bring hate crime under the umbrella of criminal law. Hall offers a helpful discussion of the intricacies associated with these legal changes in covering the "international geography of hate".

In 2007 in England and Wales various agencies within the criminal justice system, including the police, the Crown Prosecution Service, and the Prison Service, formulated a definition of hate crime based on the five strands of disability, gender identity, race, religion, and sexual orientation, to allow accurate recording and monitoring of this form of violence. Thus, in England and Wales a hate crime is a notifiable offence committed against a person or property that is motivated by hostility based on the victim's disability, race, religion, gender identity, or sexual orientation (Home Office, 2012).

Given these definitional issues, it is not surprising that that there have been difficulties in estimating the number of hate crimes.

Hate crime statistics

Victim surveys such as the British Crime Survey (BCS) produce valuable information about the levels of, often unrecorded, crime. However, for a victim to say that they have been a victim of a hate crime they must necessarily perceive the hateful intentions of the offender. While in some cases the offender's intentions are perfectly obvious, in other situations this may not always be the case. If the victim does not actually see the perpetrator or understand the context of an attack, as with say arson directed at their home by an unknown assailant, how are they to report it as a hate crime?

Nonetheless, the BCS does offer some indication of the extent of hate crime. Smith, Lader, Hoare, and Lau (2012) analysed the BCS figures from the 2009/2010 and 2010/2011 surveys to produce an annual estimate of over a quarter of a million hate crimes in England and Wales. Those individuals at the greatest risk of hate crime victimisation were aged between 16 and 24 years, single and unemployed, long-term ill or disabled, and belonged to an ethnic group other than white. Some individuals were victimised more than once: Smith et al. estimate that approximately one-third of victims experienced repeated hate crimes.

The official crime statistics invariably show lower figures than are seen in victim surveys for most types of crime. The variation in the frequency with which the different types of race crime are recorded by the police in England and Wales is shown in Box 4.1, with race hate crimes by far the majority (Home Office, 2012). These figures account for approximately 1% of all the crimes recorded by the police during 2011–2012.

Box 4.1   Police-Recorded Hate Crimes 2011–2012
in England and Wales

The total number of hate crimes recorded by the police in 2011 to 2012 was
43,748. This may be broken down as:

35,816	(82%)	were race hate crimes
4,252	(10%)	were sexual orientation hate crimes
1,621	(4%)	were religion hate crimes
1,744	(4%)	were disability hate crimes
315	(1%)	were transgender hate crimes

Source: Home Office, 2012.

The likelihood that the numbers of officially recorded hate crimes will rise over
time is illustrated by figures given by Moody and Clarke (2004): they note that in
Scotland the number of racially aggravated crimes recorded by the police rose from
386 in 1999, to 917 in 2000, then to 1,588 in 2001, and finally to 2,371 in 2002.
However, these figures do not necessarily indicate that racially aggravated crimes are
actually increasing. It is possible that an increased sensitivity to racially motivated
attacks means that victims and witnesses are more willing to report such crimes to
the police, so leading to more successful prosecutions and a rise in the crime statistics.

Craig (2008) notes that there are three areas to consider in seeking to understand
hate crime: (1) the motives of the perpetrators of this type of crime; (2) the characteristics of the victims; (3) the wider cultural, social, and economic conditions which
provide the setting in which hate crimes arise.

Perpetrators and victims of hate crime

By definition, hate crimes occur because of the individual's prejudice against some
personal characteristic of their victim. It is not difficult to make the link between
prejudice and stereotype, at the level of both the collective and the individual, such
that the hated group is perceived in global and overly simplistic terms. Cox, Abramson,
Devine, and Hollon (2012) provide an example: "If dark skin is the defining feature
for being Black, then the link between dark skin and the Black racial group is not a
stereotype. But, a link between *Black* and *poor* is a stereotype, even if there is a correlational, causal, or cultural connection" (p. 429). Thus, stereotyping is the process of
assuming that one characteristic accurately predicts another characteristic.

The early investigation of those who hold extreme stereotypes led to the
development of the concept of an authoritarian personality (Adorno, Frenkel-
Brunswik, Levinson, & Sanford, 1950). Peterson and Zurbriggen (2010) note that

"Those scoring high on authoritarianism (1) adhere strongly to conventional moral values, (2) are submissive to established authorities, and (3) are willing to aggress against others if they are perceived as unconventional or threatening" (p. 1802). Given that one of the features of hate crime is extreme prejudice towards and aggression against another group, it may be anticipated that features of the authoritarian personality will be a characteristic of those who commit hate crimes.

If we look first at the prejudiced individual, there is evidence to suggest that the constructs of right-wing authoritarianism and social dominance may be used to understand prejudice towards minority groups (Ekehammar, Akrami, Gylje, & Zakrisson, 2004) as well as animal exploitation (Dhont & Hodson, 2014). Right-wing authoritarianism is manifest as a strong preference for conventional values and authoritarian aggression. Social dominance refers to an individual's preference for hierarchical supremacy, as opposed to equality, in the various groups that form a society (Pratto, Sidanius, Stallworth, & Malle, 1994).

In terms of social organisation, it is likely that those holding similar prejudices will see themselves as belonging to a social group, however defined, and so base their social identity on the values espoused by that group. Indeed, one of the features of hate crime is that the perpetrators may form a cohesive social group based around their common resentment and hate of another group. The members of such groups may act together when committing an offence based on this hatred, with the consequence that many hate crimes are committed by multiple perpetrators. An obvious example of this type of group is the Ku Klux Klan, now a minority group but at times during American history a force for white supremacy over black citizens (Wade, 1987).

Social groups with strong but fundamentally opposed identities, sometimes linked to political values, are likely to come into open conflict. These points are highlighted, for example, by the highly polarised views with respect to immigration which are evident in different social groups (Oyamot, Fisher, Deason, & Borgida, 2012). In the UK there have been, for example, violent public clashes between members of Unite Against Fascism, with its roots in left-wing politics, and the ring-wing British National Party.

While violent crime can have severe effects on its victims, there may be an extra dimension to the harm caused by hate crime. Alongside the pain and fear that an individual victim may experience following a violent incident, other members of the victim's group, whether that group is sexually, racially, or otherwise defined, may develop a heightened awareness of their own vulnerability to attack and so become suspicious of others and censor their own movements. Yet further, if a group feels under threat from another group, then vigilante groups may form leading to retaliations.

Social, economic, and political forces   The social conditions of fear and retaliation can act to generate a wider sense of social unease, felt by all those living in a neighbourhood. This more widespread, diffuse sense of social unease may be the tinder against which a single incident becomes the spark for a blaze of community violence in which diverse groups are pitched against each other and against the police as they seek to impose law and order. In the worst-case scenario, as was seen in

England in 2011 (Bridges, 2012), these types of civil disturbance can escalate, enabled in part by social media (Baker, 2012), to become full-scale riots which spread from city to city.

Social climate is an important consideration in understanding hate crime. It is evident that at certain periods authoritarian social and political ideologies are in the ascendency. The most obvious example is the rise of the National Socialist German Workers' Party in Germany in the 1920s with its policies based on racial supremacy alongside the annihilation of so-called degenerate and asocial groups defined on the basis of their race, religion, or sexual preference.

The appearance and growth in popularity of political parties which champion group conflict is most likely to occur when there is political unrest and economic hardship. While the Nazis are an extreme case, there are recent examples in Europe of the emergence of political parties—such as the British National Party (BNP) in the UK, the Front National (FN) in France, Golden Dawn in Greece, and Nieuw Rechts (NR) in The Netherlands—based on nationalism and which argue for the expulsion of groups on the basis of their race. As noted above, such conditions provide the setting for clashes between diametrically opposing groups.

There is a long-held association between economic hardship and a rise in the incidence of hate crime (Hovland & Sears, 1940). This association does not infer a direct causal link between economic conditions and hate crime (Green & Strolovitch, 1998); rather, it argues that unfavourable economic conditions can provide the backdrop against which hatreds may be played out. While the association between personality and political attitudes is complex at an individual level (Verhulst, Eaves, & Hatemi, 2012; Verhulst, Hatemi, & Martin, 2010), there can be little doubt that there are periods where the political climate shifts to accommodate divisive authoritarian opinion. The degree to which such periods of social unrest see a rise in the incidence of hate crime is as yet unknown and, rather like the putative link between unemployment and crime (Phillips & Land, 2012), difficult to establish conclusively.

Kidnapping and Abduction

In England and Wales three offences are grouped within the category of kidnapping: the first is *kidnapping*, which is taking a person by force or trickery without their consent; the second is *false imprisonment*, unlawfully detaining or restraining a person's liberty; the third is *hijacking*, which includes unlawfully taking control of an aircraft or train, causing damage to or destroying an aircraft or train, or endangering an aircraft's safety.

Kidnapping

Kidnapping is not a common offence: the *Offender Management Caseload Statistics 2008* (Ministry of Justice, 2009) recorded 57 kidnappings/abductions that resulted in a conviction in 2007–2008, falling to 21 in 2008–2009. The *Caseload Statistics* note that in England and Wales in 2008 the number of people in prison was 98,820, of which 217 (208 men and 9 women) had been convicted of kidnapping, so accounting for 0.23% of the prison population.

Using official records, Soothill, Francis, and Ackerley (2007) reviewed the criminal histories of the 7,042 males and 545 females who had been convicted of kidnapping between 1979 and 2001. The average age of the kidnappers was the mid-twenties: over one-half of the males and one-third of the females had previous convictions, mainly for theft and violent offences, but only 10 men and 14 women had more than one conviction for kidnapping. The majority of the kidnappings had sexual and violent motives rather than financial gain.

Child abduction

Erikson and Friendship (2002) reviewed police records at New Scotland Yard to identify 149 cases which had resulted in a conviction for child abduction between 1993 and 1995. The analysis of these cases was based on their classification according to the offender's motivation for taking the child and their relationship with the child. Erikson and Friendship reported three main types of child abduction, which they called *sexual* (60% of cases), *custodial* (18%), and *maternal desire* (12%). The remaining 10% of cases involved a range of circumstances such as abducting a child for religious motives and stealing a car which contained children.

The *sexually motivated* offenders were the only ones who had previously abducted a child and they were the most criminal group, with convictions for both sexual and violent offences. In the cases with a sexual motivation the children were mostly female and had an average age of 10 years, making them the oldest of all the abduction victims. The *custodial dispute* cases were child custody disagreements involving estranged parents; most of these abductions were by the child's father. The offenders falling into the *maternal desire* classification were all female and were not related to the child: these women were the youngest perpetrators and abducted the youngest children, seemingly to satisfy a maternal drive.

A similar analysis, this time of 798 cases of child abduction in England and Wales from 2002 to 2003, was reported by Newiss and Fairbrother (2004). They found three main types of abduction involving children with an average of 9 years of age and who were mainly male (56%): the three types were (1) a stranger unsuccessfully attempting to abduct a child (47%); (2) parental abduction (23%); (3) abduction by a stranger (9%).

There are rare cases where a child is abducted, sexually assaulted, and then murdered. A review of the literature on sexually motivated child abductions was reported by Heide, Beauregard, and Myers (2009). They concluded that this particular type of abduction is most often perpetrated by someone who is a stranger to both the child and their family. The offender is not likely to misuse substances, is likely to use pornography, and may plan the offence by going to settings such as schools and parks where children gather, although the choice of victim may be spontaneous.

The killing may be by physical force, such as strangling, rather than with the use of a weapon. The child's body is likely to be left, sometimes roughly concealed, close to the scene of the murder.

An American study by Beasley et al. (2009) compared 311 cases of abduction where the child was later found alive with 439 cases where the abducted child was murdered or missing presumed dead. Overall, the majority of the abductions were carried out by men. Of the 41 abductions by women there were 31 cases where the child was recovered alive. Most of the child abductors had lengthy criminal histories, including convictions for various types of acquisitive offence, drug offences, kidnapping, violent offences including weapon law violations, and sex offences.

Arson

Arson is primarily a property crime which occurs when a fire is deliberately started with the aim of damaging a commercial or domestic property. However, fire is dangerous and at times uncontrollable, and may, either intentionally or unintentionally, endanger life. The Office for National Statistics (ONS) reports that in 2013 the police recorded 18,698 instances of arson in England and Wales (ONS, 2014b). While the majority of these fires will have primarily involved property, such as a factory, a school, a car, or even a rubbish skip, rather than a dwelling, these figures nonetheless translate to 55 injuries and two deaths caused by arson in an average week in England and Wales. The highest toll on life is when the fire is in a home and a group of adults and children die in the same fire.

As will be also be seen with offending by homicide perpetrators, not all arsonists follow the same pattern of setting fires; some arsonists start a single fire while others will set multiple fires. There are *mass arsonists* who light several fires over a very short period of time, typically hours, in the same general location. In contrast, a *spree arsonist* lights several fires over longer period, typically a day, in different locations. A *serial arsonist* sets fires in a variety of locations over an extended period of weeks, months, or years. As with other violent crimes, arson may be carried out for instrumental purposes, for example with the intention of a making a fraudulent insurance claim, or in a hostile manner in order to exact revenge against an adversary.

The research into arson suggests that there are three broad groups of individuals who set fires. These three are juvenile firesetters, adult arsonists, and mentally disordered firesetters.

Juvenile firesetters

As arson is a crime and some juveniles involved in firesetting are below the age of criminal responsibility it can be inappropriate to use the term *juvenile arsonist*, and *juvenile firesetter* is preferred. A substantial number of studies have investigated the demographic, psychological, and social characteristics of juvenile firesetters

(Hollin, Epps, & Swaffer, 2002; Kennedy, Vale, Khan, & McAnaney, 2006; Martin, Bergen, Richardson, Roeger, & Allison, 2004; McCarty & McMahon 2005; Pollinger, Samuels, & Stadolnik, 2005); see Lambie and Randell (2011) for a review.

Juvenile firesetters are most likely to be male, although some female juveniles do set fires: Hickle and Roe-Sepowitz (2010) found that the characteristics of 114 female juveniles charged with arson were similar to those seen in males, although the females appeared particularly to target schools and on occasions they acted in a group. Juvenile firesetters may well be involved in more than one incident of firesetting and display a childhood fascination with fire, as seen in playing with matches and deliberately setting off fire alarms. They are also likely to display a range of problem behaviours including violent behaviour, animal cruelty, and substance abuse as well as psychiatric issues such as anxiety and depression. The psychological factors associated with juvenile firesetting include poor interpersonal skills, impulsivity, high levels of anger, and poor assertion and problem-solving skills. Juvenile firesetters are also likely to experience social difficulties such as a disturbed education and family life characterised by parental conflict and experience of abuse. These young people may attend several schools over a short period of time alongside breaks in family life spent in foster care and in residential childcare homes.

Adult arsonists

The majority of adult arsonists set fires for pragmatic purposes such as covering up evidence of another crime, say a burglary or a murder, or for financial gain, for example, to make a false insurance claim. This group includes "professional" arsonists who are paid to set fires and may well be expert in practices such as the use of accelerants like glue, butane, and petrol (Flanagan & Fisher, 2008; Heath, Kobus, & Byard, 2011).

Canter and Fritzon (1998) analysed crime reports and witness statements from 175 cases in which the perpetrator had been convicted of arson. They reported two broad types of arson: one in which the intent is to damage or destroy a building, the other where the intent is to harm a person—this can be either self-harm or harm of another person. Canter and Fritzon also noted that arson directed against people tended to be carried out by individuals with a psychiatric history, while arson attacks intended to damage buildings tended to be carried out by serial arsonists. A Finnish study reported by Häkkänen, Puolakka, and Santilla (2004) investigated 189 cases of arson and reported a similar pattern to Canter and Fritzon, additionally noting that the most frequent motive arsonists gave for setting the fire was revenge, hatred, or jealously.

In developing scales to assess the factors associated with adult firesetting, Gannon and Barrowcliffe (2012) found that self-reported firesetters experienced high levels of fascination with and arousal by fire. The supporting longitudinal evidence is lacking, but it is plausible to suggest that the fascination with fire evident in adults is a continuation of the same trait from childhood.

Recidivism   Do convicted arsonists continue to set fires after serving their sentence? Soothill and Pope (1973) conducted a 20-year follow-up of 74 individuals, of whom only one was a woman, convicted for arson in 1951 in England and Wales. At 5% of the sample, there was a very low rate of reconviction for further crimes of arson, but almost one-half of the arsonists did receive a later conviction for another offence unrelated to arson. This study was replicated by Soothill, Ackerley, and Francis (2004) by looking at the criminal careers of three cohorts of convicted arsonists in England and Wales: 1,352 in 1963–1965; 5,584 in 1980–1981; and 3,335 in 2000–2001. These later figures indicate a remarkable rise in the number of convictions for arson when set against the 1951 figure; however, this rise may, as Soothill et al. suggest, be due to more successful prosecutions rather than more offending. The 1980s arsonists were more likely to be reconvicted for a criminal offence after their initial sentence. The rate of reconviction for another offence of arson remained relatively small at about 11% of the sample. As Soothill et al. note, the rise from three recidivistic arsonists in the 1951 group to an annual average of 300 from the 1980–1981 group points to a problem that is on the rise.

Mentally disordered firesetters

The figures from several European countries—including Finland (Repo, Virkkunen, Rawlings, & Linnoila, 1997), Sweden (Fazel & Grann, 2002), and the United Kingdom (Coid, Kahtan, Gault, Cook, & Jarman, 2001)—indicate that about one in ten admissions to forensic psychiatric services are of people who have committed arson. The risk posed by these patients is a cause of great professional concern to psychiatrists—particularly when the fire was started in occupied premises with the associated danger to life (Sugarman & Dickens, 2009)—and raises a raft of theoretical, practical, and legal issues (Dickens, Sugarman, & Gannon, 2012).

There are, as discussed below, a range of mental disorders associated with arson. However, there is one mental disorder, *pyromania*, specifically concerned with pathological firesetting.

Pyromania   The diagnostic criteria for pyromania, as given by the American Psychiatric Association (2000), are intended for those individuals who deliberately set more than one fire. This is a rare condition and classified as an impulse-control disorder: it is characterised by an undue curiosity for and fascination with fire which leads the person impulsively to start fires not for the usual reasons of financial gain or personal revenge but rather to release psychological tension or for excitement.

Lindberg, Holi, Tani, and Virkkunen (2005) looked at the medical and forensic examination of 401 arsonists referred to Helsinki University Hospital, Finland, for psychiatric assessment prior to a court appearance. Within this group there were 90 arsonists, all male, responsible for two or more fires. Lindberg et al. used APA diagnostic criteria (DSM-IV-TR) to look for the incidence of pyromania.

Of the 90 male arsonists, only three met the full diagnostic criteria for pyromania. Thus, these three individuals, all working as volunteer firefighters and referred to by Lindberg et al. as "pure arsonists", account for less than 1% of the original cohort of 401 arsonists. It is clear that pyromania is a rare phenomenon which leads to the question: What types of mental disorder are frequently associated with arson?

Characteristics of mentally disordered arsonists   A Canadian study by Rice and Harris (1991) looked at 243 male firesetters, including 145 repeat firesetters, admitted to a maximum security psychiatric facility. The repeat firesetters had a more disturbed background which included several other types of criminal behaviour. The most common diagnoses were personality disorder, evident in over one-half of the sample, followed by schizophrenia in about one-third of the sample. In keeping with Lindberg et al. (2005), only one individual met the diagnostic criteria for pyromania.

From their 1981 data, Rice and Harris (1996) identified four groups of firesetter: (1) *psychotics* formed the largest group, characterised by a high rate of both schizophrenia and alcohol abuse; (2) *unassertives*: were men with a stable background who had atarted a fire for revenge or in anger; (3) *multifiresetters*: these were the youngest patients with the most disturbed backgrounds and had set several fires in different places; (4) *criminals*: these had the most extensive criminal history, including other violent crimes.

Rice and Harris (1996) then considered the outcomes for their sample of 243 male firesetters. They found that there was a 16% chance of another arson at almost eight years follow-up after discharge—in terms of criminal recidivism this figure is on the low side. The patients in the *criminals* group were the most likely to set fires as well as to commit other offences after release.

Diagnoses   A Swedish study by Enayati, Grann, Lubbe, and Fazel (2008) looked at 214 arsonists, 59 women and 155 men, who had been referred for inpatient psychiatric assessment. The most frequently observed diagnoses, for both males and females, were substance use disorders, personality disorders, and psychosis (typically schizophrenia). A similar study with 167 male and female adult arsonists referred to psychiatric services in England found that personality disorder and learning disability were more frequent among multiple firesetters than among those who had set a single fire (Dickens et al., 2009).

Schizophrenia is often associated with serious crime, including arson, and particularly so for women who start fires (Gannon, Tyler, Barnoux, & Pina, 2012; Jamieson, Butwell, Taylor, & Leese, 2000). A Swedish study by Anwar, Långström, Grann, and Fazel (2011) compared the incidence of schizophrenia in a sample of 1,340 male and 349 female arsonists with a control group drawn from the general population. They reported that the probability of being diagnosed with schizophrenia was 20 times greater for the arsonists than for the controls, with a higher rate of schizophrenia among the female arsonists.

A study carried out in a maximum security forensic hospital in The Netherlands by Labree, Nijman, van Marle, and Rassin (2010) compared 25 arsonists with 50 patients in the same institution who had committed other serious offences. They found that just over one-quarter of the arsonists were diagnosed with a major psychotic disorder compared to over one-half of the controls. However, a study of patients admitted to a medium secure psychiatric unit in England reported by Hollin et al. (2013) found that from a population of 595 admissions over a 20-year period there were 129 patients, 93 males and 36 females, with a conviction for arson. The psychiatric profile of the arsonists indicated high levels of mental illness, including schizophrenia, for both males and females.

Intellectual disability is also often associated with arson (Devapriam & Bhaumik, 2012). In a typical study, Dickens et al. (2008) looked at a sample of 202 male and female arsonists referred for psychiatric assessment. In all, 88 of the arsonists had an IQ of 85 or below and the low IQ arsonists set more fires than those with a higher IQ.

Understanding Arson

All the major psychological theories have been applied to formulate an understanding of arson. Thus, Freud (1932) suggested a link between interest in fire and sexual desire, although recent research has found little empirical support for the idea that those who set fires find the act to be sexually arousing (Quinsey, Chaplin, & Upfold, 1989). The application of learning theory to consider the reinforcing consequences of firesetting was employed by Jackson, Glass, and Hope (1987) in providing a functional analysis of arson. In this approach the consequences of firesetting are seen as positively reinforcing the behaviour: for example, a fire started with peers in a group context may provide social rewards, or the actions of other people and the presence of firefighters may be rewarding and so increase the likelihood of more firesetting. Alternatively, firesetting may be negatively reinforcing by helping the perpetrator to avoid a problem, such as debt or bankruptcy; or burning down a school is effective in the short term as a way of avoiding the demands of education and so leads to more firesetting when a similar situation to be avoided arises in the future. This functional analysis approach was drawn on in the development of SAFARI (St Andrew's Fire and Arson Risk Instrument; Long, Banyard, Fulton, & Hollin, 2013) an assessment tool for use with mentally disordered firesetters.

Social learning theory suggests that there may be models which make fire appear attractive and exciting, particularly to children. Curri et al. (2003) carried out a study in an American national toy store looking at images of fire on the packaging of toys. They found over 404 toys, mainly toy vehicles and video games targeted at young boys, which used pictures of fire on the packaging. As Curri et al. note, the message being conveyed is that fire is fun and enjoyable. A similar study by Greenhalgh and Palmieri (2003) looked at accounts of fire and its consequences in the American popular media including both printed material and television programmes. As did Curri et al., Greenhalgh and Palmieri suggest that images of flames are mainly used in advertising, typically for clothes, skateboards, and hot rods, directed at boys and young men. Thus, Greenhalgh and Palmieri argue that the media may influence the behaviour of children and adults by depicting fire as fun and having little real consequence. Once the child copies these models, the real-life rewarding consequences may act to strengthen the behaviour and lead to its reoccurrence.

While arson may serve one or more functions for the arsonist, it does have a place in the context of interpersonal violence. As the statistics reveal, the use of fire as an act of hostility or revenge towards another person can have serious consequences, be they physical, psychological, or social, for the victims.

Taking Another Person's Life

In Britain, the Homicide Act 1957 defines three forms of killing: these are murder, manslaughter, and infanticide. *Murder* is the *intentional* taking of another person's life. The element of intent is critical: if there is no premeditation then the act cannot be murder, although it may be *manslaughter*. It may be a matter for the criminal courts to determine if a killing was premeditated and therefore murder rather than manslaughter. It follows that the accused must legally be seen to be competent with respect to forming the intent to kill. A person may not be seen as liable for their actions if, for example, they are under the age of criminal responsibility—which is 10 years in England and Wales but 8 in Scotland—or if they are mentally disordered as defined by the Mental Health Act.

In law, *manslaughter* has two basic forms: (1) in *voluntary manslaughter* there is intent to kill but there may be mitigating circumstances such as provocation or diminished responsibility; (2) *involuntary manslaughter* may take the form of an act, such as dangerous driving, which is grossly negligent, or an unlawful or negligent act, such as failure to exercise professional care, which similarly results in death. The offence of *corporate manslaughter* occurs when managerial failings, such as the failure properly to maintain equipment, cause a person's death. Finally, *infanticide* is the murder of a child which, as discussed below, may be of a number of types.

Number of homicides

The Criminal Statistics for England and Wales released on 13 February 2014 (Office for National Statistics, 2014a) show that homicide is not a common crime. The Home Office Homicide Index for in England and Wales recorded 551 homicides in 2012–2013. This figure is 21 higher than the 530 recorded in the previous year due to a rise, from 47 to 67, in homicides by those under 16 years of age.

The low numbers of homicide is at variance with the image projected by the popular media, where murder is a regular form of entertainment. Brown, Hughes,

McGlen, and Crichton (2014) compared the number of murders over several years in the fictional television series *Midsomer Murders* with the real number recorded by the Lothian and Borders police in Scotland. The television series contained 217 homicides carried out by 105 perpetrators as compared to 55 homicides by 53 perpetrators over a similar period in the real world. (Thus making the sleepy county of Midsomer the single most dangerous place in England!) There were also variations in the details of the murders: the fictional accounts had more serial killings and planned homicides involving shooting and poisoning than in real life. In the mundane world of the Lothian and Borders police the large majority of murders were unplanned single killings involving intoxicated perpetrators armed with kitchen knives and their own fists and feet.

Homicide: The Details

The majority of murderers will kill one person. However, there are other murderers, *multiple murderers*, who kill more than once. Multiple murderers may be one of three types—mass murderers, spree murderers, or serial murderers—as defined by the amount of time between killings (Gresswell & Hollin, 1994).

Mass murderers

The mass murderer kills a substantial number of people in a very short period of time. The American mass murderer James Huberty, armed with submachine gun, a pump-action 12-gauge shotgun, and a pistol, entered a McDonalds restaurant in San Diego and shot and killed 21 people in a sustained act of violence lasting 77 minutes. In a similar case, Thomas Hamilton entered a primary school in Dunblane, Scotland, and opened fire with four handguns. Within minutes he had killed 16 children and one teacher before fatally shooting himself.

Spree murderers

The spree murderer also kills several people but typically over a number of hours in several different locations. On 19 August 1987, armed with a handgun and two semi-automatic rifles, Michael Ryan went on a killing spree in the town of Hungerford, Berkshire. Ryan walked around the town shooting people on the street, in their cars, on the town common, and in their homes. He killed his first victim just after noon, and in the following seven hours he killed another 15 people, including his own mother, and wounded five people before fatally shooting himself. A similar episode took place on 2 June 2010 in several locations in the county of Cumbria, when Derrick Bird, armed with a rifle and a shotgun, killed 12 people and injured 11 others before killing himself.

Serial murderers

In contrast to mass and spree killers, the serial murderer kills over an extended period of time, sometimes years. There are many serial murderers in English criminal history (Jenkins, 1988), although it is highly unlikely that there are substantial numbers of active serial murderers at any one time. The most recent British case at the time of writing involved Dr Harold Shipman, a general practitioner practising in Hyde near Manchester, who is estimated to have killed over 250 of his patients (Gunn, 2010). The number of Shipman's victims is an estimate because it is difficult to know exactly how many people are murdered by a serial killer. The serial killer Peter Sutcliffe, known as the "Yorkshire Ripper"—many serial killers attract a moniker in the popular press—murdered 13 women in the English city of Leeds and attacked and injured seven other women. It is thought that Sutcliffe's offences took place between 1976 and 1981, although it is possible that they took place over a much longer period and that there are other, unknown, victims.

Some serial killers commit their crimes in pairs with, as Gurian (2013) notes, variations on this theme. There are same-sex pairs who work together in committing the murders: Kenneth Bianchi and Angelo Buono—together known as "The Hillside Strangler" as it was initially thought that there was a single killer—abducted, tortured, sexually assaulted, and killed 10 women in Los Angeles, California, between 1977 and 1979. There are also mixed-sex pairs such as Ian Brady and Myra Hindley, the so-called "Moors Murderers", who between 1963 and 1965 killed five children aged between 10 and 17 years, four of whom are known to have been sexually assaulted. Brady and Hindley are known as the Moors Murderers because they buried several of their victims (not all the bodies have been found) on Saddleworth Moor near Manchester, England. Gurian also points to the phenomenon of *folie à deux*, a state of affairs where there is a pathological intermingling of two people's fantasies and delusions which they then act upon to turn into reality. This form of shared psychotic disorder (Enoch & Ball, 2001) may drive violent and homicidal behaviour, including serial murder.

Murder followed by suicide

Some murderers kill themselves very soon after they have killed. The phenomenon of murder followed by suicide was noted above as a characteristic of spree murderers, but it is perhaps most commonly seen when a parent kills their own children and immediately or very soon afterwards commits suicide. This variation in the act of murder has been documented in several countries, including Australia, several European counties, Hong Kong, Japan, and the USA (Liem, 2010), while its incidence varies from country to country, from a low in England and Wales (Flynn et al., 2009) to a high in Japan (Hata et al., 2001).

Who Kills and Why?

Who is most likely to kill another person and why? A number of surveys give some insight into the types of situation where homicide occurs. These surveys also allow a glimpse of the varied patterns of the interpersonal dynamics which culminate in the death of one or more of those involved.

Roberts, Zgoba, and Shahidullah (2007) analysed 336 homicides dealt with by the New Jersey Department of Corrections, from which they produced a typology of homicide offences: (1) the act was in context of an interpersonal conflict such as an argument; (2) the killing was in the context of another crime; (3) the homicide was related to domestic violence; (4) the homicide followed an accident. This fourfold typology provides a starting point for an overview of homicide.

Interpersonal conflict

In an analysis of 588 homicide victims and 621 homicide offenders in Philadelphia, Wolfgang (1958) found that one-third of the homicides followed a trivial exchange, such as an argument or an insult, between two people. In a typical exchange the offender, generally a male under the age of 35 years with a criminal record, and the victim, again generally a male, were acquainted and likely to have been drinking. If present, a knife was the most frequently used weapon.

A survey carried out in England and Wales by Shaw et al. (2006) looked at 1,594 homicide perpetrators convicted between 1996 and 1999. As might be anticipated, 90% of the perpetrators were male, aged from 10 to 77 years, and about one-half of the victims were men aged between 18 and 35 years whose relationship with their killer was most often family member, current or former partner, or acquaintance. There was a high frequency of drinking at the time of the offence, and stabbing was the most frequent means of killing.

These homicides fit the type described by Luckenbill (1977) in which a sequence of situated transactions is antecedent to the killing (see Box 1.3 above). It may be expected that a fine-grained analysis of the homicides reported by Wolfgang and by Shaw et al. would reveal such transactions.

Homicide with another crime

As Roberts et al. note, "felony homicides" are those which occur, for example, during the commission of a crime such as theft or kidnapping. There are two situations in which violence is connected with another crime: (1) the violence or threat of violence is a fundamental and premeditated part of the crime; (2) the violence is unplanned but occurs during a crime. The first type is seen in robbery, the second, for example, when a domestic burglary is interrupted by a householder who confronts the burglar.

Robbery   There are two types of robbery: the first is robbery from a business property such as a bank or a post office; the second is robbery from the person. The act of robbery from the person, an act of interpersonal violence, may happen in a public place. Bennett and Brookman (2010) suggest that street robbery is typically targeted at money, bags, jewellery, and mobile telephones. The majority of street robberies are perpetrated by young men and the majority of victims are also young men. Homicide is unusual in this type of robbery, although the chances are increased if the robber is carrying a weapon.

Theft   A common example of homicide during theft occurs when a householder attempts to apprehend a burglar and a fight takes place. If the burglar is carrying a weapon the resident may be seriously or fatally injured. A similar scenario may be seen with other crimes such as mugging or car theft. The risk of death for the victim who fights back is greatest for elderly people or those with a physical complaint such as a heart condition.

Domestic homicide

As discussed above, all those resident within a household are at risk of violence with an associated chance of fatality. Thus, children may be killed by their parents, a sibling may kill a parent or their sibling, and adults may kill each other. Honour killings are a particular type of domestic homicide which occur in certain cultures, Ozdemir, Celbis, and Kaya (2014) explain that:

> Honor killings can be defined as acts of murder of women or men who had an extramarital affair, and are killed by the family members. The murderer is usually the victim's husband or male relatives such as father, brother, brother-in-law, etc. Victims of honor killings are believed to bring shame on the name of family and accused of fouling the family's honor with "black-stain". These homicides are aimed to clean the family's reputation of any dishonorable accusations. (p. 198)

As illustrated by Ozdemir et al. (2013) with graphic photographs, this type of killing, often carried out with a knife, can be particularly brutal and may inflict a large number of wounds upon the victim, who can be either male or female.

A domestic homicide may take place in the presence of a child. Katz (2014) interviewed children living in Israel, aged 4 to 7 years, who had witnessed their father killing their mother. The interviews revealed four themes which ran through the children's accounts of what they had observed. The first theme Katz calls "The domestic homicide as the dead end of domestic violence", referring to the fact that the children had previously witnessed incidents of domestic violence but would do so no longer. The second theme, "What I did when daddy killed mommy" indicates that the children said that the fatal incident was no different to previous incidents of domestic violence. In some cases, there was a family routine that preceded the assault where children protected their siblings by taking them to another room. The third theme, "The time that daddy killed mommy", hints at the children's traumatic memories of the time when in the family home their father strangled or stabbed their mother. Finally, "Mommy will feel better and will go back home" speaks to the children's apparent lack of understanding of what they have seen: some children said they were waiting for the mother to return from the doctor's so that all would be well in the future. As with other instances of observing interpersonal violence, it is plain that witnessing their mother's death is deeply disturbing, even traumatic, for the young child.

Infanticide   Infanticide is the murder of a child and is to be found in many countries (see for example Baralic et al., 2010; Benítez-Borrego, Guàrdia-Olmos, & Aliaga-Moore, 2013; Makhlouf & Rambaud, 2014; Putkonen et al., 2011; Somander & Rammer, 1991) and understandably leads to much soul-searching among the helping professions (Pritchard, Davey, & Williams, 2013).

The special case of a parent killing their own child is called *filicide*, or *neonaticide* if the child is killed within the first 24 hours of its life (Bourget, Grace, & Whitehurst, 2007). Neonaticide is most commonly committed by mothers, as are homicides during the child's first week of life, with boys and girls at equal risk. However, filicides after the first week are likely to involve the father or stepfather, sometimes in the context of child abuse (Cavanagh, Dobash, & Dobash, 2007).

McKee and Egan (2013) reviewed 21 UK cases of maternal filicide, beginning with the dreadful statistic that: "A UK child is killed by their parents every ten days, whereas a baby is killed every two weeks" (p. 753). They found that most of the women who killed their children were in their twenties and were experiencing a range of problems, including mental health problems, and difficulties with their intimate relationship. McKee and Egan suggest that the mother's emotional distress and despair at her circumstances were critical factors in the child's death.

The murder of a child within a family may take the form of *filicide* or *neonaticide*, as discussed above, or *siblicide*, when the killing is carried out by close biological relatives (Gebo, 2002): to be more exact, *sororicide* is the killing of a sister and *fratricide* the killing of a brother. However, many more murders of infants take place outside the family than within it: indeed, infants under 1 year of age of are at the highest risk of being a victim of homicide of any age group in England and Wales (Brookman & Nolan, 2006).

Flynn, Shaw, and Abel (2007) reviewed 112 cases of infant homicide between 1996 and 2001 in England and Wales. The majority of perpetrators were the child's parents: they were generally in their mid-twenties and the man was most likely to commit the fatal act. Neonaticide was the exception, with seven of the eight cases carried out by young mothers aged from 14 to 25 years; a high rate of mental disorder, most often depression and schizophrenia, was evident among the child murderers.

Adult family members   The murder of a child may be the culmination of a period of parental abuse or it may be the outcome of a single violent event. The same is true of other types of family homicide: thus, killing an intimate partner may follow a prolonged period of abuse or it may be a solitary violent act (Goussinsky & Yassour-Borochowitz, 2012). Similarly, the prolonged physical abuse of an older adult may result in *eldercide*; alternatively a single eruption of violence may be fatal for a weakened older person (Krienert & Walsh, 2010). It is also the case that children can kill their parents, an act termed *parricide* (Malmquist, 2010).

In their reviews of the literature on homicide of women both Campbell, Glass, Sharps, Laughton, and Bloom (2007) and Jordan et al. (2010) note that a woman is more likely than a man be killed by an intimate partner. They estimate that in almost one-third of cases where the homicide victim is female the murderer is a husband, ex-husband, or boyfriend. In contrast, only 3% of male homicide victims were killed by their wife, ex-wife, or girlfriend. Campbell et al. (2007) suggest that the major risk factor for homicide by an intimate partner is where there are previous occurrences of abuse: this singularly important risk factor is amplified by "Estrangement, perpetrator gun ownership, perpetrator unemployment, a highly controlling abuser, threats to kill, threats with a weapon or use of a weapon, forced sex, violence during pregnancy, attempted strangulation, a stepchild in the home (her biological child, not his), and the perpetrator avoiding arrest for domestic violence" (p. 264).

While agreeing that prior partner abuse is an important risk factor for partner homicide, a Finnish study by Weizmann-Henelius et al. (2012) suggested that the risk factors for homicide differ by gender. In particular, intoxication increased the odds that a woman would kill her partner but decreased the odds for men. However, Weizmann-Henelius et al. suggest that this finding may not generalise given the, albeit changing, national "drinking culture" in Finland. The complexity of domestic homicide is further illustrated by the finding that, looking beyond the confines of the home, levels of economic deprivation are strongly related both to intimate partner homicide as well as to filicide (Diem & Pizarro, 2010).

Accident homicide

As the name suggests, Roberts et al. formulated this category for those homicides which are typically the result of an automobile accident when the driver, generally a male, was driving under the influence of drink or drugs.

Commonalities across homicide types

The picture which emerges of a typical homicide is of a violent act that often involves two people who know each reasonably well or are related. The setting is likely to be one in which an argument, possibly accompanied by drinking, takes place. In terms of gender, a prominent point to emerge from the homicide literature is that, as with violence generally, it is most likely that the homicide perpetrator will be male. This point is reinforced by the findings of Agha (2009), who looked at the homicide arrest figures from 48 countries. With some marked variations between countries, males were involved in homicide more often than females. Yourstone, Lindhome, and Kristiansson (2008) compared 43 male and 43 female homicide perpetrators. The females were more likely to have killed a person to whom they were closely related. While both males and females had disturbed histories in terms of family life, education, and mental health, the males were more likely to have a criminal background, while the females had higher levels of physical and sexual abuse.

The gender differences in connection with homicide are also apparent when looking at juvenile killers.

Juvenile perpetrators

A survey of over 4,000 homicide convictions in England and Wales between 1996 and 2004 revealed that 363 of the convictions were for homicides carried out by juveniles aged 17 years and under (Rodway et al., 2011). In 331 of these 363 cases the perpetrators were white males, as were most of the victims, and were acquainted with their victim: however, in only 35 cases was the victim a family member. The most common means of inflicting death was by using a sharp instrument, followed by hitting and kicking, with the use of firearms a rarity.

The small number of female juvenile perpetrators were more likely than their male counterparts to kill either a female or a family member; in the latter case this was mainly their own child. While one-half of the juveniles, more males than females, had a previous conviction, this was principally for acquisitive offences, although some did have a conviction for a violent offence. Thus, as with many other violent acts, a general picture emerges in which the perpetrator knew their victim, the killing typically involved a knife which was used in the context of an argument, and the fatal act took place in a setting where drink was available.

Farrington, Loeber, and Berg (2012) used longitudinal data from the Pittsburgh Youth Study to identify risk factors for adolescent homicide. They found several significant factors across a range of environmental, socioeconomic, and individual measures. The most important behavioural risk factors were school suspension, a disruptive behaviour disorder, and holding an attitude favourable towards delinquency. However, as Farrington et al. point out, in this sample the majority of the convicted homicide offenders were African American, leaving open the question of the generalisability of the findings to other jurisdictions.

Alcohol

Given the high degree of association between violence and alcohol it is not surprising that alcohol is implicated in many homicides. A survey by Shaw et al. (2006) looked at alcohol and drug use among 1,594 individuals convicted of homicide in England

and Wales between 1996 and 1999. In terms of a known history of substance use, Shaw et al. reported that around 40% of the convicted murderers had a history of alcohol misuse or dependence, or drug misuse or addiction. Shaw et al. also found that alcohol or drug use, in the latter case mostly often cannabis, was a contributory factor in 40% of the cases.

Mental illness

Flynn, Abel, While, Menta, and Shaw (2011) note that in England and Wales a long history of mental illness is evident in about one-third of homicides. They reviewed the cases of 446 women and 4,126 men convicted of homicide in England and Wales between 1997 and 2004. They found that significantly more women than men in the sample had a lifetime history of mental illness and were more likely to be mentally ill at the time of offence. In particular the women were more likely than the men to be diagnosed with affective disorder, alcohol dependence, or personality disorder.

Weapons

The use of a weapon in a violent exchange dramatically increases the chances of a homicide. Felson and Messner (1996) suggest that, when compared to violence that does not involve weapons, the presence of firearms increases the probability of death 40 times while a knife increases it four times. Given these odds, as Brennan and Moore (2009) state, it follows that in both the USA and in the UK weapons are used in the majority of homicides. The killing may be intentional, with the weapon carried specifically for that purpose: in extreme cases, such as the mass murders and spree murders discussed above, high-powered firearms are taken to the scene as part of the plan to wreak the maximum possible amount of damage.

As noted throughout, there are some settings that are more likely than others to engender interpersonal violence. It follows that the availability of a gun in those particular settings increases the likelihood of homicide (Hepburn & Hemenway, 2004; Stroebe, 2013; Wiebe, 2003). This point can be demonstrated, from the macro level of the country to the micro level of the home.

It is a fact that the availability of firearms varies from country to country. Brent, Miller, Loeber, Mulvey, and Birmaher (2013) show that across six high-income countries—Australia, Canada, Finland, Switzerland, the United Kingdom, and the United States—the rate of gun homicide is highest in the United States followed by Finland and Canada, while the highest rates of civilian gun ownership are, in order, the United States, Finland and Canada. It is also possible for there to be variations *within* a single country. Felson and Pare (2010) cite American data showing that white people in the southern states are much more likely to be victims of gun homicide than white people in the northern states.

However, the relationship between the availability of firearms and the homicide rate is not straightforward. Felson, Berg, and Rogers (2014) make the suggestion that guns beget guns: in other words, if your opponent, who could be another criminal or a police officer, has a gun then you get one too which, in turn, increases the chances of homicide. The emphasis here is on firearms, not knives or other types of weapon: if you have a knife and your adversary has a gun then the outcome of an altercation is almost certainly going one way. Thus, Felson et al. point to the "adversary effect": "Offenders are more likely to have lethal intent when they believe their adversaries have firearms. Killing an armed adversary eliminates the threat. At the same time the tendency of offenders to use firearms reduces the frequency of violence without firearms. People do not rely on knives or fists when they anticipate a gun fight" (p. 87).

The point that guns beget guns is illustrated by Papachristos, Wildeman, and Roberto (2015), who looked at patterns of nonfatal gunshot wounds in Chicago. They found that there was a concentration of nonfatal wounding, with 70% of victims part of offending networks who accounted for less than 6% Chicago's population. The force of this finding is seen in Papachristos et al.'s summary that "While the overall rate of gunshot victimization in Chicago is 62.1 per 100,000, the rate is 740.5 for individuals in a co-offending network, more than twelve times higher than the overall city rate" (p. 139). Thus, being wounded or killed by gunshot is not a random event: people who know gunshot victims as part of their social network are themselves at a much greater risk of similar wounding.

A further problem arises when mental disorder is added to the equation: there have been several cases which have attracted a great deal of publicity and reinforced calls to limit by law access to guns by people with a mental illness (Chappell, 2014). The dangers inherent in gun ownership by those with a mental illness are to be seen in two case studies, one European the other American.

In 2011 in the Norwegian capital of Oslo, Anders Behring Breivik planted car bombs by government buildings, so causing the deaths of eight people. As the bombs exploded he travelled 24 miles northwest of Oslo to the island of Utøya where, armed with a carbine and a pistol, he shot and killed 69 people, mostly teenagers attending a Workers' Youth League camp. Breivik claimed to hold extreme right-wing views which included a hatred of Islam and opposition to feminism (Pantucci, 2011).

Breivik was assessed by two teams of forensic psychiatrists: the first diagnosed him as a paranoid schizophrenic; the second suggested he was not psychotic but did have a narcissistic personality disorder. In August 2012 the Oslo District Court reached the view that, within the meaning of the law, Breivik was sane and he was found guilty of terrorism, causing a fatal explosion, and the murder of 77 people. He received a sentence of 21 years in prison with the option that the period of incarceration be prolonged for as long as he is judged to be a danger to society.

While there was some debate over Breivik's sanity and responsibility for his actions within the meaning of mental health law, the same is not true in other cases. In 2007 in America, Seung-Hui Cho, aged 23 years, went on a shooting spree, armed with two high-power semi-automatic pistols, on the Virginia Tech campus where he was a student. He killed 32 people and wounded 17 others before taking his own life. Although he had a long-standing mental disorder of sufficient severity that he had previously been assessed as mentally ill and in need of hospitalisation (though he was not admitted), Cho was free to purchase firearms.

Homicide Recidivism

The recidivism rate for homicide is very low. The number of people convicted of homicide who serve a sentence, typically a long prison sentence, and then commit a subsequent murder is generally small. Thus, Roberts, Zgoba, and Shahidullah (2007) found that after five years none of their sample of 336 homicide offenders had killed again. The Criminal Statistics for England and Wales released on 13 February 2014, as cited above (Office for National Statistics, 2014a), record that in 2012–2013 there were three convictions for homicide for individuals who had a previous homicide conviction. This low figure was also the case in 2011–2012, when there were two people with a previous conviction for homicide who committed another homicide. A similar study reported by Liem, Zahn, and Tichavsky (2014), based on figures gathered in Philadelphia spanning the period 1977 to 1983, also found a low level of recidivism for homicide in the sample of 92 paroled homicide offenders. They found that while over one-half of the sample committed more crimes, principally property, drugs, and traffic offences, there were just three offenders who committed another homicide. A very similar pattern emerges for juvenile homicide offenders (Vries & Liem, 2011).

The issue of whether recidivism is related to the type of homicide offender is con-sidered in Liem's (2013) review of homicide offender recidivism. Liem considered a wide literature in reviewing the recidivism of female homicide offenders, juvenile homicide offenders, psychotic homicide offenders, sexual homicide offenders, and spousal homicide offenders. Of course, as Liem notes, like any other offender group, homicide offenders may recidivate by committing any type of offence, including but not limited to another homicide. However, if the focus is maintained on a further homicide, Liem's review reveals that the rate is, as suggested above, very low. The exception is to be found in a Russian study of 133 psychotic homicide offenders with an 11% recidivism rate specifically for homicide at a 30-year follow-up (Golenkov, Large, Nielssen, & Tsymbalova, 2011).

Conclusion

Criminal violence has a great deal in common with other forms of violence. It occurs in the same types of setting as other kinds of violence and engages similar perpetra-tors, victims, and third parties. The motivations of profit, revenge, and the exercise of power over another person are all to be found. The exception is to be found in the comparatively rare act of homicide where, unlike other forms of violence, the victim pays the ultimate price. As seen in the formulation of criminal law, society offers little by way of acceptance or tolerance of this particular form of violence.

5

Sexual Violence

The focus in this chapter is on violent crimes where a sexual element is attached to the violence.

Sexual violence is a criminal offence and so the criminal law guides our understanding of what society will and will not tolerate. To the extent that criminal law reflects a society's moral values, it follows that the laws governing acceptable sexual behaviour can change over time. In England and Wales since the mid-1950s, for example, there have been changes in the law regarding the criminalisation of homosexuality and in the lowering of the age of consent (Myhill & Allen, 2002). The legal definition of a sexual offence varies from country to country, posing problems for comparisons across different jurisdictions. In England and Wales the sexual behaviours prohibited by criminal law are given in the Sexual Offences Act 2003 (Stevenson, Davies, & Gunn, 2003).

Legal Definition

As shown in Box 5.1, the Sentencing Council Guidelines for the 2003 Sexual Offences Act describe various types of sexual offending (Sentencing Guidelines Secretariat, 2007).

At one extreme there are non-contact offences such as exhibitionism and voyeurism which like Internet sex offending do not involve direct physical contact: these contactless offences can cause distress to the victims and for a small number of individuals may be a precursor to contact sexual offending (McNally & Fremouw, 2014). At the other extreme the offence is marked by life-threatening physical violence. However, the Sexual Offences Act does not capture all offensive

The Psychology of Interpersonal Violence, First Edition. Clive R. Hollin.
© 2016 John Wiley & Sons, Ltd. Published 2016 by John Wiley & Sons, Ltd.

Box 5.1   Sexual Offences in the 2003 Act

Non-Consensual Offences
Rape and assault by penetration
Sexual assault
Causing or inciting sexual activity
Other non-consensual offences

Offences Involving Ostensible Consent
Offences involving children
Offences against vulnerable adults

Preparatory Offences
Sexual grooming
Committing another offence with intent
Trespass with intent
Administering a substance with intent

Other Offences
Sex with an adult relative
Sexual activity in a public lavatory
Exposure
Voyeurism
Intercourse with an animal
Sexual penetration of a corpse

Exploitation Offences
Indecent photographs of children
Abuse of children through prostitution and pornography
Exploitation of prostitution
Trafficking

Source: After Sentencing Guidelines Secretariat, 2007.

acts with a sexual connation. Sexual harassment, as may be evident in the workplace in the form of offensive sexual jibes or suggestive nonverbal behaviours, is not, legally speaking, a sexual offence as it is dealt with through the Sex Discrimination Act 1975 (Pina, Gannon, & Saunders, 2009). Yet further, there is sexual murder, a term that is in common use but which is not defined in criminal law (Carter & Hollin, 2010). Finally, as in other areas of law, such as copyright law and the electronic distribution and playing of music and films, changes in technology require a change in legislation with respect to sexual crimes. The impact of technology is evident in sex offending as, for example, in offences against children involving the Internet.

Criminal Statistics for Sex Offending

Official figures

A child or adult who is the victim of a sexual offence may be unwilling to report the crime to the police. The victim may feel ashamed or humiliated and not wish to answer questions about what has happened, or they may fear reprisals from the aggressor if they go to the police, while parents may remain silent in order to protect their children. The failure to report sexual crimes—it is estimated that only approximately 11% of victims of a serious sexual assault report the crime to the police (Hoare & Jansson, 2007)—has a detrimental effect on the official crime statistics (Kelly, Lovett, & Regan, 2005). Thus, if only 1 in 10 offences are reported to the police and given that in 2008–2009 the police recorded 12,129 offences of rape against women (Ministry of Justice, 2010c), and then the official figure is just the tip of a substantial iceberg. Nonetheless, official figures for England and Wales (Ministry of Justice, Home Office, & Office for National Statistics, 2013) note that: "It is estimated that 0.5 per cent of females report being a victim of the most serious offences of rape or sexual assault by penetration in the previous 12 months, equivalent to around 85,000 victims on average per year. Among males, less than 0.1 per cent (around 12,000) report being a victim of the same types of offences in the previous 12 months" (p. 6).

The United Nations Office on Drugs and Crime (UNODC) website presents statistics for sexual violence, including "rape and sexual assault including offences against children": 2008 the rate of such offences stood at almost 75 children per 100,000 of the population in England and Wales.

While the majority of sexual offences are perpetrated by men against women and children, as well as against other men (Scarce, 1997), there are women who commit sexual offences (Gannon & Cortoni, 2010). Sexual offences, typically against children, may also be committed by juveniles (Barbaree & Marshall, 2008; Hunter, Hazelwood, & Slesinger, 2000). Indeed, Hudson and Ward (2001) state that adolescents may account for between 20% and 30% of rapes and between 30% and 60% of offences against children. Krahé, Tomaszewska, Kuyper, and Vanwesenbeeck (2014) conducted a review of the prevalence of sexual aggression, considering both perpetration and victimisation, among young people. This review, based on figures from 27 European countries, reported high rates of sexual aggression among both male and female young people. Finally, sex offences may be carried out by multiple perpetrators as, for example, with gang rape and child sex rings (Harkins & Dixon, 2010).

The weight of the literature considers sexual offences against children and against adults, and these two areas are addressed below.

Sexual Offences Against Children

There are particular problems in conducting research into sex offences against children which may impair a full understanding of this crime. Young children may not comprehend the offence in which they are involved or they may be afraid of the consequences for their family should they report their abuse. Nonetheless, it is safe to say that female children are at greater risk of sexual assault than males given that there is a range of individual and social factors, including low family income, behavioural problems, and special educational needs, which heighten the risk of sexual assault for girls under 18 years of age (Butler, 2013).

Sexual assaults may take place against children of any age but there are peaks of vulnerability at age 6–7 years and at prepubescence from 10 to 12 years (Finkelhor, 1986). Moreno (2013) examined the medical records of sexual assault victims over a two-year period in a region of Spain. The records were considered across the three age groups of children, adolescents, and adults. The degree of physical injury suffered by the victim was strongly associated with age group: sexual assaults with penetration, which cause the greatest physical injury, were more frequent with older age groups. In four-fifths of cases the assault was perpetrated by someone known to the victim, and the likelihood of sexual assault by a stranger increased with age. A British survey by Cawson, Wattam, Brooker, and Kelly (2000) similarly found that in cases involving children the perpetrator is often acquainted with the victim.

Finkelhor (1984, 1986) interviewed men and women who had been abused as children. In many instances the sexual abuse was a single episode following which the child avoided the adult or reported the incident to their parents. However in a minority of instances there was regular abuse over a period of weeks, months, or years. Genital fondling, with either hand or mouth, was the most common sexual act, followed by exposure and masturbation: as with the Moreno study, penetrative sex was less common, which appears to be a stable characteristic of sexual abuse of children (Negriff, Schneiderman, Smith, Schreyer, & Trickett, 2014).

A forensic medical study of 138 children, modal age 15 years, involved in sexual abuse allegations was presented by Davies and Jones (2013). The child's use of drugs and alcohol was a strong risk factor, particularly for the older children. The offender was most frequently an acquaintance, followed by a relative.

The sexual abuse of children, which has been happening for centuries, is a global issue prevalent across all the world's continents: Stoltenborgh, van IJzendoorn, Euser, and Bakermans-Kranenburg (2011) conclude their meta-analysis of the worldwide prevalence of child sexual abuse (CSA) with the statement that: "The global prevalence of CSA was estimated to be 11.8% or 118 per 1000 children, based on 331 independent samples with a total of 9,911,748 participants" (p. 87). Stoltenborgh et al. found that the lowest rates of sexual abuse for girls and boys were in Asia, with the highest rate for girls in Australia and in Africa for boys. A meta-analysis of studies of child sexual abuse in China reported by Ji, Finkelhor, and Dunne (2013) found that compared to international norms there was a lower rate of sexual abuse of females but a higher rate of abuse of males. However, a series of three American telephone surveys of children aged from 2 to 9 and from 10 to 17 years and their caregivers, carried out in 2003, 2008, and 2011 suggested a downward trend in rates of many different forms of abuse (Finkelhor, Shattuck, Turner, & Hamby, 2014). In particular, the decline was notable for physical assault, physical intimidation, and sexual victimisation. Finkelhor et al. suggest that the decline in abuse is in accord with the overall fall in the American national crime statistics.

Poly-victimisation

As noted in Chapter 3, some children experience several different forms of abuse; this compound form of abuse is known as *poly-victimisation*. An American study by Turner, Finkelhor, and Ormrod (2010) gathered information from telephone interviews with a nationally representative sample of 4,053 children aged from 2 to 17 years and their caregivers. The survey asked respondents about their experience of a wide range of types of victimisation, including bullying, witnessing family violence, and physical and sexual assault. It was found that almost two-thirds of the sample reported more than one type of victimisation, one-third reported five or more types, and 1 in 10 said their lifetime experience was of 11 or more different types of victimisation. Those children who had been sexually victimised were at high risk of poly-victimisation compared to the other victimised children.

Pérez-Fuentes et al. (2013) reported a survey of an American national sample of 34,000 adults aged 18 years and above. They found that the overall self-reported prevalence of child sexual abuse stood at 10.14%: of those reporting abuse, almost one-quarter were men and just over three-quarters women. In keeping with Turner, Finkelhor, and Ormrod (2010), other forms of abuse, including neglect and physical abuse, were more prevalent among those who had experienced child sexual abuse.

A similar survey of 5,940 15–17-year-old school pupils in Sweden was reported by Annerbäck, Sahlqvist, Svedin, Wingren, and Gustafsson (2012). This survey included questions about bullying, physical abuse, exposure to parental intimate violence, and being forced to participate in sexual acts. Among the younger children, those around 15 years of age, 5.3% reported forced sexual activity; this percentage rose to 6.1% for the older children aged around 17 years. There were more female pupils (8.7%) than male pupils (2.6%) who reported forced sexual acts, with males reporting more frequent bullying.

As might be anticipated, poly-victimisation leads to multiple behavioural and mental health issues in both childhood and adolescence (Cater, Andershed, & Andershed, 2014).

Child sexual abuse and the Internet

The "Internet sex offender" poses a particular set of issues because while the abuse is real, as Sheldon and Howitt (2007) point out, in cyberspace the offender is not restricted by the traditional forces of law or order. Beech, Elliott, Birgden, and

Findlater (2008) describe four ways in which the sexual abuse of children can be facilitated by the use of the Internet: (1) distribution of sexualised images; (2) formation of virtual social networks for communication between individuals with a sexual interest in children; (3) enabling sexual communication with children; (4) as a means of locating vulnerable children.

The distribution of sexual images of children raises two issues: first, it presents children in a sexual manner, potentially playing to a wider stereotype of children sometimes seen in advertising, cinema, and so on; second, the making of the images, often in the form of "collections", may have involved child abuse (Sheehan & Sullivan, 2010; Taylor & Quayle, 2006). Taylor, Holland, and Quayle (2001) produced a typology of such picture collections, ranging from children dressed in normal everyday clothes, to children in explicit poses, then to extreme images of sexual assault, sadism, and bestiality. The distribution of sets of images has led to the practice of "collecting", with the purchase or exchange of images from a set which are stored on a computer. These collections can be large: Niveau (2010) notes that child pornography offenders may download over a thousand images.

While difficult if not impossible to quantify, the practice of grooming potential victims has, given the widespread availability of access to the Internet, understandably become a cause of considerable concern (Kloess, Beech, & Harkins, 2014). In their review of online grooming, Whittle, Hamilton-Giachritsis, Beech, and Collings (2013) note that the adult may use several techniques to groom the child, such as bribery, flattery, or making threats, in order to increase the child's compliance with their wishes. The child may become ever more ensnared by regular online communication with someone they do not know but whom they begin to see as a friend rather than a stranger, sharing personal information, sending photographs, and even going so far as arranging a meeting.

Seto, Hanson, and Babchishin (2011) reviewed the literature on the degree to which men with online sex offences committed contact sexual offences. They found that that at the time of their index offence, about 12% of online offenders had an official record of contact sexual offending; this percentage rose to over 50% when measured by self-report. When considering recidivism over a 1.5- to 6-year follow-up period, Seto, Hanson, and Babchishin reported that 4.6% of online offenders committed a new sexual offence: for these new offences, 2.0% of offenders committed a contact sexual offence while 3.4% committed a new child pornography offence.

As with cyberbullying, there is some debate about whether Internet sex offenders are simply traditional sex offenders using advances in technology or whether they represent a new type of sex offender. Babchishin, Hanson, and Hermann (2011) conducted a meta-analysis of the literature comparing the demographic and psychological characteristics of online and traditional "offline" sexual offenders. They reported that the marginally younger online offenders were more likely than the offline offenders to be Caucasian and had greater victim empathy, attached greater importance to impression management (the degree to which individuals present themselves in a positive way), and greater sexual deviancy than offline offenders. However, both groups of offenders reported a higher rate of physical and sexual childhood abuse than is evident in the general population. Babchishin, Hanson, and Hermann suggested that the differences between the two groups may be explained by online offenders having greater self-control alongside psychological barriers to enacting their deviant sexual interests. However, the distinction between online and offline offenders may become blurred as some child pornography offenders will become contact offenders (Houtepen, Sijtsema, & Bogaerts, 2014).

Family factors   Family factors may be associated with child sexual abuse in two ways: (1) the abuse is perpetrated by a family member; (2) the family to which the abused child belongs has a particular range of characteristics.

The sexual abuse of a child by a member of his or her family, traditionally known as *incest*, is referred to in the Sexual Offences Act 2003 for England and Wales as *intrafamilial* in order to reflect the diversity of the contemporary family unit. Thus, in this broader sense, the family may be taken to consist of those living in the same household, male and female, who have a position of trust or authority over a child. This position of trust extends to blood relatives and adoptive and foster parents, and includes civil as well as married relationships. Intrafamilial sexual abuse is most frequently recorded between fathers and daughters and between brothers and sisters (Cyr, Wright, McDuff, & Perron, 2002; Yildirim et al., 2014). The frequency with which this type of abuse takes place is impossible to measure accurately (Horvath, Davidson, Grove-Hills, Gekoski, & Choak, 2014).

The familial factors associated with a heightened risk of child sexual abuse include disruption of the family due to parental conflict or separation and low levels of attachment between the child and their parents (Aspelmeier, Elliott, & Smith, 2007; Hamill, Newman, Todd, & Peck, 2014). Some abusive parents will have been abused themselves with, as discussed below, subsequent mental health and substance use problems; some abusive families will be struggling with financial problems, low-quality housing, and long-term unemployment. The abuse of children within a family should therefore be seen in the context of a plethora of economic, psychological, and social problems.

Consequences of child sexual abuse

Short-term consequences   The consequences of sexual abuse for the child may be both immediate and evident over the longer term. The immediate effects may be physical injury, especially in those less frequent cases where penetration has occurred, which is more likely for female children (Maikovich-Fong & Jaffee, 2010), and changes in behavioural and psychological functioning. The child may become withdrawn and fearful, displaying a range of emotional and behavioural difficulties including developmental problems such as enuresis and difficulties at school (Trickett & McBride-Chang, 1995). The sexually abused child may display a range of psychiatric problems including anxiety disorder, conduct disorder, depression, eating disorder, post-traumatic stress disorder (PTSD), engaging in risky sexual practices, sleep disorders, substance misuse, and suicide attempts (Chen et al., 2010; Ford Elhai, Connor, & Frueh, 2010; Soylu & Alpaslan, 2013; Walsh, Latzman, & Latzman, 2014). The abusive experience may have a different effect on males and females: for example, Coohey (2010) found that abused boys had more pronounced internalising problems, such as withdrawal, somatic complaints, depression, and anxiety, than abused girls. Further, the effects of the abuse may be attenuated by the young person's favoured coping mechanism: Shapiro, Kaplow, Amaya-Jackson, and Dodge (2012) found that avoidant coping, where the memories of the abuse are suppressed and avoided, was predictive of psychiatric symptoms.

Long-term consequences For the sexually abused child the short-term consequences of the abuse may reach into adult life disturbing their psychological functioning, health, social functioning, and relationships, and increasing the risk of further victimisation (Messman-Moore & Brown, 2004; Paolucci, Genuis, & Violato, 2001).

A typical study of the effects of childhood sexual abuse on adult psychological health was reported by Cutajar at al. (2010). A comparison was made of the medical records of 2,759 sexually abused children with a matched control group drawn randomly from public records. It was found that sexual abuse in childhood increased the risk of a range of adverse outcomes, including anxiety, depression and other affective disorders, personality disorder, psychosis, and substance abuse. In addition, it was found that the risk of psychopathology increased when the sexual abuse occurred at an older age, or involved penetration, or when there were multiple perpetrators of the abuse.

Drawing on data collected in a sample of over 7,000 adults in an English household survey, Jonas et al. (2011) reported a significant relationship between childhood sexual abuse and later anxiety disorders, depression, alcohol and drug abuse, post-traumatic stress disorder, and eating disorders. The relationships were especially strong when the abuse involved non-consensual sexual intercourse. Childhood abuse was also associated with an increased likelihood of revictimisation as an adult.

A string of meta-analyses has confirmed the relationship between the experience of childhood sexual abuse and adult psychopathology (e.g., Chen et al., 2010). As noted by Hillberg, Hamilton-Giachritsis, and Dixon (2011) in their overview of these meta-analyses, there are some limitations and inconsistencies in the evidence base. However, the overall picture, for both males and females, is that childhood sexual abuse is a risk factor for adult psychopathology. Further, for populations in which the risk of psychosis is already present, childhood sexual abuse further compounds the degree of risk (Thompson et al., 2014).

As well as mental health, childhood sexual abuse may affect adult physical health, including neurological functioning (Gould et al., 2012; Heim, Shugart, Craighead, & Nemeroff, 2010). A meta-analysis of 31 studies conducted by Irish, Kobayashi, and Delahanty (2010) found that childhood sexual abuse was associated with poor general health in adulthood as well as with specific complaints including gastrointestinal problems, gynaecological and reproductive functioning, cardiopulmonary symptoms, and obesity.

The other sequelae of childhood sexual abuse are seen in an increased likelihood of adolescent pregnancy. A meta-analysis of 21 studies reported by Noll, Shenk, and Putnam (2009) revealed that compared to women who were not sexually abused in childhood, women who were sexually abused were more than twice as likely to become pregnant during adolescence. Noll et al. suggest that the sexual abuse may adversely change the child's normal development processes, disturbing the acquisition of emotional and social-cognitive skills. This developmental disturbance, in turn, may distort perceptions of self-worth and of the intentions of other people and so confuse the establishment of sexual boundaries and understanding of appropriate sexual behaviours and risky sexual acts (Walsh, Latzman, & Latzman, 2014). This point is reinforced by the finding that childhood sexual abuse is a strong predictor of continued sexual abuse in later life (Chan, 2011b; Reese-Weber & Smith, 2011; Van Bruggen, Runtz, & Kadlec, 2006) which may, as the cycle turns, relate to the parenting practices of mothers sexually abused in their own childhood (Kim, Trickett, & Putnam, 2010).

There are individual differences in reactions to the experience of abuse and some people use more effective strategies than others in coping with adverse experiences (Walsh, Fortier, & DiLillo, 2010). Yancey and Hansen (2010) suggest that the later outcomes of child sexual abuse may be dependent upon personal, familial factors, and abuse-specific factors. The personal factors include age, gender, and how the victim attributes the cause of abuse; familial factors include a parental history of abuse, with all the associated negative connotations, and parental reaction to the abuse and their support of the child. The abuse-specific factors are the severity and duration of the abuse and the nature of the perpetrator's relationship with the child.

How do the effects of childhood sexual abuse persist into later life? Do the effects of childhood sexual abuse form a specific, unique syndrome? Paolucci et al. (2001) are clear that their meta-analysis favours a model based on the effects of trauma rather than a specific syndrome. Similarly, Wall and Quadara (2014) argue strongly that complex trauma provides the best means by which to comprehend the effects of sexual victimisation. The place of trauma in understanding interpersonal violence is addressed further in Chapter 6.

Sexual Offending Against Adults

The focus here is on three very different types of sexual offence: the first, stalking, is a strange form of interpersonal violence given its detached aspect; there is no doubt that the second offence, rape, is an act of violence which can cause great damage to the victim; and finally, while not an offence specifically defined in law, the act of sexual murder is one in which the victim pays the ultimate price.

Stalking

Stalking is a form of sexual harassment that includes obscene and threatening communications either by writing, telephone, or email; following, watching, or waiting at the victim's home or place of work; or tampering with personal property (Baum, Catalano, Rand, & Rose, 2009; Pina et al., 2009). As with other sexual offences it is impossible to know the exact figures with regard to stalking. However, the available statistics, mainly gathered through surveys, suggest that a considerable number of people experience stalking. The 2012–2013 Crime Survey for England and Wales revealed that for adults aged between 16 and 59 just over 4% of women and just less than 2% of men reported an experience of stalking (Ministry of Justice, 2014). Similar concerns about the prevalence of stalking have been expressed by various commentators, including those from Australia (Purcell, Pathé, & Mullen, 2002), Austria (Stieger, Burger, & Schild, 2008), Germany (Dressing, Kuehner, & Gass, 2005), Italy (De Fazio, 2011), Sweden (Strand & McEwan, 2011), and the United States (Baum et al., 2009). The victims of stalking may be those in the public eye such as celebrities and politicians (Phillips, 2007) or simply members of the general public.

Consequences of stalking

Sheridan and Lyndon (2012) conducted a survey of 1,214 self-reported victims of stalking on the basis of which they described four consequences of stalking. At an individual level the victim's physical health may suffer, as seen by fluctuations in appetite and weight, sleep disturbance and tiredness, and ailments such as headaches and nausea. There may be accompanying psychological changes such as anxiety, panic attacks and fear, depression and suicidal thoughts or attempts, and anger and aggression. Women reported more psychological and physical symptoms than men.

Alongside these individual costs, the victim of stalking may find that their social life changes as they abandon social activities, so losing touch with friends and even family, are forced to change employment, seek anonymity by changing their telephone number and email address, or even leave their home to move to a new residence. As may be imagined, these individual and social changes are not economically neutral, and for many victims they are a source of lost money. Sheridan and Lyndon state that:

> Just over half the respondents (52.5%) said they had lost money as a direct result of being stalked. Financial losses ranged from $10 to $55,000 (M = $3,583, SD = $8,451). If they did lose money, most victims (86.4%) lost more than $1,000. There were two modal values, namely $350 and $3,000. Those reporting losses of $350 were most likely to describe losses due to stalker vandalism and therapy-related expenses, while those with losses of $3,000 were most likely to ascribe these to legal costs. (p. 344)

Inspection of the fine details of these economic costs reveals a great deal about how the stalking changed victims' lives as they faced bills due to losing employment or being forced to take time off work; or the costs of repairing or replacing a vandalised car, fixing damaged property and installing security systems, and paying for counselling and legal advice.

Rape

Rape is a worldwide problem affecting millions of people (Abrahams et al., 2014). Three aspects of rape are discussed below: (1) the location of the offence; (2) victim characteristics; (3) the consequences of rape for the victim.

Offence location   A rape may take place in any of a number of locations—including the victim's home, a public place, and even a motor vehicle—depending in part on the relationship between the offender and the victim. Myhill and Allen (2002) reported that rape in the victim's own home was the case for over one-half of rapes in England and Wales; Ploughman and Stensrud (1986) noted a similar figure for New York. The home is often a location for rape because in almost one-half of cases the rape is carried out by the victim's partner or ex-partner; alternatively, the victim may have become acquainted with the attacker socially or through work. Thus, the attacker may have been freely admitted by the victim or have their own means of access to the victim's home. However, as Myhill and Allen note, a public place is often the setting for a rape committed by someone who is a stranger to the victim. In addition, rape most frequently occurs on Saturdays between 8 p.m. and 2 a.m., a peak period for social interaction and drinking that includes a period of darkness with obvious advantages for the perpetrator. Ceccato's (2014) analysis of "rape places" illustrates the complexity of the interactions between features of the urban landscape—such as railway lines and arterial roads, and the layout of public spaces such as streets and parks—and population movement in familiar places at different times for different purposes. A serial sex offender is likely to use a limited range of sites selected not just on the basis of their familiarity but also of the availability of potential victims in those locations and the opportunity to carry out an attack (Deslauriers-Varin & Beauregard, 2014).

The importance of the economic standing of the community as a backdrop to child victimisation is seen in a study by Mustaine et al. (2014), who analysed 1,172 child sexual assault incidents, subdivided as preteen and teen, reported to law enforcement agencies in Orange County, Florida, from 2004 to 2006. They looked at how the incidents were clustered in different parts of the location according to community characteristics such as economic disadvantage, levels of violent crime, population density, and social cohesion. The levels of economic disadvantage and housing density were positively related to the quantity of preteen and teen sexual assault. The presence of registered sex offenders was a risk factor for assault against teens but not younger children.

As well as the community, closed institutions, such as prisons, may also offer opportunities for same-sex rape. The exact figures for prison rape are impossible to establish and will vary from country to country (Neal & Clements, 2010).

The rape victim   There is general agreement across the literature that rape victims are typically aged from 16 to 25 years and likely to be single with a low income or unemployed (Feist, Lawrence, McPhee, & Wilson, 2007; Myhill & Allen, 2002; Ploughman & Stensrud, 1986). As was the case with the location where rape takes place, there is a tangle of details underpinning the profile of the typical rape victim. Thus, a single woman may be more frequently exposed to situations in which there is a higher risk of attack: these situations include living alone, travelling alone on public transport, residing in a lower-income, high-crime area, and a lifestyle characterised by regular social interaction with young men aged under 25 years in settings where alcohol and drugs are available. Feist et al. note that in some rape cases the victim had been deliberately incapacitated by being given spiked drinks or being forced to take drugs.

Consequences of rape   The consequences of rape may be far-reaching, affecting the victim's physical health, psychological state, and relationships and lifestyle (Culbertson & Dehle, 2001; Jonas et al., 2011).

The fine detail of the damaging and diverse effects of rape is to be seen in a study by Perilloux, Duntley, and Buss (2014). Perilloux et al. found that women who were victims of rape experienced the cost of rape across no fewer than 13 personal domains—value as a romantic partner, sexual reputation, frequency of sex, long-term relationships, attractiveness, social reputation, health, sexual desire, family relationships, social life, work life, enjoyment of sex, and self-esteem—so touching every aspect of their lives, as well as the lives of their family and friends. Yet further, the victim's relationship with their attacker may moderate the impact of the assault, with closer relationships such as cohabitation or marriage having a more marked effect (Culbertson & Dehle, 2001).

Given the ubiquity of rape across countries, it is appropriate that the World Health Organization (2013) should make the comment that "Violence against women is a significant public health problem, as well as a fundamental violation of women's human rights" (p. 2).

Yet further, the costs of rape may be exacerbated by the continued promulgation of rape myths which work against a widespread understanding of the effects of rape, thereby reducing consideration for the issues faced by the victim. As shown in Box 5.2, rape myths are prevalent for both men (Turchik & Edwards, 2012) and women (Edwards, Turchik, Dardis, Reynolds, & Gidycz, 2011).

However, contrary to some rape myths, a sexual assault on a man may have harmful effects. Peterson, Voller, Polusny, and Murdoch (2011) conclude their review by noting that: "Although the data are mixed as to whether the consequences of male ASA are comparable to the consequences of female ASA, there is relatively

> ### Box 5.2　Examples of Rape Myths for Men and Women
>
> *Men*
> It is impossible for a man to rape a man.
> "Real" men can defend themselves against rape.
> Only gay men are victims and/or perpetrators of rape.
> Men are not affected by rape; or not as much as women.
> Male rape only happens in prisons.
> Sexual assault by someone of the same sex causes homosexuality.
>
> *Women*
> A lot of women lead a man on and then cry rape.
> Husbands cannot rape their wives.
> If a woman does not physically fight back it is not really rape.
> If a woman is raped while she is drunk, she is responsible for letting things get
> out of control.
> It is usually only women who dress suggestively who are raped.
> Women enjoy rape.

convincing evidence that male sexual assault victims experience higher rates of psychological disturbance than men who have not been assaulted" (p. 19).

Sexual homicide

"Sexual murder" does not exist as a specific crime defined in law: however, sexual activity is clearly present in some homicides, and a body of research has investigated the circumstances in which sex may be attached to murder (Carter & Hollin, 2010; James & Proulx, 2014; Kerr, Beech, & Murphy, 2013; Meloy, 2000; Proulx, Beauregard, Cusson, & Nicole, 2005). There is a range of explanations for sexual murder: the man may be seeking revenge against a particular woman or against women in general; an attack that started as a sexual assault ends in homicide as the attacker attempts to silence the woman during the offence or kills her afterwards to avoid detection; the man may be acting out his violent, sadistic, fantasies (Maniglio, 2010).

The majority of sexual murderers are men in their twenties or thirties—although cases of female sexual murderers have been documented (Chan & Frei, 2013)—typically with childhoods characterised by physical and sexual abuse, social isolation, and difficulties at home and at school. In adult life sexual murderers may have a criminal record and a history of contact with the psychiatric services. When committing the offence the perpetrator will probably be heavily using drugs or alcohol and is most likely to kill by strangulation, followed by stabbing or physical beating, but is unlikely to use firearms (Chan & Heide, 2008). A small number of sexual murderers may kill more than once, sometimes driven by extremes of sexual sadism (Knoll & Hazelwood, 2009).

The Sex Offender

A great deal of research has been carried out looking at the characteristics of sex offenders. The majority of studies gather data from known or convicted samples of sex offenders, which runs the risk of introducing a systematic bias into the literature should meaningful differences exist between detected and undetected offenders (Neutze, Grundmann, Scherner, & Beier, 2012). The research is summarised below by looking first at perpetrators of stalking, then sex offenders against children, and finally sex offenders against adult women. However, the starting point is the longitudinal studies which consider the developmental factors and processes that lead an individual to sex offending.

Developmental factors

It is firmly established that criminal careers may take a variety of forms: for example, some individuals start and stop offending in adolescence, while other adolescents will continue offending throughout adulthood (Moffitt, 1993). Piquero, Farrington, Jennings, Diamond, and Craig (2012) used data from the Cambridge Study in Delinquent Development to investigate the onset and persistence of sex offending. (The Cambridge Study in Delinquent Development is a longitudinal study of a cohort of 411 South London males followed from early childhood to adulthood.) Piquero et al. found very few convicted sex offenders, with just 10 of the cohort convicted for a total of 13 offences. Thus, while 41% of the cohort had been convicted for a criminal offence by the age of 50 years, only 2.5% of the males had a conviction for a sex offence; looked at another way, by the age of 50 years the cohort were responsible for a total of 808 convictions of which 13 (1.6%) were for sex offences. There was not a consistent pattern in the emergence of sex offending: 13 sex offences occurred at various ages with four offences committed between 10–15 years, two offences between 16–20 years, five between 31–40 years, and two between 41–50 years. As Piquero et al. note, the very low base rate of sex offending in the Cambridge data is consistent with the findings of two separate American longitudinal studies.

A Danish study by Christoffersen, Soothill, and Francis (2005) reported results from a prospective study of all boys born in Denmark in 1966. The study compared the 96 males with a conviction for rape of rape when aged between 15 and 27 years with the remainder of the population (n = 43,307) identifying risk factors for the offence. The distinguishing characteristics of the sex offenders at a family level were parental mental illness and a father with no vocational training; at an individual level the risk factors were having been in residential care, a history of violence, no vocational training and experience of mental illness. As Christoffersen, Soothill, and Francis point out, these risk factors are similar to those for violence, emphasising the point that rape is a violence offence.

A Canadian study reported by Mathesius and Lussier (2014) investigated the offending histories of 332 first-time convicted adult male sex offenders. The majority of the offenders said that they started sex offending as young adults aged from 25 to 35 years, although in the main they were not arrested until later in middle adulthood. These men committed a large number of sex offences, ranging from 1 to 91, with a mean of over 2 victims per offender.

It appears that sex offending may typically start as early as adolescence or as late as middle-age. Seto and Lalumière (2010) conducted a meta-analysis of 59 studies which compared male adolescent sex offenders with male adolescent non-sex offenders. The analysis strongly suggested that adolescent sex offending is not just another manifestation of general antisocial propensities. The adolescent sex offenders differed from the non-sex offenders in that they had less extensive criminal histories and fewer antisocial peers but greater problems with substance use. An explanation for the offending couched in terms of the adolescent's own sexual history was supported: the sex offenders were more likely to have a background which encompassed sexual and other forms of abuse as well as exposure at a young age to pornography and sexual violence; the sex offenders were more likely to show atypical sexual interests such as an interest in coercive sex and sex with children, to be socially isolated, and to be anxious and have low self-esteem. The most marked differences between the offenders and non-offenders were evident for atypical sexual interests and sexual abuse history.

The nature of the variations in developmental experience between sex offenders against children and against adults is seen in a study by Simons, Wurtele, and Durham (2008). The offenders against children were more likely to report sexual abuse, early exposure to pornography before 10 years of age, and experience of sexual acts involving animals. The rapists were more likely to report physical and emotional abuse, parental violence, and cruelty to animals.

A meta-analysis by Jespersen, Lalumière, and Seto (2009) looked specifically at abuse in the backgrounds of adult sex offenders and non-sex offenders. The sex offenders were more likely to have a history of sexual abuse but not physical abuse. In terms of victim type, a history of sexual abuse was more likely to be seen in sex offenders against children as compared to adults, while the opposite was found for physical abuse, supporting the view that sexual abuse increases the probability of becoming a sexual abuser. However, not all sex offenders will have been abused so the abuse is not itself a complete explanation for the offending.

Against the potential backdrop of a history of abuse there are specific factors which may be associated with each of stalking, sex offences against children, and sex offences against adult women.

Stalkers

The complexities of stalking are evident in the findings reported by Spitzberg (2002) from a meta-analysis of 103 studies involving a total of 70,000 people who had been stalked, over three-quarters of whom were women. In the majority of cases the stalker and the victim knew each other, sometimes having had a romantic relationship. The stalking lasted on average for two years and in some cases was accompanied by a threat of violence. The likelihood of violence is heightened when there is a previous sexually intimate relationship (Douglas & Dutton, 2001; Meloy, Davis, & Lovett, 2001) and when the stalker belongs to a clinical and forensic sample, as may be found in a secure hospital (Spitzberg & Cupach, 2007). The majority of stalkers are adult males, although stalking by young people (Ravensberg & Miller, 2003) and by women (Purcell, Pathé, & Mullen, 2001) has also been recorded.

Miller (2012a) suggests that the stalker may have several reasons for following their selected victim: these motivations include a delusional romantic belief, wanting to recover a previous relationship, and an aggressive wish to make the victim suffer. Miller notes that some stalkers may be mentally disordered, typically personality disordered, psychotic, or delusional: this type of stalker may exhibit a "Psychotic overidentification with the (often famous) victim and the resultant desire to become him by eliminating and replacing him" (p. 503).

Sex Offenders Against Children

As with most crime, sex offenders against children are predominantly male although, as discussed below, there are some female sex offenders. There are two main strands within the research on the perpetrators of sex offences against children: first, typologies of the abuser; second, the cognitive processes characteristic of abusers.

Typologies

Miller (2013) provides an overview as typologies of sex offenders against children which is summarised in Box 5.3, which also shows three different typologies of collectors of child pornography.

Henry, Mandeville-Norden, Hayes, and Egan (2010) present a threefold typology of Internet sexual offenders based on the results of a battery of psychometric tests, which included measures of cognitive distortions, victim empathy, loneliness, and impulsiveness, completed by a large sample of male offenders convicted for Internet sexual offences. The first type were called "normal" offenders as they were more emotionally stable and held attitudes less supportive of offending. The "inadequate" offenders showed emotional problems, low self-esteem, and emotional loneliness. Finally, the "deviant" offenders were characterised by very marked attitudes in favour of offending.

Box 5.3 Typologies of Sex Offenders Against Children
(after Miller, 2013)

Contact Offenders

Preferential child molester. As the name implies, this type of offender has a stable sexual preference for children.

Situational child molester. Does not have a preferential interest in children but will sexually victimise children, along with other vulnerable groups such as the disabled or elderly, if the opportunity arises.

Sadistic paedophile. A violent child molester, likely to commit other types of violence, whose sexual appetite involves sadistic aggression. Carried out with a high degree of planning: the child is abducted, tortured, sexually assaulted, and mutilated. The child may die or be left alive highly damaged both physically and psychologically.

Child Pornography Collectors

Hartman, Burgess, and Lanning (1984) typology:

Closet collectors accumulate images in secret and typically do not seek sexual contact with children.

Isolated collectors gather images, perhaps of their own sexual contact with children, to strengthen their sexual contact with real children.

Cottage collectors belong to networks where images are traded and shared, which provides contact with other collectors as well as enabling them to refine their collections.

Commercial collectors sell images for financial profit.

Sullivan and Beech (2004) typology:

Type 1 offenders collect images as an activity within a range of sexual offending including contact with children.

Type 2 offenders collect images as they have a sexual interest in children which may develop into seeking contact.

Type 3 offenders search for images out of curiosity or because of sexual interest in children but do not make contact.

Alexy, Burgess, and Baker (2005) typology:

Traders swap or sell images online.

Travellers use the internet to find and make contact with potential victims.

Trader-travellers combine trading in images with using the internet to find victims.

Typologies are informative as they provide a way of configuring the diversity of factors grouped under the generic term "child sex offender". However, the typologies do not necessarily capture all the relevant information, such as the gender of the offender, the nature of their occupation, or the setting in which the abuse takes place: for example, Miller (2013) makes particular note of child sexual abuse perpetrated by members of the clergy and by childcare providers alongside the abuse which takes places in institutions.

Although typologies can sort perpetrators into categories such as, say, sadistic and non-sadistic, they do not give details of the psychological processes that may underpin the categories. However, the development of typologies may provide the starting point for research into variations across categories. A separate body of work has looked particularly at the cognitive processes associated with sex offending against children.

Cognitive processes

An understanding of the thinking of perpetrators of sex offences is a logical step from both a theoretical and an applied perspective. The research investigating the cognitive distortions of sex offenders against children has shed light on the role of cognitions in sexual offending.

Cognitive distortions   Abel, Becker, and Cunningham-Rather (1984) used the term *cognitive distortion* to refer to the attitudes and beliefs expressed by child offenders about their offences. Such cognitions serve a variety of functions for the individual: they minimise the sexual act ("Genital fondling is not really sex so no harm is done"); they alleviate feelings of guilt ("Children don't tell because they enjoy the sex"); and they deny that the behaviour is deviant ("Society will eventually see that sex with a child is acceptable").

The *Abel and Becker Cognitions Scale* was devised to aid the assessment of 29 offence-supportive cognitive distortions (Abel et al., 1989). There is some empirical support for the role of cognitive distortions in offending (Gannon & Polaschek, 2006), particularly attitudes supportive of sexual offending (Helmus, Hanson, Babchishin, & Mann, 2013).

Studies of Internet sex offenders have also revealed details about the beliefs associated with offences against children. Winder and Gough (2010) describe how convicted adult males serving prison sentences for the possession and/or distribution of indecent images of a child were able to distance themselves from their offences. The distortion-like statements made by the offenders rejected the view that they were responsible for creating child victims or that they were offenders, and presented what they did as relatively harmless when set against contact crimes. Similarly, DeLong, Durkin, and Hundersmarck (2010) reported three types of cognitive distortion, described in Box 5.4, used by men to deny the seriousness of their involvement in online solicitation of sex with children.

Box 5.4   Cognitive Distortions in Internet Sex Offenders Against Children

Justification/rationalisation occurs when the offender invents spurious explanations for their actions: e.g., "I was only going to watch a movie with her" and "I was only going to see if she was alone, and if she was alone then I was going to call the police".

Minimisation is denial of the extent of the offence and of the intent to commit an offence: e.g., "I knew what I was saying was not right but I had no intention of having sex with her" and "She was the one who brought up sex, I just wanted to chat".

Refutation is complete denial of the offence, the facts associated with the offence, the offender's own behaviour, and the effect on the victim: e.g., "This was all a set up" and "She was saying she was 19".

Source: After DeLong et al., 2010.

In addition to statements of the type discussed above, men apprehended for accessing child pornography may claim to suffer from psychological problems such as addiction to the Internet or addiction to pornography (Seto, Reeves, & Jung, 2010).

Understanding sex offences against children

While cognitions are important, a complete model of sexual offending against children must collate an array of cultural, economic, individual, and social variables. Finkelhor (1984) developed one of the most influential multifactor theories to account for sex offences against children. Finkelhor's approach, called the *Precondition Model*, is concerned with four complementary processes—each including individual, physiological, and sociocultural variables—all of which must occur in sequence before the individual acts to abuse children.

Finkelhor's Precondition Model

The first precondition is the individual's *motivation to sexually abuse children*. Finkelhor suggests that there are three aspects to this motivation: first, *emotional congruence* in that the individual finds children a source of emotional gratification perhaps because children are not threatening or because of the individual's low self-esteem and immaturity; second, *being sexually aroused by* children which may be a consequence of early learning, including sexual abuse, or the use of child pornography; third, *blockage* in seeking adult partners, perhaps because of social anxiety or poor social skills, leading to children becoming sexual outlets.

Once an individual has acquired the motivation to abuse children, the second precondition lies in their overcoming *internal inhibitors*. It is one thing to be sexually attracted by children; it is quite another thing to act on that attraction. The offender must overcome both their own moral restraints against such behaviour and the strong social disapproval of such actions. There are several routes to *disinhibition*, such as alcohol use and high levels of stress, which may act in a given situation to mitigate inhibitions and allow the offence to take place. The third precondition, *overcoming external inhibitors*, lies in creating the conditions in which the offence takes place. There are several ways in which this precondition may be contrived by the offender, such as gaining a family's trust, grooming a child, or planning to gain access to a child when they are alone or unsupervised.

The fourth precondition, once the other three are satisfied, lies in *overcoming the child's resistance*. The individual may seek to overcome the child's resistance to sexual contact by gaining their trust and gradually introducing them to the idea of sex, or by creating a context where the child emotionally depends on them as an adult, or by misusing a position of authority.

Finkelhor's precondition model is important because it seeks to understand the process by which sexual offence takes place, drawing on social as well as individual factors. The social factors range from children left unsupervised because of the absence of social support for families or parents' work patterns due to financial pressures, and the availability of child pornography on the Internet.

Sexual Offences Against Women

Rape is committed by men of all ages with, as Feist et al. (2007) point out, a strong positive correlation between the ages of the victim and the suspect. In terms of a broad typology, Groth (1979) studied 500 rapists and defined three types of relationship between violent and sexual behaviour. In the first type, *anger rape*, the sexual attack follows a soured relationship with a woman which has left the offender feeling wrongly treated and angry. The offender seeks to vent his anger through injuring the victim by the use of excessive physical force: the rape may be a means of inflicting pain and humiliation rather than a sexual act per se. Groth suggested that 40% of the sample were of the anger rape type.

The *power rape* is characterised by the use of a degree of physical force necessary to force the woman to comply with the man's sexual demands. Thus, unlike anger rape, the sexual element is at the forefront although, Groth suggests, it is the experience of power, not sexual gratification, which drives the offender to display his strength, proclaim his heterosexuality and so relieve his anxieties. Groth suggested that 55% of the sample were of the power rape type. In the third type, *sadistic rape*, violence and sex become fused so that the woman's fear and suffering are sexually arousing to the attacker. The rape is characterised by brutal acts of torment, torture, and sexual abuse: it is the most uncommon type accounting for 5% of the sample.

The basis of Groth's typology of rapists lies not so much in sexual gratification but in the exercise of physical authority for reasons such as seeking revenge and self-affirmation of manhood. These themes of dominance and power are also to be found in other explanations of rape based on men's accounts of their offence (e.g., Mann & Hollin, 2007; Scully & Marolla, 1985).

A narrower typology, specifically for stranger rape, was developed by Canter, Bennell, Alison, and Reddy (2003) based on victim statements made to the police in 112 rape cases in which the offender was found guilty. The cases were considered in terms of the levels of four factors—(1) *hostility*, the level of violence in the assault; (2) *control*, the degree to which efforts are made to immobilise the victim physically; (3) *theft*, stealing from the victim; (4) *involvement* in the sense of seeking social contact and intimacy—as originally put forward by Canter (1994). In almost three-quarters of the cases a dominant theme was evident: 32% of cases were classified as involvement; 26% as hostile; 10% as control; and 5% as theft. Thus, Canter et al. suggest that stranger rapes may be more concerned with hostility and seeking pseudo-intimacy than with the exercise of power and control.

Cognitive distortions

Ryan (2004) argues that cognitions lie at the heart of any explanation of rape: for example, men provide justifications for rape in terms of sexual narcissism, that women are complicit in rape, that men are entitled to sex. These cognitions may also play a part in the rapist's denial and minimisation of their acts. An enduring concep-tualisation of cognitions in this context lies in the notion of *rape myths*: Burt (1980) notes that: "Examples of rape myths are 'only bad girls get raped'; 'any healthy woman can resist a rapist if she really wants to'; 'women ask for it'; 'women "cry rape" only when they've been jilted or have something to cover up'; 'rapists are sex-starved, insane, or both'" (p. 217). The formal assessment of rape myths for both research and applied purposes has been aided by the development of scales such as the *Attitudes Towards Sex and Violence Scale* and the *Rape Myth Acceptance Scale* (Burt, 1980) and the *Illinois Rape Myth Acceptance Scale* (Payne, Lonsway, & Fitzgerald, 1999). The major issue associated with rape myths is that they may function to shift the blame for the offence from the aggressor to the victim, which may lead to further distress for the woman and potentially influence proceedings within the criminal justice system (Grubb & Turner, 2012; Perilloux, Duntley, & Buss, 2014; Suarez & Gadalla, 2010).

Implicit theories

Ward (2000) suggested that cognitive distortions are a product of the offender's schema (schema are outside our conscious awareness, hence the term *implicit*) with reference to the sex offender's views about themselves and other people (Mann &

Hollin, 2010). Polaschek has described five implicit theories characteristic of rapists (Polaschek & Gannon, 2004; Polaschek & Ward, 2002).

1 *Women are unknowable.* As women are not the same as men they cannot be understood by men; heterosexual relations are therefore confrontational, with women trying to deceive men about their true intentions.
2 *Women are sex objects.* While women do not realise it they are always amenable to the sexual needs of men.
3 *The male sex drive is uncontrollable.* Men must have sexual release or their sexual energy may rise to dangerous levels.
4 *Entitlement.* A man's needs have primary importance, meaning that men are entitled to sexual access to women. If that access is not given it follows that men are entitled to take by force what they need.
5 *Dangerous world.* The world is a hostile environment requiring anticipatory action to avoid rejection and hostility from others.

The association between cognitive distortions and rape myths is clearly seen in the notion of male entitlement to sex. Bouffard (2010) states that "Sexual entitlement refers to a view that men have strong, and often uncontrollable, sexual needs that must be fulfilled and that women must serve that purpose" (p. 871). There is evidence to support the role of entitlement in aggression generally (Moeller, Crocker, & Bushman, 2009) and sexual aggression specifically (Bouffard, 2010).

Understanding sex offences against women

As with sex offences against children, an understanding of sexual offending against women must involve a range of cultural, economic, individual, and social variables. There are several approaches to the development of such a model, including feminist theories (e.g., Brownmiller, 1975) and evolutionary theories (e.g., McKibbin, Shackelford, Goetz, & Starratt, 2008). The more overtly psychological explanations, as Ward, Polaschek, and Beech (2006) point out, fall into single factor and multifactor types.

Single-factor approaches   A wide range of psychological and individual factors are associated with sex offending: these factors include cognitive distortions, deviant sexual fantasy, deficits in victim empathy, deviant sexual functioning with respect to the cues the offender finds sexually preferable and arousing, some features of social functioning as with relationship skills, and the use of alcohol and other substances (Ward, Polaschek, & Beech, 2006).

A single-factor approach emphasises the role of specific characteristics which may play a prominent role in sexual offending. However, a highly complex event such as rape cannot be explained by one aspect of the offender's functioning. The interactions between a variety of individual and social factors must necessarily be involved in a full account of rape.

Multifactor approaches   There are several multifactor theories of rape (see Gannon, Collie, Ward, & Thakker, 2008), of which Marshall and Barbaree's *Integrated Theory* is an excellent example (Marshall, Anderson, & Fernandez, 1999; Marshall & Barbaree, 1990; Marshall & Marshall, 2000). The approach taken by Marshall and Barbaree seeks to accommodate early experience, biological and psychological functioning, and immediate situational factors in the context of the political and economic climate. This theory takes the stance that sex offending is a consequence of psychological vulnerabilities developed during childhood as set against the social and biological changes which take place during puberty. Thus, various psychological vulnerabilities, such as poor interpersonal skills and difficulties with emotional self-regulation, can develop from adverse early experience. Once formed, these vulnerabilities increase the chances of the individual experiencing problems in forming social, emotional, and sexual attachments to others. The adolescent male with psychological vulnerabilities may develop poor social skills which, in turn, lower his chances of being successful in genuine attempts at sexual intimacy. The rejected adolescent develops deviant sexual fantasies which may become potent if the individual fails to learn how to distinguish feelings of aggression and of sexual interest. A sexual offence occurs when the man's vulnerabilities interact with emotional disinhibitors such as alcohol use, anger, sexual frustration or rejection, loneliness, the situational availability of a victim, and the opportunity to offend. Repeated sex offending is a consequence of direct reinforcement of the sexual offence in conjunction with the cognitive distortions used by the offender to rationalise his actions.

Parenthetically, it is notable that, as with other forms of violence, alcohol may play a role in sexually violent behaviour. There may be alcohol consumption by either the attacker or the victim, or both (Abbey, 2011; Monk & Jones, 2014), with a greater severity of outcome for the victim associated with greater levels of consumption by the perpetrator (Parkhill, Abbey, & Jacques-Tiura, 2009).

"Crossover" Offenders

The majority of sex offenders have a specific, fixed sexual interest which both determines and limits their offending to, say, teenage boys or female adults. However, it has been known for some time that a minority of sex offenders cross the boundaries defined by the victim's age, gender, or their biological relationship with the victim (Abel et al., 1987). The term *crossover offender* has been used to describe such undiscriminating offenders (Heil, Ahlmeyer, & Simons, 2003).

Cann, Friendship, and Gozna (2007) investigated the criminal histories of 1,345 adult male sex offenders who had committed two or more offences involving several victims. They reported that 330 offenders, all convicted in England and Wales, showed some evidence of crossover: 108 had both child and adult victims; 121 had female and male victims; and 189 had victims both within and outside their own family. In addition, 74 sex offenders had crossed two boundaries, most frequently age and biological relationship, while 7 offenders had crossed all three boundaries of age, gender, and relationship.

Sim and Proeve (2010) looked at a sample of 128 Australian adult male sexual offenders who had offended against several children. They found that over one-half of the offenders were crossover offenders: crossover offending against children of different ages (grouped as preschool, 6–12 years, and 13 years and above) was the most frequent, followed by relationship to victim, then the gender of the victim.

Female Sex Offenders

As with most criminal behaviour, sex offences are predominantly the province of men. However, since the early 1980s there has been a growing realisation that there is an under-reporting of sex offences perpetrated by females. The first, mainly American, studies suggested that female sex offenders are likely to be in the age range 26–36 years, to be white and single, to have a low socio-economic status and with a high probability of a substance abuse problem (e.g., Allen, 1991). The increasing amount of research evidence over the past two decades has allowed Sandler and Freeman (2007) to formulate a typology of female sex offenders which is summarised in Box 5.5.

The knowledge base continues to expand with several reviews now available (Fisher & Pina, 2013; Gannon & Cortoni, 2010; Tsopelas, Spyridoula, & Athanasios, 2011). Following the pathway set by research on male sex offenders, the psychological research on female sex offenders has been concerned with the sequence of event leading up to the offence.

Offence pathway

Gannon, Rose, and Ward (2008) conducted interviews with 22 convicted female sex offenders, from which they devised a three-phase model of the temporal steps that culminated in the offence. This model, outlined in Box 5.6, orders the factors of importance as background variables, the period before the offence, and finally the offence and its aftermath.

This ordering of clusters of factors according to their temporal order—Nietzel, Hasemann, and Lynam (1999) conducted a similar exercise, as discussed in Chapter 1—has the strength of allowing a picture to emerge of the developmental sequences that lead to the offence. The temporal flow of events also prompts further questions about issues such as the nature of the accompanying psychological processes. In this light, Gannon and Alleyne (2013) reviewed the literature regarding the cognitive processes associated with female sexual offending. Gannon and

Box 5.5 Sandler and Freeman's (2007) Typology
of Female Sex Offenders

1 *Heterosexual nurturers.* Women of average age 30 years, victims young males about 12 years of age. The women have a lack of intimacy in their lives and are trying to find emotional compensation from the offence.
2 *Non-criminal homosexual offender.* Women of average age 32 years with no criminal history, victims typically females about 13 years of age. These women are not likely to become recidivists.
3 *Female sexual predators.* Women of average age 29 years with a preference for male victims about 11 years of age. These women have a high likelihood of reoffending.
4 *Young adult child exploiters.* The youngest offenders of average age 28 years, likely to be arrested for sexual assault of child victims, with no preference for gender, about 7 years of age. The woman is likely to have a relationship with the child victim (possibly its mother) and does not display a preference for either male or female victims.
5 *Homosexual criminals.* These women are older, as are their victims, both typically in their mid-thirties and upwards. These offenders have a criminal history and may force the victim into prostitution for their own financial profit.
6 *Aggressive homosexual offenders.* These women are older and favour assaulting adult victims about 30 years of age. The women generally have an established relationship with the victim and the assault may occur in the context of domestic violence.

Alleyne suggest that, as with male sex offenders, female sex offenders hold beliefs which are supportive of their actions. However, the research base is limited and, as Gannon, Tyler, Barnoux, and Pina (2012) state, assuming that there is a direct match between the cognitive processes of male and female sex offenders is unwarranted.

Sex Offender Recidivism

There are several difficulties inherent in measuring recidivism generally: first, different jurisdictions may have a different legal understanding and practice (which may also change over time) regarding sex offences which creates difficulties in comparing studies conducted in different countries; second, when recidivism is measured by official statistics there remain undetected offences (indeed, official statistics may be seen as a measure of the likelihood of an offender being caught again); third, the time at risk varies across studies so that comparing across studies may not be comparing like with like.

Box 5.6   Offence Pathway for Female Sex Offenders

Background Factors: Childhood to Early Adulthood
Early family environment; any abusive experiences; resultant adaptive or mal-adaptive lifestyle in late adolescence and early adulthood; level of vulnerability due to social and personal characteristics; life stressors due, for example, to abusive partner(s), childcare responsibilities.

Proximal Planning: The Minutes Immediately Prior to the Offence
Three planning patterns emerged: (1) *implicit disorganized planning* refers to situations where the women had previously planned the offence but as it drew close they became disorganized and their plan fragmented; (2) *directed proximal planning* occurs when the immediate planning style is directed by a coercive male who is also taking part in the offence; (3) *explicit precise planning* occurs when the offence follows precisely a distal explicit plan.

Offence and Post-offence Period
Offence. The offences fell into four broad styles: (1) *maternal approach*, in which the woman takes a coercive but nonaggressive direct approach to her, mainly teenage male, victim sometimes by engaging in a sexual relationship; (2) *maternal avoidant approach*, where the woman adopts a coercive but non-aggressive approach to her victim and may not wish to offend but does so under pressure from an abusive partner; (3) *aggressive approach*, refers to offences where the woman treats her victim in an aggressive manner, some-times with the aim of causing humiliation; (4) *operationalized approach*, refers to those offences, such as sex trafficking, where the sexual element is seen as part of the wider context.

Post-offence. The women's responses immediately after the offence were *affective*, as in feelings of pleasure or anger; *cognitive* in their thoughts about themselves and their victims; and *behavioural* with respect to a controlled response as the final part of their plan such as taking steps to avoid detection, or uncontrolled and passive by simply carrying on as normal.

Source: After Gannon et al., 2008.

Cann, Falshaw, and Friendship (2004) conducted a 21-year follow-up looking at the reconviction rates for sexual, violent, and general offences of 419 male sex offenders released from prison in England and Wales during 1979. It was found that 103 offenders were reconvicted for a sexual offence, 91 for a violent crime, and 259 were reconvicted for other offences. The highest rates of reconviction for a sexual offence (i.e., the same offence at first and second conviction) were for indecent exposure with intent to assault any female (75% reconviction), offences involving buggery (39.3%), and indecent assault on a female aged 16 and over (28.1%): of the 68 men convicted for rape, 9 (13.2%) were reconvicted for a further rape. The benefits of a long follow-up period were seen in the finding that some of the offenders received their first reconviction for a sex offence up to 15 years after leaving prison. Cann et al. point out that their findings are in accord with other studies both in other countries (e.g., Prentky, Lee, Knight, & Cerce, 1997), and previously in England and Wales (e.g., Soothill & Gibbens, 1978).

Male sex offenders appear to recidivate at a higher rate than female sex offenders. An American study reported by Sandler and Freeman (2009) looked at reconviction for a sample of 1,466 female sex offenders. At a 5-year follow-up after their first conviction, 1.9% of the sample had been reconvicted for a sexual offence. This low rate of reconviction was confirmed as typical in a meta-analysis of 10 studies reported by Cortoni, Hanson, and Coache (2010). However, "crossover sex offenders" have been shown to have a significantly higher risk of reoffending than non-crossover offenders (Hanson & Thornton, 1999), as is also the case with mentally disordered sex offenders (e.g., Rice, Quinsey, & Harris, 1991).

In considering these findings it is important to take into account the degree of variability in offending by individual sex offenders. Lussier, Bouchard, and Beauregard (2011) note that one-half of their sample of 553 sex offenders, all serving custodial sentences in a Canadian maximum security institution, were caught after three or fewer assaults with a single victim. At the other end of the spectrum, about 1 in 10 offenders survived arrest for more than 16 years and with a maximum of 13 victims.

Factors associated with recidivism

Hanson and Morton-Bourgon (2005) conducted a meta-analysis of 82 empirical studies of sex offender recidivism, the majority of which were conducted in the United States, Canada, and the United Kingdom. The analysis revealed that for both adult and adolescent sexual offenders there were two strong predictors of sex offence recidivism: Hanson and Morton-Bourgon titled these two predictors *antisocial orientation* and *deviant sexual preferences*. Antisocial orientation, more apparent in rapists than in sex offenders against children, refers to the offender's history of rule violation, the presence of any traits, such as impulsivity, associated with antisocial behaviour, and a history of substance abuse and unemployment. Deviant sexual preferences refers, for example, to sexual interest in children, paraphilias, and a partiality to forcing sexual compliance through the use of actual and threatened violence.

Hanson and Morton-Bourgon suggest that the antisocial orientation factors recognise that sex offenders are, indeed, offenders who, like most other offenders, are willing to harm other people. It appears that the gratification of deviant sexual preferences is then one arena among others—the sex offenders also had a high recidivism rate generally, including for nonsexual violence—in which the antisocial individual acts illegally. Hanson and Morton-Bourgon also make the point that there are other problems, such as an adverse family background and psychological problems, which are frequently found among sexual offenders while not being predictive of sexual reoffending. It is possible that some features of an adverse family background, such as being a victim of some form of child abuse, may help in part to explain the development of both an antisocial orientation and deviant sexual preferences. However, having played a formative role, these individual features are not the driving force that underpins repeated sexual offending in later life.

Conclusion

There are several points to note from considering the research investigating sex offending. There is a similarity between sex offending and other forms of violent behaviour in terms of the reasons for the offence. As with, say, bullying, the sex offender seeks to hurt another person as an exercise in displaying dominance and power. The rewards for the offender, as for example with inter-partner violence, may be feelings of dominance or relief from anxiety or angry arousal. The situational context may be similar to, say, physical assault in that the offence may occur in a public place or in private, sometimes after one or both of those involved have been drinking. Yet further, there is also a cyclical aspect: while not all sex offenders have been victims of sexual assault, although some clearly have, the background and developmental experiences of sex offenders show similarities with those of violent offenders.

6

Where To Next?

The standout point to emerge from the previous chapters is that the topic of interpersonal violence is both extensive in range and complex in nature. The extensive range of interpersonal violence is evident from the many settings in which it may occur and the variety of forms it can take. Interpersonal violence is complex in the sense that the evidence points to this form of behaviour as being a basic constituent of our character as a species. If this is the case then finding a complete explanatory framework for interpersonal violence, not to say a theory, becomes a daunting task. The big picture, as seen in expansive models such as that produced by Nietzel, Hasemann, and Lynam (1999), lays bare the extent of the theoretical challenge in accounting for the wide range of influences which culminate in violent behaviour. Of course, meeting such a large-scale theoretical challenge would include psychology but must necessarily extend to a panoply of disciplines ranging from biology to zoology, criminology to law, and economics to sociology.

The contribution to date of psychology to the unfolding of theoretical understanding has been twofold: first, the application of general, mainstream psychological theories, such as social learning theory (Bandura, 1978), to produce an account of interpersonal violence; second, the formulation of specific theories, such as the *General Aggression Model* (Anderson & Bushman, 2002), which offer an account built on the complexities of individual and social functioning. It is in the nature of theoretical advancement that things change, with old ideas modified or even discarded as new conceptual connections are forged and fresh empirical data emerges (Hamby, 2011). The process of theoretical change may take various routes, one of which involves the formation of closer ties between extant theories to produce a fuller, more expansive theory. Alternatively, the point may be arrived at where current theories are completely discarded—a radical degree of change sometimes

The Psychology of Interpersonal Violence, First Edition. Clive R. Hollin.
© 2016 John Wiley & Sons, Ltd. Published 2016 by John Wiley & Sons, Ltd.

referred to as a *paradigm shift*—in order to make way for a new, different approach to emerge. An example of a theory falling from favour is to be found in the field of addictions with the call to put to rest the "stages of change" model as, arguably, it had outlived its usefulness (West, 2005).

Binding Current Theories

As discussed in Chapter 1, there is a range of theories which aim to provide a psychologically informed account of interpersonal violence. It is not difficult to see points of overlap between theories from different disciplines. The notion of situated transactions taken from criminology (Luckenbill, 1977), for example, provides an effective means of describing the interactions which precede interpersonal violence. The nature of these transactions could be further elaborated by, say, expounding on the role of cognitive processes and angry arousal in these transactions; once this exercise is completed another variable, say the effects of alcohol on such cognitions, could be added to increase the theory's explanatory power. In this way a fuller and fuller picture of the interpersonal exchanges that result in violence could be constructed as more factors are more fully explained. The process of combining theories, referred to as "theory knitting" (Chovan, 2002), may lead to incremental shifts towards addressing the big picture as portrayed in expansive models as presented by Nietzel, Hasemann, and Lynam (1999).

Towards New Theories

The alternative to incremental change is to be seen when a theory is completely discarded in favour of a new approach. This is seen in the proposal advanced by Ferguson and Dyck (2012) that "The Time Has Come to Retire the General Aggression Model". Ferguson and Dyck suggest that it is time for a paradigm shift in the way aggression is understood because, they argue, some of the basic assumptions that underpinned the original model now longer hold true and the theory does not thoroughly account for real-world acts of violence. Ferguson and Dyck suggest that the stress-diathesis model may offer a better alternative. The stress-diathesis model is a theoretical approach, to be found across several areas of psychological research, which attempts to explain a specific behaviour such as, say, depression or schizophrenia, in terms of an individual vulnerability, or diathesis, in association with specific stressful life events. When looked at in this way progress has evidently been made in terms of identifying some of the individual vulnerabilities associated with violent behaviour. The same point holds for the life events associated with interpersonal violence. Thus, for example, in reading across a wide range of material in preparing this book I found that several topics—such as the place of alcohol in the perpetration of acts of violence (e.g., McMurran, 2013), the phenomenon of victim to offender (e.g., Jennings, Piquero, & Reingle, 2012), and cycles of violence (e.g., Widom, 2014)—repeatedly appear in the literature. These and some of the other factors which contribute to interpersonal violence have been carefully researched and their role is now reasonably well understood.

The immediate caveat to such a positive view is, of course, that we don't know everything and it is likely that research will continue to identify new issues to consider. In this light, an emerging topic associated with individual vulnerability lies in the nature of the psychological impact of interpersonal violence on those involved. The utility of the notion of post-traumatic stress as an explanatory vehicle to account for the psychological effects of involvement in violence is attracting attention and may well prove to be of significance in adding to our understanding of interpersonal violence.

Post-traumatic Stress

The application of the notion of post-traumatic stress to help understand interpersonal violence raises several issues: (1) What is post-traumatic stress? (2) What is the evidence for the association between violence and post-traumatic stress? (3) How might understanding the association add to theory? These three points will be considered in turn.

What is post-traumatic stress?

The DSM-IV-TR criteria for post-traumatic stress disorder (American Psychiatric Association, 2000) are intended for use when an individual has experienced a traumatic event—such as being involved in a natural disaster such as a fire, or surviving a man-made event such as an aeroplane crash—which involves the threat of serious personal harm or death. The fear and helplessness immediately after the traumatic event are followed, in the longer term, by repeated intrusive and distressing thoughts and images of the event which last for longer than a month. These intrusive cognitions may occur when the person is asleep and dreaming or, when awake, as hallucinations and flashbacks. The distress brought about by the intrusive cognitions leads the person to avoid anything they associate with the trauma which, in turn, may impair personal and social functioning. The PTSD is said to be *acute* if the symptoms have been experienced for under three months and *chronic* if they have been present for over three months. The PTSD has a *delayed onset* if it occur six months or more after the event.

The DSM-IV-R criteria were modified slightly in DSM-V (American Psychiatric Association, 2013) and three new symptoms were added: (1) persistent and distorted blame of self or others; (2) a persistent negative emotional state; (3) reckless or destructive behaviour.

The association between violence and post-traumatic stress

It has long been evident that involvement in acts of violence may lead to a cluster of symptoms similar to those seen in PTSD. The descriptions of soldiers returning from the First World War (e.g., Merskey, 1995) as "shell-shocked" or suffering from "war neuroses" we would now recognise as describing the symptoms of PTSD. More recent conflicts, such as the war in Iraq (e.g., Milliken, Auchterlonie, & Hoge, 2007), have produced similar concerns about the effects of combat on the military personnel involved. Of course, it is not only military personnel who are involved in war: there is every likelihood that civilians caught up in a conflict, children and adults alike, may suffer PTSD (Thabet, Tawahina, Eyad, & Vostanis, 2008).

The presence of PTSD symptomatology in military personnel, even in the role of aggressor, illustrates the psychological impact of involvement in violence. In the context of interpersonal violence, is it possible that the aggressor might experience the symptoms of post-traumatic stress? This question actually divides into two sub-questions: (1) Has the perpetrator previously been exposed to situations which may have resulted in trauma and which relate to their violent actions? (2) Has the perpetration of a specific violent act resulted in trauma for the aggressor? In order to answer these questions researchers have turned to populations of known offenders.

PTSD in offender populations   A systematic literature review by Goff, Rose, Rose, and Purves (2007) noted high levels of PTSD in offenders, with higher rates seen for women offenders. This same pattern is evident in more recent studies. An Australian study of stress symptomatology in 291 incarcerated young offenders, 256 males and 35 females, was reported by Moore, Gaskin, and Indig (2013). A range of measures revealed that 20% of the young offenders, with significantly more females than males, met the criteria for a diagnosis of PTSD. In addition, 60% of the young offenders reported experiencing abuse or neglect as a child. The most significant correlate of diagnosis of PTSD was experiencing three or more types of maltreatment as a child. The female offenders were almost 10 times more likely to report three or more types of severe child maltreatment. Gunter, Chibnall, Antoniak, McCormick, and Black (2012) found a history of traumatic life experiences and high levels of PTSD in both male and female adult prisoners admitted to an American state prison. Ruzich, Reichert, and Lurigioc (2014) reported that 21% of men admitted to an urban American jail met the criteria for PTSD.

The rate of PTSD in offender populations is above what would be expected in the general population. An American survey of a national sample of over 10,000 adolescents conducted by McLaughlin et al. (2013) reported a PTSD rate of 4.7%, with a significantly greater rate for females (7.3%) than males (2.2%). This high rate of PTSD may, partly at least, be explained by the fact that offender populations are likely to contain a high proportion of individuals who have experienced poly-victimisation (Ford, Grasso, Hawke, & Chapman, 2013). As high levels of poly-abuse in childhood are consistent with the notion of a cumulative effect of trauma in childhood and into adolescence (Hodges et al., 2013), so as the trauma "dosage" increases so the likelihood of PTSD increases (Cougle, Resnick, & Kilpatrick, 2009). The higher rate of stress symptomatology in females may point to a particular effect of experiencing emotional abuse (Van Vugt, Lanctôt, Paquette, Collin-Vézina, & Lemieux, 2014) and to higher levels of poly-victimisation.

How does post-traumatic stress relate to interpersonal violence?

The interplay between trauma, stress, and violent offending raises a raft of conceptual and legal issues (Miller, 2012b) including the nature of the association between the traumatic stress and the commission of acts of violence.

There is evidence indicating that some young offenders do experience trauma symptomatology as a consequence of their violent conduct, which may be as extreme as taking a life (Evans, Ehlers, Mezey, & Clark, 2007; Welfare & Hollin, 2012). Despite the likelihood that some of these young people will previously have been victimised as children resulting in enduring traumatic symptomatology (Widom, 1999), we know remarkably little about the psychological functioning of this group of violent young people and their development in adulthood. A Chinese study has suggested that violent, traumatised young people experience cognitive difficulties in executive functioning (Zou et al., 2013) which are a potentially important avenue of research. If traumatised violent offenders do experience deficits in executive functioning then this will impair their judgement and decision-making in interpersonal relations, potentially acting as a risk factor for further violence. Yet further, while some people may recover from PTSD, with different recovery rates for males and females (Blain, Galovski, & Robinson, 2010), it is not known if this holds true for violent offenders. As with psychological functioning, recovery from PTSD among violent offenders is another risk factor which could be used to inform decision-making in, say, parole hearings regarding release from custody.

Conclusion

While much is known about interpersonal violence a great deal remains to be understood. There are two aspects to consider for the future: first, there is much to reflect upon in terms of what is known and how that may influence theory; second, a coherent strategy for researching emerging topics, such as PTSD, would have many advantages in terms of positively advancing knowledge. Finally, in the words of Kurt Lewin, one of the founders of applied psychology, "There is nothing more practical than a good theory" (Lewin, 1952, p. 169). One goal of research and theory should be to advance knowledge which can be put to use to reduce the damaging effects of interpersonal violence in all its many forms.

References

Abbey, A. (2011). Alcohol's role in sexual violence perpetration: Theoretical explanations, existing evidence and future directions. *Drug and Alcohol Review, 30*, 481–489.

Abel, G. G., Becker, J. V., & Cunningham-Rather, J. (1984). Complications, consent, and cognitions in sex between children and adults. *International Journal of Law and Psychiatry, 7*, 89–103.

Abel, G. G., Becker, J. V., Mittelman, M., Cunningham-Rathner, J., Rouleau, J. L., & Murphy, W. D. (1987). Self-reported sex crimes of nonincarcerated paraphiliacs. *Journal of Interpersonal Violence, 2*, 3–25.

Abel, G. G., Gore, D. K., Holland, C. L., Camp, N., Becker, J. V., & Rathner, J. (1989). The measurement of the cognitive distortions of child molesters. *Annals of Sex Research, 2*, 135–153.

Aber, J. L., & Cicchetti, D. (1984). The social-emotional development of maltreated children. In B. M. Lester & M. W. Yogman (Eds.), *Theory and research in behavioral pediatrics* Vol. *1* (pp. 147–205). New York: Plenum Press.

Abrahams, N., Devries, K., Watts, C., Pallitto, C., Petzold, M., Shamu, S., & García-Moreno, C. (2014). Worldwide prevalence of non-partner sexual violence: A systematic review. *The Lancet, 383*(9929), 1648–1654.

Adachi, P. J. C., & Willoughby, T. (2011). The effect of violent video games on aggression: Is it more than just the violence? *Aggression and Violent Behavior, 16*, 55–62.

Adkins, K. S., & Dush, C. M. K. (2010). The mental health of mothers in and after violent and controlling unions. *Social Science Research, 39*, 925–937.

Adorno, T. W., Frenkel-Brunswik, E., Levinson, D. J., & Sanford, R. N. (1950). *The authoritarian personality*. New York: Harper & Row.

Agha, S. (2009). Structural correlates of female homicide: A cross-national analysis. *Journal of Criminal Justice, 37*, 576–585.

Alden, A., Brennan, P., Hodgins, S., & Mednick, S. (2007). Psychotic disorders and sex offending in a Danish birth cohort. *Archives of General Psychiatry, 64*, 1251–1258.

The Psychology of Interpersonal Violence, First Edition. Clive R. Hollin.
© 2016 John Wiley & Sons, Ltd. Published 2016 by John Wiley & Sons, Ltd.

Alexandre, C. G., Nadanovsky, P., Moraes, C. L., & Reichenheim, M. (2010). The presence of a stepfather and child physical abuse, as reported by a sample of Brazilian mothers in Rio de Janeiro. *Child Abuse & Neglect, 34*, 959–966.

Alexy, E. M., Burgess, A. W., & Baker, T. (2005). Internet offenders: Traders, travelers, and combination trader-travelers. *Journal of Interpersonal Violence, 20*, 804–812.

Ali, P. A., & Naylor, P. B. (2013a). Intimate partner violence: A narrative review of the feminist, social and ecological explanations for its causation. *Aggression and Violent Behavior, 18*, 611–619.

Ali, P. A., & Naylor, P. B. (2013b). Intimate partner violence: A narrative review of the biological and psychological explanations for its causation. *Aggression and Violent Behavior, 18*, 373–382.

Allen, C. M. (1991). *Women and men who sexually abuse children: A comparative analysis.* New York: The Safer Society Press.

Allred, K. G. (2000). Anger and retaliation in conflict. In T. M. Deutsch & P. T. Coleman (Eds.), *The handbook of conflict resolution: Theory and practice* (pp. 236–255). San Francisco, CA: Jossey-Bass.

American Psychiatric Association. (2000). *Diagnostic and statistical manual of mental disorders* (4th ed.). Text-Revision (DSM-IV-TR). Washington, DC: APA.

American Psychiatric Association. (2013). *Diagnostic and statistical manual of mental disorders* (5th ed.). Washington, DC: APA.

Amin, K. (2011). Concussions in ice hockey: Is it time to worry? *The Meducator, 1*(20), Article 8. Available at: http://digitalcommons.mcmaster.ca/meducator/vol1/iss20/8

Anderson, C. A. (1989). Temperature and aggression: Ubiquitous effects of heat on occurrence of human violence. *Psychological Bulletin, 106*, 74–96.

Anderson, C. A., Berkowitz, L., Donnerstein, E., Huesmann, L. R., Johnson, J. D., … & Wartella, E. (2003). The influence of media violence on youth. *Psychological Science in the Public Interest, 4*, 81–110.

Anderson, C. A., & Bushman, B. J. (2002). Human aggression. *Annual Review of Psychology, 53*, 27–51.

Anderson, C. A., Shibuya, A., Ihori, N., Swing, E. L., Bushman, B. J., … & Saleem, M. (2010). Violent video game effects on aggression, empathy, and prosocial behavior in eastern and western countries: A meta-analytic review. *Psychological Bulletin, 136*, 151–173.

Annas, G. J. (1983). Boxing: Atavistic spectacle or artistic sport? *American Journal of Public Health, 73*, 811–812.

Annerbäck, E. M., Sahlqvist, L., Svedin, C. G., Wingren, G., & Gustafsson, P. A. (2012). Child physical abuse and concurrence of other types of child abuse in Sweden—Associations with health and risk behaviors. *Child Abuse & Neglect, 36*, 585–595.

Anwar, S., Långström, N., Grann, M., & Fazell, S. (2011). Is arson the crime most strongly associated with psychosis? A national case-control study of arson risk in schizophrenia and other psychoses. *Schizophrenia Bulletin, 37*, 580–586.

Arluke, A., & Luke, C. (1997). Physical cruelty toward animals in Massachusetts, 1975–1996. *Society and Animals, 5*, 195–204.

Ascione, F. R. (1998). Battered women's reports of their partner's and their children's cruelty to animals. *Journal of Emotional Abuse, 1*, 119–133.

Ascione, F. R., & Lockwood, R. (2001). Cruelty to animals: Changing psychological, social, and legislative perspectives. In D. J. Salem & A. N. Rowan (Eds.), *The state of the animals 2001* (pp. 39–53). Washington, DC: Humane Society of the United States.

Askeland, I. R., Evang, A., & Heir, T. (2011). Association of violence against partner and former victim experiences: A sample of clients voluntarily attending therapy. *Journal of Interpersonal Violence, 26,* 1095–1110.

Aspelmeier, J. E., Elliott, A. N., & Smith, C. H. (2007). Childhood sexual abuse, attachment, and trauma symptoms in college females: The moderating role of attachment. *Child Abuse & Neglect, 31,* 549–566.

Atria, M., Strohmeier, D., & Spiel, C. (2007). The relevance of the school class as social unit for the prevalence of bullying and victimization. *European Journal of Developmental Psychology, 4,* 372–387.

Aucoin, K. J., Frick, P. J., & Bodin, S. D. (2006). Corporal punishment and child adjustment. *Journal of Applied Developmental Psychology, 27,* 527–541.

Babchishin, K. M., Hanson, R. K., & Hermann, C. A. (2011). The characteristics of online sex offenders: A meta-analysis. *Sexual Abuse: A Journal of Research and Treatment, 23,* 92–123.

Babcock, J. C., Green, C. E., & Webb, S. A. (2008). Decoding deficits of different types of batterers during presentation of facial affect slides. *Journal of Family Violence, 23,* 295–302.

Babcock, J. C., Tharp, A. L. T., Sharp, C., Heppner, W., & Stanford, M. S. (2014). Similarities and differences in impulsive/premeditated and reactive/proactive bimodal classifications of aggression. *Aggression and Violent Behavior, 19,* 251–262.

Bachi, K. (2012). Equine-facilitated psychotherapy: The gap between practice and knowledge. *Society and Animals, 20,* 364–380.

Bailey, S. L., Flewelling, F. L., & Rosenbaum, D. P. (1997). Characteristics of students who bring weapons to school. *Journal of Adolescent Health, 20,* 261–270.

Baillien, E., De Cuyper, N., & De Witte, H. (2011). Job autonomy and workload as antecedents of workplace bullying: A two-wave test of Karasek's Job Demand Control model for targets and perpetrators. *Journal of Occupational and Organizational Psychology, 84,* 191–208.

Baker, C. K., Billhardt, K. A., Warren, J., Rollins, C., & Glass, N. E. (2010). Domestic violence, housing instability, and homelessness: A review of housing policies and program practices for meeting the needs of survivors. *Aggression and Violent Behavior, 15,* 430–439.

Baker, S, A. (2012). From the criminal crowd to the "mediated crowd": The impact of social media on the 2011 English riots. *Safer Communities, 11,* 40–49.

Baker, W. J. (1983). The state of British sport history. *Journal of Sport History, 10,* 53–66.

Balci, Y. G., & Ayranci, U. (2005). Physical violence against women: Evaluation of women assaulted by spouses. *Journal of Clinical Forensic Medicine, 12,* 258–263.

Baldry, A. C. (2003). Animal abuse and exposure to interparental violence in Italian youth. *Journal of Interpersonal Violence, 18,* 258–281.

Balducci, C., Cecchin, M., Fraccaroli, F., & Schaufeli, W. B. (2012). Exploring the relationship between workaholism and workplace aggressive behaviour: The role of job-related emotion. *Personality and Individual Differences, 53,* 629–634.

Balkmar, D., & Joelsson, T. (2012). Feeling the speed: The social and emotional investments in dangerous road practices. In M. Jansdotter Samuelsson, C. Krekula, & M. Åberg (Eds.), *Gender and change: Power, politics and everyday practices* (pp. 37–52). Karlstad: Karlstad University Press.

Bandura, A. (1978). Social learning theory of aggression. *Journal of Communication, 28,* 12–29.

Bannister, J., Pickering, J., Batchelor, S., Burman, M., Kintrea, K., & McVie, S. (2010). *Troublesome youth groups, gangs and knife carrying in Scotland*. Edinburgh: The Scottish Centre for Crime and Justice Research.

Baralic, I., Savic, S., Alempijevic, D. M., Jecmenic, D. S., Sbutega-Milosevic, G., & Obradovic, M. (2010). Child homicide on the territory of Belgrade. *Child Abuse & Neglect, 34*, 935–942.

Barbaree, H. E., & Marshall, W. L. (Eds.). (2008). *The juvenile sex offender*. New York: Guildford Press.

Barker, E. D., Arseneault, L., Brendgen, M., Fontaine, N., & Maughan, B. (2008). Joint development of bullying and victimization in adolescence: Relations to delinquency and self-harm. *Journal of the American Academy of Child and Adolescent Psychiatry, 47*, 1030–1038.

Barlas, J., & Egan, V. (2006). Weapons carrying in British teenagers: The role of personality, delinquency, sensational interests, and mating effort. *Journal of Forensic Psychiatry and Psychology, 17*, 53–72.

Barlett, C. P., & Gentile, D. A. (2012). Attacking others online: The formation of cyberbullying in late adolescence. *Psychology of Popular Media Culture, 1*, 123–135.

Barnes, J. C., TenEyck, M., Boutwell, B. B., & Beaver, K. M. (2013). Indicators of domestic/intimate partner violence are structured by genetic and nonshared environmental influences. *Journal of Psychiatric Research, 47*, 371–376.

Barron P., Hassiotis A., & Banes, J. (2002). Offenders with intellectual disability: The size of the problem and therapeutic outcomes. *Journal of Intellectual Disability Research, 46*, 454–463.

Bartels, L. (2010). *Emerging issues in domestic/family violence research*. Research in Practice no. 10. Canberra: Australian Institute of Criminology.

Bartholow, B. D., Anderson, C. A., Carnagey, N. L., & Benjamin, A. J. (2005). Interactive effects of life experience and situational cues on aggression: The weapons priming effect in hunters and nonhunters. *Journal of Experimental Social Psychology, 41*, 48–60.

Bartlett, J. D., Raskin, M., Kotake, C., Nearing, K. D., & Easterbrooks, M. A. (2014). An ecological analysis of infant neglect by adolescent mothers. *Child Abuse & Neglect, 38*, 723–734.

Baum, K., Catalano, S., Rand, M., & Rose, K. (2009). *Stalking victimization in the US*. US Department of Justice National Crime Victimisation Survey. NCJ 224527.

Beasley, J. O., Hayne A. S., Beyer, K., Cramer, G. L., Berson, S. B., Muirhead, Y., & Warren, J. I. (2009). Patterns of prior offending by child abductors: A comparison of fatal and non-fatal outcomes. *International Journal of Law and Psychiatry, 32*, 273–280.

Beech, A. R., Elliott, I. A., Birgden, A., & Findlater, D. (2008). The internet and child sexual offending: A criminological review. *Aggression and Violent Behavior, 13*, 216–228.

Beirne, P. (2009). *Confronting animal abuse: Law, criminology, and human-animal relationships*. Lantham, ML: Rowman & Littlefield.

Bell, P. A., & Baron, R. A. (1976). Aggression and heat: The mediating role of negative affect. *Journal of Applied Social Psychology, 6*, 18–30.

Benítez-Borrego, S., Guàrdia-Olmos, J., & Aliaga-Moore, Á. (2013). Child homicide by parents in Chile: A gender-based study and analysis of post-filicide attempted suicide. *International Journal of Law and Psychiatry, 36*, 55–64.

Benjet, C., & Kazdin, A. E. (2003). Spanking children: The controversies, findings, and new directions. *Clinical Psychology Review, 23*, 197–224.

Bennett, S., Farrington, D. P., & Huesmann, L. R. (2005). Explaining gender differences in crime and violence: The importance of social cognitive skills. *Aggression and Violent Behavior, 10,* 263–288.

Bennett, T., & Brookman, F. (2010). Street robbery. In F. Brookman, M. Maguire, H. Pierpoint, & T. Bennett (Eds.), *Handbook on crime* (pp. 270–289). Cullompton, Devon: Willan Publishing.

Berger, A., Wildsmith, E., Manlove, J., & Steward-Streng, N. (2012). *Relationship Violence Among Young Adult Couples* (Research Brief). Washington, DC: Child Trends.

Bhattacharjya, H., & Deb, D. (2014). Intimate partner violence against women during pregnancy in Tripura: A hospital based study. *International Journal of Research in Medical Sciences, 2,* 84–90.

Bichler, S., & Nitzan, J. (2014). No way out: Crime, punishment and the capitalization of power. *Crime, Law and Social Change, 61,* 251–271.

Biggs, S., Manthorpe, J., Tinker, A., Doyle, M., & Erens, B. (2009). Mistreatment of older people in the United Kingdom: Findings from the First National Prevalence Study. *Journal of Elder Abuse & Neglect, 21,* 1–14.

Bijleveld, C. C. J. H., & Wijkman, M. (2009). Intergenerational continuity in convictions: A five-generation study. *Criminal Behaviour and Mental Health, 19,* 142–155.

Birkbeck, C., & LaFree, G. (1993). The situational analysis of crime and deviance. *Annual Review of Sociology, 19,* 113–137.

Bjorkqvist K. (1994). Sex differences in physical, verbal, and indirect aggression: A review of recent research. *Sex Roles, 30,* 177–188.

Blain, L. M., Galovski, T. E., & Robinson, T. (2010). Gender differences in recovery from posttraumatic stress disorder: A critical review. *Aggression and Violent Behavior, 15,* 463–474.

Bo, S., Abu-Akel, A., Kongerslev, M., Haahr, U. H., & Simonsen, E. (2011). Risk factors for violence among patients with schizophrenia. *Clinical Psychology Review, 31,* 711–726.

Boesch, C., & Boesch, H. (1989). Hunting behavior of wild chimpanzees in the Tai' National Park. *American Journal of Physical Anthropology, 78,* 547–573.

Boles, S. M., & Miotto, K. (2003). Substance abuse and violence: A review of the literature. *Aggression and Violent Behavior, 8,* 155–174.

Bonta, J., Blais, J., & Wilson, H. A. (2014). A theoretically informed meta-analysis of the risk for general and violent recidivism for mentally disordered offenders. *Aggression and Violent Behavior, 19,* 278–287.

Bonta, J., Law, M., & Hanson, K. (1998). The prediction of criminal and violent recidivism among mentally disordered offenders: A meta-analysis. *Psychological Bulletin, 123,* 123–142.

Bouffard, L. A. (2010). Exploring the utility of entitlement in understanding sexual aggression. *Journal of Criminal Justice, 38,* 870–879.

Bourget, D., Grace, J., & Whitehurst, L. (2007). A review of maternal and paternal filicide. *Journal of the American Academy of Psychiatry and the Law, 35,* 74–82.

Bowes, N., & McMurran, M. (2013). Cognitions supportive of violence and violent behavior. *Aggression and Violent Behavior, 18,* 660–665.

Brackenridge, C. H., Bishopp, D., Moussali, S., & Tapp, J. (2008). The characteristics of sexual abuse in sport: A multidimensional scaling analysis of events described in media reports. *International Journal of Sport and Exercise Psychology, 16,* 385–406.

Brackenridge, C. H., Bringer, J. D., & Bishopp, D. (2005). Managing cases of abuse in sport. *Child Abuse Review, 14*, 259–274.

Bragado-Jimenez, M. D., & Taylor, P. J. (2012). Empathy, schizophrenia and violence: A systematic review. *Schizophrenia Research, 141*, 83–90.

Braham, L. G., Trower, P., & Birchwood, M. (2004). Acting on command hallucinations and dangerous behavior: A critique of the major findings in the last decade. *Clinical Psychology Review, 24*, 513–528.

Branas, C. C., Elliott, M. R., Richmond, T. S., Culhane, D., Ten Have, T. R., & Wiebe, D. (2009). Alcohol consumption, alcohol outlets, and the risk of being assaulted with a gun. *Alcoholism: Clinical and Experimental Research, 11*, 906–915.

Breetzke, G. D., & Cohn, E. G. (2012). Seasonal assault and neighborhood deprivation in South Africa: Some preliminary findings. *Environment and Behavior, 44*, 641–667.

Brennan, I. R., & Moore, S. C. (2009). Weapons and violence: A review of theory and research. *Aggression and Violent Behavior, 14*, 215–225.

Brennan, I. R., & Moore, S. C., & Shepherd, J. P. (2010). Aggression and attitudes to time and risk in weapon-using violent offenders. *Psychiatry Research, 178*, 536–539.

Brent, D. A., Miller, M. J., Loeber, R., Mulvey, E. P., & Birmaher, B. (2013). Ending the silence on gun violence. *Journal of the American Academy of Child & Adolescent Psychiatry, 52*, 333–338.

Bridges, L. (2012). Four days in August: The UK riots. *Race & Class, 54*, 1–12.

Brookman, F., & Nolan, J. (2006). The dark figure of infanticide in England and Wales: Complexities of diagnosis. *Journal of Interpersonal Violence, 21*, 869–889.

Brooks-Gunn, J., Schneider, W., & Waldfogel, J. (2013). The Great Recession and the risk for child maltreatment. *Child Abuse & Neglect, 37*, 721–729.

Brown, J., Hughes, N. S., McGlen, M. C., & Crichton, J. H. M. (2014). Misrepresentation of UK homicide characteristics in popular culture. *Journal of Forensic and Legal Medicine, 23*, 62–64.

Brown, J. R., Aalsma, M. C., & Ott, M. A. (2013). The experiences of parents who report youth bullying victimization to school officials. *Journal of Interpersonal Violence, 28*, 494–518.

Brown, V., Clery, E., & Ferguson, C. (2011). *Estimating the prevalence of young people absent from school due to bullying*. London: National Centre for Social Research.

Brownmiller, S. (1975). *Against our will: Men, women and rape*. New York: Simon & Schuster.

Bucci, S., Birchwood, M., Twist, L., Tarrier, N., Emsley, R., & Haddock, G. (2013). Predicting compliance with command hallucinations: Anger, impulsivity and appraisals of voices' power and intent. *Schizophrenia Research, 147*, 163–168.

Bunting, L., Webb, M. A., & Healy, J. (2010). In two minds? Parental attitudes toward physical punishment in the UK. *Children and Society, 24*, 359–370.

Burt, M. R. (1980). Cultural myths and supports for rape. *Journal of Personality and Social Psychology, 38*, 217–230.

Buse, G. J. (2006). No holds barred sport fighting: A 10 year review of mixed martial arts competition. *British Journal of Sports Medicine, 40*, 169–172.

Bushman, B. J., Wang, M. C., & Anderson, C. A. (2005). Is the curve relating temperature to aggression linear or curvilinear? Assaults and temperature in Minneapolis reexamined. *Journal of Personality and Social Psychology, 89*, 62–66.

Bussmann, K., Erthal, C., & Schroth, A. (2011). The effect of banning corporal punishment in Europe: A five-nation comparison. In A. B. Smith & J. Durrant (Eds), *Global *pathways to abolishing physical punishment: Realizing children's rights* (pp. 299–322). New York: Routledge.

Butler, A. C. (2013). Child sexual assault: Risk factors for girls. *Child Abuse & Neglect, 37,* 643–652.

Butters, J. E., Mann, R. E., & Smart, R. G. (2006). Assessing road rage victimization and perpetration in the Ontario adult population: The impact of illicit drug use and psychiatric distress. *Canadian Journal of Public Health, 97,* 96–99.

Byrne, C. A., Resnick, H. S., Kilpatrick, D. G., Best, C. L., & Saunders, B. E. (1999). The socio-economic impact of interpersonal violence on women. *Journal of Consulting and Clinical Psychology, 67,* 362–366.

Caldwell, J. E., Swan, S. C., & Woodbrown, V. D. (2012). Gender differences in intimate partner violence outcomes. *Psychology of Violence, 2,* 42–57.

Calvete, E., Orue, I., Estévez, A., Villardón, L., & Padilla, P. (2010). Cyberbullying in adolescents: Modalities and aggressors' profile. *Computers in Human Behavior, 26,* 1128–1135.

Calvete, E., Orue, I., & Gámez-Guadix, M. (2013). Child-to-parent violence: Emotional and behavioral predictors. *Journal of Interpersonal Violence, 28,* 755–772.

Campbell, J. C., Glass, N., Sharps, P. W., Laughon, K., & Bloom, T. (2007). Intimate partner homicide: Review and implications of research and policy. *Trauma, Violence & Abuse, 8,* 246–269.

Campbell, M. A. (2005). Cyber bullying: An old problem in a new guise? *Australian Journal of Guidance and Counselling, 15,* 68–76.

Cann, J., Falshaw, L., & Friendship, C. (2004). Sexual offenders discharged from prison in England and Wales: A 21-year reconviction study. *Legal and Criminological Psychology, 9,* 1–10.

Cann, J., Friendship, C., & Gozna, L. (2007). Assessing crossover in a sample of sexual offenders with multiple victims. *Legal and Criminological Psychology, 12,* 149–163.

Cannon, E. A., Bonomi, A. E., Anderson, M. L., & Rivara, F. P. (2009). The intergenerational transmission of witnessing intimate partner violence. *Archives of Pediatric and Adolescent Medicine, 163,* 706–708.

Canter, D. V. (1994). *Criminal shadows.* London: HarperCollins.

Canter, D. V., Bennell, C., Alison, L. J., & Reddy, S. (2003). Differentiating sex offences: A behaviorally based thematic classification of stranger rapes. *Behavioral Sciences and the Law, 21,* 157–174.

Canter, D., & Fritzon, K. (1998). Differentiating arsonists: A model of firesetting actions and characteristics. *Legal and Criminological Psychology, 3,* 73–96.

Cao, L., Zhang, Y., & He, N. (2008). Carrying weapons to school for protection: An analysis of the 2001 school crime supplement data. *Journal of Criminal Justice, 36,* 154–164.

Carabellese, F., Rocca, G., Candelli, C., & Catanesi, R. (2014). Mental illness, violence and delusional misidentifications: The role of Capgras' syndrome in matricide. *Journal of Forensic and Legal Medicine, 21,* 9–13.

Carbone-Lopez, K., Esbensen, F., & Brick, B. T. (2010). Correlates and consequences of peer victimization: Gender differences in direct and indirect forms of bullying. *Youth Violence and Juvenile Justice, 8,* 332–350.

Card, N., Stucky, B., Sawalani, G., & Little, T. (2008). Direct and indirect aggression during childhood and adolescence: A metaanalytic review of gender differences, intercorrelations, and relations to maladjustment. *Child Development, 79,* 1185–1229.

Carlo, G., Mestre, M. V., Samper, P., Tur, A., & Armenta, B. E. (2010). Feelings or cognitions? Moral cognitions and emotions as predictors of prosocial and aggressive behaviors. *Personality and Individual Differences, 48*, 872–877.

Carmo, R., Grams, A., & Magalhães, T. (2011). Men as victims of intimate partner violence. *Journal of Forensic and Legal Medicine, 18*, 355–359.

Carney, M., Buttell, F., & Dutton, D. (2007). Women who perpetrate intimate partner violence: A review of the literature with recommendations for treatment. *Aggression and Violent Behavior, 12*, 108–115.

Carter, A. J., & Hollin, C. R. (2010). Characteristics of non-serial sexual homicide offenders: A review. *Psychology, Crime, & Law, 16*, 25–45.

Cater, Å. K., Andershed, A., & Andershed, H. (2014). Youth victimization in Sweden: Prevalence, characteristics and relation to mental health and behavioral problems in young adulthood. *Child Abuse & Neglect, 38*, 1290–1302.

Cavanagh, K., Dobash R. E., & Dobash, R. P. (2007). The murder of children by fathers in the context of child abuse. *Child Abuse & Neglect, 31*, 731–746.

Cawson, P., Wattam, C., Brooker, S., & Kelly, G. (2000). *Child maltreatment in the United Kingdom: A study of the prevalence of abuse and neglect.* London: NSPCC.

Ceccato, V. (2005). Homicide in Sao Paulo, Brazil: Assessing spatial-temporal and weather variations. *Journal of Environmental Psychology, 25*, 307–321.

Ceccato, V. (2014). The nature of rape places. *Journal of Environmental Psychology, 40*, 97–107.

Chakraborti, N., & Zempi, I. (2012). The veil under attack: Gendered dimensions of Islamophobic victimization. *International Review of Victimology, 18*, 269–284.

Chan, H. C., & Frei, A. (2013). Female sexual homicide offenders: An examination of an underresearched offender population. *Homicide Studies, 17*, 96–118.

Chan, H. C., & Heide, K. M. (2008). Weapons used by juveniles and adult offenders in sexual homicides: An empirical analysis of 29 years of US data. *Journal of Investigative Psychology and Offender Profiling, 5*, 189–208.

Chan, K. L. (2011a). Gender differences in self-reports of intimate partner violence: A review. *Aggression and Violent Behavior, 16*, 167–175.

Chan, K. L. (2011b). Association between childhood sexual abuse and adult sexual victimization in a representative sample in Hong Kong Chinese. *Child Abuse & Neglect, 35*, 220–229.

Chan, Y-C., & Yeung, J. W-K. (2009). Children living with violence within the family and its sequel: A meta-analysis from 1995–2006. *Aggression and Violent Behavior, 14*, 313–322.

Chappell, D. (2014). Firearms regulation, violence and the mentally ill: A contemporary Antipodean appraisal. *International Journal of Law and Psychiatry, 37*, 399–408.

Chen, L. P., Murad, M. H., Paras, M. L., Colbenson, K. M., Sattler, A. L., Goranson, E. N., … & Zirakzadeh, A. (2010). Sexual abuse and lifetime diagnosis of psychiatric disorders: Systematic review and meta-analysis. *Mayo Clinic Proceedings, 85*, 618–629.

Ching, H., Daffern, M., & Thomas, S. (2012). Appetitive violence: A new phenomenon? *Psychiatry, Psychology and Law, 19*, 745–763.

Choi, N. G., Kulick, D. B., Mayer, J. (1999). Financial exploitation of elders: Analysis of risk factors based on County Adult Protective Services data. *Journal of Elder Abuse & Neglect, 10*, 39–62.

Chokkanathan, S., & Lee, A. E. Y. (2005). Elder mistreatment in urban India: A community based study. *Journal of Elder Abuse & Neglect, 17*, 45–61.

Chovan, W. (2002). Theory knitting reconsidered. *American Psychologist, 57,* 1127–1128.

Christodoulou, G. N. (1991). The delusional misidentification syndromes. *British Journal of Psychiatry, 14,* 65–69.

Christoffersen, M. N., Soothill, K., & Francis, B. (2005). Who is most at risk of becoming a convicted rapist? The likelihood of a rape conviction among the 1966 birth cohort in Denmark. *Journal of Scandinavian Studies in Criminology and Crime Prevention, 6,* 39–56.

Cleckley, H. (1941). *The mask of sanity.* St Louis, MO: Mosby.

Clements, K., & Schumacher, J. A. (2010). Perceptual biases in social cognition as potential moderators of the relationship between alcohol and intimate partner violence: A review. *Aggression and Violent Behavior, 15,* 357–368.

Coid J., Kahtan, N., Gault, S., Cook, A., & Jarman, B. (2001). Medium secure forensic psychiatry services: Comparison of seven English health regions. *British Journal of Psychiatry, 178,* 55–61.

Collins, R. (2008). *Violence: A micro-sociological theory.* Princeton, NJ: Princeton University Press.

Collins, R. E. (2013). The effect of gender on violent and nonviolent recidivism: A meta-analysis. *Journal of Criminal Justice, 38,* 675–684.

Collins, R. (2012). Entering and leaving the tunnel of violence: Micro-sociological dynamics of emotional entrainment in violent interactions. *Current Sociology, 61,* 132–151.

Combs-Orme, T., & Cain, D. S. (2008). Predictors of mothers' use of spanking with their infants. *Child Abuse & Neglect, 32,* 649–657.

Coohey, C. (2010). Gender differences in internalizing problems among sexually abused early adolescents. *Child Abuse & Neglect, 34,* 856–862.

Cook-Daniels, L. (1998). Lesbian, gay male, bisexual and transgendered elders: Elder abuse and neglect issues. *Journal of Elder Abuse & Neglect, 9,* 35–49.

Cooke, L. B., & Sinason, V. (1998). Abuse of people with learning disabilities and other vulnerable adults. *Advances in Psychiatric Treatment, 4,* 119–125.

Cordilia, A. (1985). Alcohol and property crime: Exploring the causal nexus. *Journal of Studies on Alcohol and Drugs, 46,* 161–171.

Cortoni, F., Hanson, R. K., & Coache, M. (2010). The recidivism rates of female sexual offenders are low: A meta-analysis. *Sexual Abuse: A Journal of Research and Treatment, 22,* 387–401.

Corvo, K., & deLara, E. (2010). Towards an integrated theory of relational violence: Is bullying a risk factor for domestic violence? *Aggression and Violent Behavior, 15,* 181–190.

Corvo, K., & Johnson, P. (2013). Sharpening Ockham's Razor: The role of psychopathology and neuropsychopathology in the perpetration of domestic violence. *Aggression and Violent Behavior, 18,* 175–182.

Cougle, J. R., Resnick, H., & Kilpatrick, D. G. (2009). Does prior exposure to interpersonal violence increase risk of PTSD following subsequent exposure? *Behaviour, Research and Therapy, 47,* 1012–1017.

Cox, W. T., Abramson, L. Y., Devine, P. G., & Hollon, S. D. (2012). Stereotypes, prejudice, and depression: The integrated perspective. *Perspectives on Psychological Science, 7,* 427–449.

Craig, I. W., & Halton, K. E. (2009). Genetics of human aggressive behaviour. *Human Genetics, 126,* 101–113.

Craig, K. M. (2008). Examining hate-motivated aggression: A review of the social psychological literature on hate crimes as a distinct form of aggression. *Aggression and Violent Behavior, 7,* 85–101.

Crapanzano, A. M., Frick, P. J., & Terranova, A. M. (2010). Patterns of physical and relational aggression in a school-based sample of boys and girls. *Journal of Abnormal Child Psychology, 38,* 433–445.

Crawley, E. (2007). Imprisonment in old age. In Y. Jewkes (Ed.), *Handbook on prisons* (p. 224–244). Cullompton, Devon: Willan Publishing.

Crick, N. R., & Dodge, K. A. (1994). A review and reformulation of social information-processing mechanisms in children's social adjustment. *Psychological Bulletin, 115,* 74–101.

Crick, N. R., & Grotpeter, J. K. (1995). Relational aggression, gender, and social-psychological adjustment. *Child Development, 66,* 710–722.

Cross, C. P., & Campbell, A. (2011). Women's aggression. *Aggression and Violent Behavior, 16,* 390–398.

Crossland, S., Burns, M., Leach, C., & Quinn, P. (2005). Needs assessment in forensic learning disability. *Medicine, Science, and Law, 45,* 147–153.

Crowley, A., & Vulliamy, C. (2002). *Listen up: Children talk about smacking.* Cardiff: Save the Children.

Crowther, S., Goodson, C., McGuire, J., & Dickson, J. M. (2013). Having to fight. *Journal of Interpersonal Violence, 28,* 62–79.

Culbertson, K. A., & Dehle, C. (2001). Impact of sexual assault as a function of perpetrator type. *Journal of Interpersonal Violence, 16,* 992–1007.

Curri, T. B., Palmieri, T. L., Aoki, T. H., Kaulkin, C. K., Lunn, M. E., Gregory, C. M., & Greenhalgh, D. G. (2003). Playing with fire: Images of fire on toy packaging. *Journal of Burn Care and Rehabilitation, 24,* 163–165.

Currie, C. L. (2006). Animal cruelty by children exposed to domestic violence. *Child Abuse & Neglect, 30,* 425–435.

Cutajar, M. C., Mullen, P. E., Ogloff, J. R. P., Thomas, S. D., Wells, D. L., & Spataro, J. (2010). Psychopathology in a large cohort of sexually abused children followed up to 43 years. *Child Abuse & Neglect, 34,* 813–822.

Cyr, M., Wright, J., McDuff, P., & Perron, A. (2002). Intrafamilial sexual abuse: Brother-sister incest does not differ from father-daughter and stepfather-stepdaughter incest. *Child Abuse & Neglect, 26,* 957–73.

Dadds, M. R., Turner, C. M., & McAloon, (2002). Developmental links between cruelty to animals and human violence. *Australian and New Zealand Journal of Criminology, 35,* 363–382.

Dadds, M. R., Whiting, C., Bunn, P., Fraser, J. A., Charlson, J. H., & Pinola-Merlo, A. (2004). Measurement of cruelty in children: The Cruelty to Animals Inventory. *Journal of Abnormal Child Psychology, 32,* 321–334.

Daly, J. M., Merchant, M. L., & Jogerst, G. J. (2011). Elder abuse research: A systematic review. *Journal of Elder Abuse & Neglect, 23,* 348–365.

Davies, E. A., & Jones, A. C. (2013). Risk factors in child sexual abuse. *Journal of Forensic and Legal Medicine, 20,* 146–150.

Davies, R., Collins, M., Netana , C., Folkes, L., Jenkins, R., Tombs, M., … Evans, C. (2011). *Exploring the motivations of perpetrators who abuse vulnerable adults: Final report.* Newport: University of Wales.

De Donder, L., Luoma, M., Penhale, B., Lang, G., Santos, A. J., Tamutiene, I., … Verte, D. (2011). European map of prevalence rates of elder abuse and its impact for future research. *European Journal of Ageing, 8,* 129–143.

De Fazio, L. (2011). Criminalization of stalking in Italy: One of the last among the current European member states' anti-stalking laws. *Behavioral Sciences & the Law, 29,* 317–323.

De Pauw, K. W., & Szulecka, T. K. (1998). Dangerous delusions: Violence and the misidentification syndromes. *British Journal of Psychiatry, 152,* 91–96.

de la Roche, R. S. (1996). Collective violence as social control. *Sociological Forum, 11,* 97–128.

Deater-Deckard, K., Lansford, J. E., Dodge, K. A., Pettit, G, S., & Bates, J. E. (2003). The development of attitudes about physical punishment: An 8–year longitudinal study. *Journal of Family Psychology, 17,* 351–360.

Deffenbacher, J. L., White, G. S., & Lynch, R. S. (2004). Evaluation of two new scales assessing driving anger: The Driving Anger Expression Inventory and the Driver's Angry Thoughts Questionnaire. *Journal of Psychopathology and Behavioral Assessment, 26,* 87–99.

Deibert, G. R., & Miethe, T. D. (2003). Character contests and dispute-related offenses. *Deviant Behavior: An Interdisciplinary Journal, 24,* 245–267.

DeLisi, M., Umphress, Z. R., & Vaughn, M. G. (2009). The criminology of the amygdala. *Criminal Justice and Behavior, 36,* 1241–1262.

DeLisi, M., Vaughn, M. G., Gentile, D. A., Anderson, C. A., & Shook, J. J. (2013). Violent video games, delinquency, and youth violence: New evidence. *Youth Violence and Juvenile Justice, 11,* 132–142.

DeLong, R., Durkin, K., & Hundersmarck, S. (2010). An exploratory analysis of the cognitive distortions of a sample of men arrested in internet sex stings. *Journal of Sexual Aggression, 16,* 59–70.

Denissen, J. J. A., Butalid, L., Penke, L., & van Aken, M. A. G. (2008). The effects of weather on daily mood: A multilevel approach. *Emotion, 8,* 662–667.

Deslauriers-Varin, N., & Beauregard, E. (2014). Consistency in crime site selection: An investigation of crime sites used by serial sex offenders across crime series. *Journal of Criminal Justice, 42,* 123–133.

Devapriam, J., & Bhaumik, S. (2012). Intellectual disability and arson. In G. Dickens, P. A. Sugarman, & T. A. Gannon (Eds.), *Firesetting and mental health* (pp. 107–125). London: Royal College of Psychiatry Publications.

Devries, K. M., Kishor, S., Johnson, H., Stöckl, H., Bacchus, L. J., Garcia-Moreno, C., & Watts, C. (2010). Intimate partner violence during pregnancy: Analysis of prevalence data from 19 countries. *Reproductive Health Matters, 18,* 158–170.

DeWall, C. N., Anderson, C. A., & Bushman, B. J. (2011). The General Aggression Model: Theoretical extensions to violence. *Psychology of Violence, 1,* 245–258.

DeWall, C. N., & Bushman, B. J. (2009). Hot under the collar in a lukewarm environment: Words associated with hot temperature increase aggressive thoughts and hostile perceptions. *Journal of Experimental Social Psychology, 45,* 1045–1047.

Dhont, K., & Hodson, G. (2014). Why do right-wing adherents engage in more animal exploitation and meat consumption? *Personality and Individual Differences, 64,* 12–17.

Dickens, G., Sugarman, P., Ahmad, F., Edgar, S., Hofberg, K., Tewari, S. (2008). Characteristics of low IQ arsonists at psychiatric assessment. *Medicine, Science, and Law, 48,* 217–220.

Dickens, G., Sugarman, P., Edgar, S, Hofberg, K., Tewari, S., & Ahmed, F. (2009). Recidivism and dangerousness in arsonists. *Journal of Forensic Psychiatry and Psychology, 20,* 621–639.

Dickens, G., Sugarman, P. A., & Gannon, T. A. (Eds.). (2012). *Firesetting and mental health.* London: Royal College of Psychiatry Publications.

Diem, C., & Pizarro, J. M. (2010). Social structure and family homicides. *Journal of Family Violence, 25,* 521–532.

Dietz, T. L. (2000). Disciplining children: Characteristics associated with the use of corporal punishment. *Child Abuse & Neglect, 24,* 1529–1542.

Dionisi, A. M., Barling, J., & Dupré, K. E. (2012). Revisiting the comparative outcomes of workplace aggression and sexual harassment. *Journal of Occupational Health Psychology, 17,* 398–408.

Dixon, J., Manthorpe, J., Biggs, S., Mowlam, A., Tennant, R., Tinker, A., & McCreadie, C. (2010). Defining elder mistreatment: Reflections on the United Kingdom Study of Abuse and Neglect of Older People. *Ageing & Society, 30,* 403–420.

Dixon, N. (2010). A critique of violent retaliation in sport. *Journal of the Philosophy of Sport, 37,* 1–10.

Dobash, R. E., & Dobash, R. P. (1984). The nature and antecedents of violent events. *British Journal of Criminology, 24,* 269–288.

Dodge, K. A. (1986). A social information processing model of social competence in children. In M. Perlmutter (Ed.), *The Minnesota symposium on child psychology* (Vol. *18,* pp. 77–125). Hillsdale, NJ: Erlbaum.

Dodge, K. A. (2006). Translational science in action: Hostile attributional style and the development of aggressive behavior problems. *Development and Psychopathology. 18,* 791–814.

Donahue, E. G., Rip, B., & Vallerand, R. J. (2009). When winning is everything: On passion, identity, and aggression in sport. *Psychology of Sport and Exercise, 10,* 526–534.

Dong, X., Chen, R., Chang, E-S., & Simon, M. (2013). Elder abuse and psychological well-being: A systematic review and implications for research and policy—A mini review. *Gerontology, 59,* 132–142.

Dong, X., Simon, M. A., & Gorbien, M. (2007). Elder abuse and neglect in an urban Chinese population. *Journal of Elder Abuse & Neglect, 19,* 79–96.

Dooley, J. J., Pyzalski, J., & Cross, D. (2009). Cyberbullying versus face-to-face bullying: A theoretical and conceptual review. *Journal of Psychology, 217,* 182–188.

Dosey, M. A., & Meisels, M. (1969). Personal space and self-protection. *Journal of Personality and Social Psychology, 11,* 93–97.

Douglas, K. S., & Dutton, D. G. (2001). Assessing the link between stalking and domestic violence. *Aggression and Violent Behavior, 6,* 519–546.

Douglas, K. S., Guy, L. S., & Hart, S. D. (2009). Psychosis as a risk factor for violence to others: A meta-analysis. *Psychological Bulletin, 135,* 679–706.

Downes, C., Fealy, G., Phelan, A., Donnelly, N., & Lafferty, A. (2013). *Abuse of older people with dementia: A review.* University College Dublin, Ireland: National Centre for the Protection of Older People.

Dressing, H., Kuehner, C., & Gass, P. (2005). Lifetime prevalence and impact of stalking in a European population: Epidemiological data from a middle-sized German city. *British Journal of Psychiatry, 187,* 168–172.

Drijber, B. C., Udo J. L., & Reijnders, M. C. (2013). Male victims of domestic violence. *Journal of Family Violence, 28,* 173–178.

Dube, S. R., Anda, R. F., Felitti, V. J., Edwards, V. J., & Williamson, D. F. (2002). Exposure to abuse, neglect, and household dysfunction among adults who witnessed intimate partner violence as children: Implications for health and social services. *Violence and Victims, 17,* 3–17.

Due, P., Holstein, B. E., Lynch, J., Doderichsen, F., Gabhain, S. N., Scheidt, P., Currie, C., & The Health Behaviour in School-Aged Children Bullying Working Group. (2005). Bullying and symptoms among school-aged children: International comparative cross-sectional study in 28 countries. *European Journal of Public Health, 15*, 128–132.

Dukes, R. L., Stein, J. A., & Zane, J. I. (2010). Gender differences in the relative impact of physical and relational bullying on adolescent injury and weapon carrying. *Journal of School Psychology, 48*, 511–532.

Durrant, J. (2012). Physical punishment of children: Lessons from 20 years of research. *Canadian Medical Association Journal, 184*, 1373–1339.

Dutton, D. G. (2012). Transitional processes culminating in extreme violence. *Journal of Aggression, Conflict and Peace Research, 4*, 45–53.

Edwards, K. M., Turchik, J. A., Dardis, C. M., Reynolds, N., & Gidycz, C. A. (2011). Rape myths: History, individual and institutional-level presence, and implications for change. *Sex Roles, 65*, 761–773.

Ehrensaft, M. K., Cohen, P., Brown, J., Smailes, E., Chen, H., & Johnson, J. G. (2003). Intergenerational transmission of partner violence: A 20–year prospective study. *Journal of Consulting and Clinical Psychology, 71*, 741–753.

Einarsen, S., Hoel, H., Zapf, D., & Cooper, C. (2003). The concept of bullying at work: The European tradition. In S. Einarsen, H. Hoel, D. Zapf & C. Cooper (Eds.), *Bullying and emotional abuse in the workplace: International perspectives in research and practice* (pp. 3–30). London: Taylor & Francis.

Ekehammar, B., Akrami, N., Gylje, M., & Zakrisson, I. (2004). What matters most to prejudice: Big Five personality, social dominance orientation or right-wing authoritarianism? *European Journal of Personality, 18*, 463–482.

Elbogen, E. B., & Johnson, S. C. (2009). The intricate link between violence and mental disorder: Results from the National Epidemiologic Survey on Alcohol and Related Conditions. *Archives of General Psychiatry, 66*, 152–161.

Elisha, E., Idisis, Y., Timor, U., & Addad, M. (2010). Typology of intimate partner homicide: Personal, interpersonal, and environmental characteristics of men who murdered their female intimate partner. *International Journal of Offender Therapy and Comparative Criminology, 54*, 494–516.

Ellison-Potter, P., Bell, P., & Deffenbacher, J. (2001). The effects of trait driving anger, anonymity, and aggressive stimuli on aggressive driving behavior. *Journal of Applied Social Psychology, 31*, 431–443.

Enayati, J., Grann, M., Lubbe, S., & Fazel, S. (2008). Psychiatric morbidity in arsonists referred for forensic psychiatric assessment in Sweden. *Journal of Forensic Psychiatry and Psychology, 19*, 139–147.

Enoch, D., & Ball, H. (2001). Folie à deux (et Folie à plusieurs). In D. Enoch & H. Ball (Eds.), *Uncommon psychiatric syndromes* (4th ed.) (pp. 134–159). London: Arnold.

Erikson, M., & Friendship, C. (2002). A typology of child abduction events. *Legal and Criminological Psychology, 7*, 115–120.

Estévez, E., Murgui, S., & Musitu, G. (2009). Psychological adjustment in bullies and victims of school violence. *European Journal of Psychology of Education, 24*, 473–483.

Evans, C., Ehlers, A., Mezey, G., & Clark, D. M. (2007). Intrusive memories and ruminations related to violent crime among young offenders: Phenomenological characteristics. *Journal of Traumatic Stress, 20*, 183–196.

Fagan, G. G. (2011). *The lure of the arena: Social psychology and the crowd at the Roman Games*. Cambridge: Cambridge University Press.

Falcão de Oliveira S., Ribeiro de Lima Cardoso, K., Possante de Almeida, C. A., Cardoso, L. R., & Gutfilen, B. (2014). Violence against women: Profile of the aggressors and victims and characterization of the injuries: A forensic study, *Journal of Forensic and Legal Medicine, 23*, 49–54.

Fallon, B., Trocmé, N., Fluke, J., MacLaurin, B., Tonmyr, L., & Yuan, Y. (2010). Methodological challenges in measuring child maltreatment. *Child Abuse & Neglect, 34*, 70–79.

Fals-Stewart, W. (2003). The occurrence of partner physical aggression on days of alcohol consumption: A longitudinal study. *Journal of Consulting and Clinical Psychology, 71*, 41–52.

Farrer, T. J., Frost, R. B., & Hedges, D. W. (2012). Prevalence of traumatic brain injury in intimate partner violence offenders compared to the general population: A meta-analysis. *Trauma, Violence, & Abuse, 13*, 77–82.

Farrington, D. P. (1989). Early predictors of adolescent aggression and adult violence. *Violence and Victims, 4*, 79–100.

Farrington, D. P. (1997). The relationship between low resting heart rate and violence. In A. Raine, P. A. Brennan, D. P. Farrington, & S. A. Mednick (Eds.), *Biosocial bases of violence* (pp. 89–105). New York: Plenum Press.

Farrington, D. P., & Baldry, A. C. (2010). Individual risk factors for school bullying. *Journal of Aggression, Conflict and Peace Research, 2*, 4–16.

Farrington, D. P., Barnes, G. C., & Lambert, S. (1996). The concentration of offending in families. *Legal and Criminological Psychology, 1*, 47–63.

Farrington, D. P., Jolliffe, D., Loeber, R., Stouthamer-Loeber, M., & Kalb, L. M. (2001). The concentration of offenders in families, and family criminality in the prediction of boys' delinquency. *Journal of Adolescence, 24*, 579–680.

Farrington, D. P., Loeber, R., & Berg, M. T. (2012). Young men who kill: A prospective longitudinal examination from childhood. *Homicide Studies, 16*, 99–128.

Farrokh-Eslamlou, H., & Oshnouei, S. (2014). Intimate partner violence during pregnancy in Urmia, Iran in 2012. *Journal of Forensic and Legal Medicine, 24*, 28–32.

Fasting, K., Brackenridge, C., & Kjølberg, G. (2013). Using court reports to enhance knowledge of sexual abuse in sport: A Norwegian case study. *Scandinavian Sport Studies Forum, 4*, 49–67.

Fazel, S., Bains, P., & Doll, H. (2006). Substance abuse and dependence in prisoners: A systematic review. *Addiction, 101*, 181–191.

Fazel, S., Buxrud, P., Ruchkin, V., & Grann, M. (2010). Homicide in discharged patients with schizophrenia and other psychoses: A national case-control study. *Schizophrenia Research, 123*, 263–269.

Fazel, S., & Danesh, J. (2002). Serious mental disorder in 23 000 prisoners: A systematic review of 62 surveys. *Lancet, 359*, 545–550.

Fazel, S., & Grann M. (2002). Older criminals: A descriptive study of psychiatrically examined offenders in Sweden. *International Journal of Geriatric Psychiatry, 17*, 907–913.

Fazel, S., Grann, M., Carlström, E., Lichtenstein, P., & Långström, N. (2009). Risk factors for violent crime in schizophrenia: A national cohort study of 13,806 patients. *Journal of Clinical Psychiatry, 70*, 362–369.

Fazel, S., Gulati, G., Linsell, L., Geddes, J. R., & Grann, M. (2009). Schizophrenia and violence: Systematic review and meta-analysis. *PLOS Medicine, 6*, 1–15.

Fazel, S., Hope, T., O'Donnell, I., & Jacoby, R. (2004). Unmet treatment needs of older prisoners: A primary care survey. *Age and Ageing, 33*, 396–398.

Fazel, S., Långström, N., Hjern, A., Grann, M., & Lichtenstein, P. (2009). Schizophrenia, substance abuse, and violent crime. *Journal of the American Medical Association, 301,* 2016–2023.

Feist, A., Lawrence, J., McPhee, J., & Wilson, R. (2007). *Investigating and detecting recorded offences of rape.* Home Office Online Report 18/07. London: Home Office.

Felson, R. B., Berg, M. T., & Rogers, M. L. (2014). Bring a gun to a gunfight: Armed adversaries and violence across nations. *Social Science Research, 47,* 79–90.

Felson, R. B., & Messner, S. F. (1996). To kill or not to kill? Lethal outcomes in injurious attacks. *Criminology, 34,* 519–545.

Felson, R. B., & Pare, P. (2010). Firearms and fisticuffs: Region, race, and adversary effects on homicide and assault. *Social Science Research, 39,* 272–284.

Felson, R. B., & Steadman, H. J. (1983). Situational factors in disputes leading to criminal violence. *Criminology, 21,* 59–74.

Felthous, A. R., & Kellert, S. R. (1986). Violence against animals and people: Is aggression against living creatures generalized? *Bulletin of the American Academy of Psychiatry and Law, 14,* 55–69.

Ferguson, C. J. (2013). Spanking, corporal punishment and negative long-term outcomes: A meta-analytic review of longitudinal studies. *Clinical Psychology Review, 33,* 196–208.

Ferguson, C. J., Cruz, A. M., Martinez, D., Rueda, S, M., & Ferguson, D. E. (2010). Violence and sex as advertising strategies in television commercials. *European Psychologist, 15,* 304–311.

Ferguson, C. J., & Dyck, D. (2012). Paradigm change in aggression research: The time has come to retire the General Aggression Model. *Aggression and Violent Behavior, 17,* 220–228.

Ferguson, C. J., Garza, A., Jerabeck, J., Ramos, R., & Galindo, M. (2012). Not worth the fuss after all? Crosssectional and prospective data on violent video game influences on aggression, visuospatial cognition and mathematics ability in a sample of youth. *Journal of Youth and Adolescence, 41,* 1–14.

Ferguson, C. J., & Kilburn, J. (2009). The public health risks of media violence: A meta-analytic review. *Journal of Pediatrics, 154,* 759–763.

Ferguson, C. J., & Kilburn, J. (2010). Much ado about nothing: The misestimation and over-interpretation of violent video game effects in Eastern and Western nations: Comment on Anderson et al. (2010). *Psychological Bulletin, 136,* 174–178.

Ferguson, C. J., San Miguel, C., Garza, A., & Jerabeck, J. M. (2012). A longitudinal test of video game violence influences on dating and aggression: A 3–year longitudinal study of adolescents. *Journal of Psychiatric Research, 46,* 141–146.

Ferns, T. (2007). Considering theories of aggression in an emergency department context. *Accident and Emergency Nursing, 15,* 193–200.

Fields, S. K., Collins, C. L., & Comstock, R. D. (2010). Violence in youth sports: Hazing, brawling and foul play. *British Journal of Sports Medicine, 44,* 32–37.

Finkel, E. J., & Eckhardt, C. I. (2013). Intimate partner violence. In J. A. Simpson & L. Campbell (Eds.), *The Oxford handbook of close relationships* (pp. 452–474). New York: Oxford University Press.

Finkelhor, D. (1984). *Child sexual abuse: New theory and research.* New York: Free Press.

Finkelhor, D. (1986). *A sourcebook on child sexual abuse.* Beverly Hills, CA: Sage.

Finkelhor, D., Ormrod R. K., & Turner, H. A. (2009). Lifetime assessment of poly-victimization in a national sample of children and youth. *Child Abuse & Neglect, 33,* 403–411.

Finkelhor, D., Shattuck, A., Turner, H. A., & Hamby, S. L. (2014). Trends in children's exposure to violence, 2003 to 2011. *JAMA Pediatrics, 168*, 540–546.

Fisher, N. L., & Pina, A. (2013). An overview of the literature on female-perpetrated adult male sexual victimization. *Aggression and Violent Behavior, 18*, 54–61.

Fitzgerald, L. F., Gelfand, M. J., & Drasgow, F. (1995). Measuring sexual harassment: Theoretical and psychometric advances. *Basic and Applied Social Psychology, 17*, 425–445.

Flanagan, R. J., & Fisher, D. S. (2008). Volatile substance abuse and crime: Data from UK press cuttings 1996–2007. *Medicine, Science, and Law, 48*, 295–306.

Flynn, C. P. (1999a). Animal abuse in childhood and later support for interpersonal violence in families. *Society & Animals, 7*, 161–172.

Flynn, C. P. (1999b). Exploring the link between corporal punishment and children's cruelty to animals. *Journal of Marriage and the Family, 61*, 971–981.

Flynn, C. P. (2001). Acknowledging the "zoological connection": A sociological analysis of animal cruelty. *Society & Animals, 9*, 71–87.

Flynn, C. P. (2002). Hunting and illegal violence against humans and other animals: Exploring the relationship. *Society & Animals, 10*, 137–154.

Flynn, S., Abel, K. M., While, D., Menta, H., & Shaw, J. (2011). Mental illness, gender and homicide: A population-based descriptive study. *Psychiatry Research, 185*, 368–375.

Flynn, S., Shaw, J. J., & Abel, K. M. (2007). Homicide of infants: A cross-sectional study. *Journal of Clinical Psychiatry, 68*, 1501–1509.

Flynn, S., Swinson, N., While, D., Hunt, I. M., Roscoe, A., Rodway, C., ... & Shaw J. (2009). Homicide followed by suicide: A cross-sectional study. *Journal of Forensic Psychology and Psychiatry, 20*, 306–321.

Foran, H. M., & O'Leary, K. D. (2008). Alcohol and intimate partner violence: A meta-analytic review. *Clinical Psychology Review, 28*, 1222–1234.

Ford, J. D., Elhai, J. D., Connor, .D. F., & Frueh, B. C. (2010). Poly-victimization and risk of posttraumatic, depressive, and substance use disorders and involvement in delinquency in a national sample of adolescents. *Journal of Adolescent Health, 46*, 545–552.

Ford, J. D., Grasso, D. J., Hawke, J., & Chapman, J. F. (2013). Poly-victimization among juvenile justice-involved youths. *Child Abuse & Neglect, 37*, 788–800.

Fox, S., & Stallworth, L. E. (2005). Racial/ethnic bullying: Exploring links between bullying and racism in the US workplace. *Journal of Vocational Behavior, 66*, 438–456.

Franklin, C. A., & Kercher, G. A. (2012). The intergenerational transmission of intimate partner violence: Differentiating correlates in a random community sample. *Journal of Family Violence, 27*, 187–199.

Freud, S. (1932). The acquisition of power over fire. *International Journal of Psychoanalysis, 13*, 405–410.

Fuller, J. M. (2009). The science and statistics behind spanking suggest that laws allowing corporal punishment are in the best interests of the child. *Akron Law Review, 42*, 257–262.

Fuller, J. (2011). Corporal punishment and child development. *Akron Law Review, 44*, 5–66.

Gaes, G. G., & McGuire, W. J. (1985). Prison violence: The contribution of crowding versus other determinants of prison assault rates. *Journal of Research in Crime and Delinquency, 22*, 41–65.

Galdston, R. (1965). Observations on children who have been physically abused and their parents. *American Journal of Psychiatry, 122*, 440–443.

Galovski, T. E., Malta, L. S., & Blanchard, E. B. (2006). *Road rage: Assessment and treatment of the angry, aggressive driver*. Washington, DC: American Psychological Association.

Gannon, T. A. (2009). Social cognition in violent and sexual offending: An overview. *Psychology, Crime & Law, 15*, 97–118.

Gannon, T. A., & Alleyne, E. K. A. (2013). Female sexual abusers' cognition: A systematic review. *Trauma, Violence & Abuse, 14*, 67–79.

Gannon, T. A., & Barrowcliffe, E. (2012). Firesetting in the general population: The development and validation of the Fire Setting and Fire Proclivity Scales. *Legal and Criminological Psychology, 17*, 105–122.

Gannon, T. A., Collie, R. M., Ward, T., & Thakker, J. (2008). Rape: Psychopathology, theory and treatment. *Clinical Psychology Review, 28*, 982–1008.

Gannon, T. A., & Cortoni, F. (Eds.). (2010). *Female sexual offenders: Theory, assessment and treatment*. Chichester, Sussex: John Wiley & Sons.

Gannon, T. A., Hoare, J. A., Rose, M. R., & Parrett, N. (2012). A re-examination of female child molesters' implicit theories: Evidence of female specificity? *Psychology, Crime & Law, 18*, 209–224.

Gannon, T. A., & Polaschek, D. L. L. (2006). Cognitive distortions in child molesters: A re-examination of key theories and research. *Clinical Psychology Review, 26*, 1000–1019.

Gannon, T. A., Rose, M. R., & Ward, T. (2008). A descriptive model of the offense process for female sexual offenders. *Sexual Abuse: A Journal of Research and Treatment, 20*, 352–374.

Gannon, T. A., Tyler, N., Barnoux, M., & Pina, A. (2012). Female arsonists and firesetters. In G. Dickens, P. A. Sugarman, & T. A. Gannon (Eds.), *Firesetting and mental health* (pp. 126–142). London: Royal College of Psychiatry Publications.

Gannon, T. A., Ward, T., Beech, A. R., & Fisher, D. (Eds). (2007). *Aggressive offenders' cognition: Theory, research and practice*. Chichester, Sussex: John Wiley & Sons.

Garcia-Moreno, C., Jansen, H. A., Ellsberg, M., Heise, L., & Watts, C. H. (2006). Prevalence of intimate partner violence: Findings from the WHO multi-country study on women's health and domestic violence. *Lancet, 368* (9543), 1260–1269.

García-Sancho, E., Salguero, J. M., & Fernández-Berrocal, P. (2014). Relationship between emotional intelligence and aggression: A systematic review. *Aggression and Violent Behavior, 19*, 584–591.

Garland, J. (2012). Difficulties in defining hate crime victimization. *International Review of Victimology, 18*, 25–37.

Gebo, E. (2002). A contextual exploration of siblicide. *Violence and Victims, 17*, 157–168.

Gershoff, E. T. (2002). Corporal punishment by parents and associated child behaviors and experiences: A meta-analytic and theoretical review. *Psychological Bulletin, 128*, 539–579.

Gershoff, E. T. (2010). More harm than good: A summary of scientific research on the intended and unintended effects of corporal punishment of children. *Law and Contemporary Problems, 73*, 31–56.

Gershoff, E. T., & Bitensky, S. H. (2007). The case against corporal punishment of children. *Psychology, Public Policy and Law, 13*, 231–272.

Gershoff, E. T., Grogan-Kaylor, A., Lansford, J. E., Chang, L., Zelli, A., Deater-Deckard, K., & Dodge, K. A. (2010). Parent discipline practices in an international sample: Associations with child behaviors and moderation by perceived normativeness. *Child Development, 81*, 487–502.

Gerstenfeld, P. B. (2011). *Hate crimes: Causes, controls, and controversies* (2nd ed.). Los Angeles, CA: Sage.

Giancola, P. R., Duke, A. A., & Ritz, K. Z. (2011). Alcohol, violence, and the alcohol myopia model: Preliminary findings and implications for prevention. *Addictive Behaviors, 36,* 1019–1022.

Gilbert, R., Fluke, J., O'Donnell, M., Gonzalez-Izquierdo, A., Brownwell, M., Gulliver, P., Janson, S., & Sidebotham, P. (2012). Child maltreatment: Variation in trends and policies in six developed countries. *Lancet, 379*(9817), 758–772.

Ginn, S. (2012). Elderly prisoners. *British Medical Journal, 345,* e6263.

Gleditsch, N. P. (2012). Whither the weather? Climate change and conflict. *Journal of Peace Research, 49,* 3–9.

Gleyzer, R., Felthous, A. R., & Holzer, C. E. (2002). Animal cruelty and psychiatric disorders. *Journal of the American Academy of Psychiatry and Law, 30,* 257–265.

Godinet, M. T., Li, F., & Berg, T. (2014). Early childhood maltreatment and trajectories of behavioral problems: Exploring gender and racial differences. *Child Abuse & Neglect, 38,* 544–556.

Goff, A., Rose, E., Rose, S., & Purves, D. (2007). Does PTSD occur in sentenced prison populations? A systematic literature review. *Criminal Behaviour and Mental Health, 17,* 152–162.

Golding, J. (1999). Intimate partner violence as a risk factor for mental disorders: A meta-analysis. *Journal of Family Violence, 14,* 99–132.

Goldman, M. S., Del Boca, F. K., & Darkes, J. (1999). Alcohol expectancy theory: The application of cognitive neuroscience. In K. E. Leonard & H. T. Blane (Eds.), *Psychological theories of drinking and alcoholism* (2nd ed.) (pp. 203–246). New York: Guildford Press.

Goldstein, A. P. (2002). *The psychology of group aggression.* Chichester, Sussex: John Wiley & Sons.

Golenkov, A., Large, M., Nielssen, O., & Tsymbalova, A. (2011). Characteristics of homicide offenders with schizophrenia from the Russian Federation. *Schizophrenia Research, 133,* 232–237.

González, K. V., Verkuyten, M., Weesie, J., & Poppe, E. (2008). Prejudice towards Muslims in The Netherlands: Testing integrated threat theory. *British Journal of Social Psychology, 47,* 667–685.

González, R. A., Kallis, C., Ullrich, S., Zhang, T. Coid, J. W. (2014). The protective role of higher intellectual functioning on violence in the household population of Great Britain. *Personality and Individual Differences, 61–62,* 80–85.

González-Méndez, R., & Santana-Hernández, J. D. (2014). Perceived risk and safety-related behaviors after leaving a violent relationship. *The European Journal of Psychology Applied to Legal Context, 6,* 1–7.

Gould, F., Clarke, J., Heim, C., Harvey, P. D., Majer, M., & Nemeroff, C. B. (2012). The effects of child abuse and neglect on cognitive functioning in adulthood. *Journal of Psychiatric Research, 46,* 500–506.

Goussinsky, R., & Yassour-Borochowitz, D. (2012). "I killed her, but I never laid a finger on her"—A phenomenological difference between wife-killing and wife-battering. *Aggression and Violent Behavior, 17,* 553–564.

Graham, K., Bernards, S., Osgood, D. W., Parks, M., Abbey, A., Felson, R. B., Saltz, R. F., & Wells, S. (2013). Apparent motives for aggression in the social context of the bar. *Psychology of Violence, 3,* 218–232.

Graham, K., Bernards, S., Wells, S., Osgood, D. W., Abbey, A., Felson, R. B., & Saltz, R. F. (2011). Behavioural indicators of motives for barroom aggression: Implications for preventing bar violence. *Drug and Alcohol Review, 30,* 554–563.

Grange, P., & Kerr, J. H. (2010). Physical aggression in Australian football: A qualitative study of elite athletes. *Psychology of Sport and Exercise, 11*, 36–43.

Grann, M., & Fazel, S. (2004). Substance misuse and violent crime: Swedish population study. *British Medical Journal, 328*(7450), 1233–1234.

Green, D. P., & Strolovitch, D. Z. (1998). Defended neighborhoods, integration and racially motivated crime. *American Journal of Sociology, 104*, 372–404.

Greenfield, L., & Henneberg, M. (2001). Victim and offender self-reports of alcohol involvement in crime. *Alcohol Research & Health, 25*, 20–31.

Greenhalgh, D. G., & Palmieri, T. L. (2003). The media glorifying burns: A hindrance to burn prevention. *Journal of Burn Care & Research, 24*, 159–162.

Gresswell, D. M., & Hollin, C. R. (1994). Multiple murder: A review. *British Journal of Criminology, 34*, 1–14.

Griffin, M. L., & Amodeo, M. (2010). Predicting long-term outcomes for women physically abused in childhood: Contribution of abuse severity versus family environment. *Child Abuse & Neglect, 34*, 724–733.

Groth, A. N. (1979). *Men who rape: The psychology of the offender.* New York: Plenum Press.

Grubb, A., & Turner, E. (2012). Attribution of blame in rape cases: A review of the impact of rape myth acceptance, gender role conformity and substance use on victim blaming. *Aggression and Violent Behavior, 17*, 443–452.

Guille, L. (2004). Men who batter and their children: An integrated review. *Aggression and Violent Behavior, 9*, 129–163.

Gullone, E. (2011). Conceptualising animal abuse with an antisocial behaviour framework. *Animals, 1*, 144–160.

Gunn, J. (2010). Dr Harold Frederick Shipman: An enigma. *Criminal Behaviour and Mental Health, 20*, 190–198.

Gunter, T. D., Chibnall, J. T., Antoniak, S. K., McCormick, B., & Black, D. W. (2012). Relative contributions of gender and traumatic life experience to the prediction of mental disorders in a sample of incarcerated offenders. *Behavioral Sciences and the Law, 30*, 615–630.

Gurian, E. A. (2013). Explanations of mixed-sex partnered homicide: A review of sociological and psychological theory. *Aggression and Violent Behavior, 18*, 520–526.

Guyll, M., & Madon, S. J. (2004). Effects of trait hostility and self-relevance on social information processing. *Basic and Applied Social Psychology, 26*, 263–276.

Häkkänen, H., Puolakka, P., & Santilla, P. (2004). Crime scene actions and offender characteristics in arsons. *Legal and Criminological Psychology, 9*, 197–214.

Hall, N. (2013). *Hate crime* (2nd ed.). London: Routledge.

Hamby, S. (2011). The second wave of violence scholarship: Integrating and broadening theories of violence. *Psychology of Violence, 1*, 163–165.

Hamby, S., Finkelhor, D., Turner, H., & Ormrod, R. (2011). Children's exposure to intimate partner violence and other family violence. *Juvenile Justice Bulletin—NCJ232272.* Washington, DC: US Government Printing Office.

Hamill, C. A., Newman, E., Todd, L., & Peck, D. (2014). Attachment and violent offending: A meta-analysis. *Aggression and Violent Behavior, 19*, 322–339.

Hansen, T. B., Steenberg, L. M., Palic, S., & Elklit, A. (2012). A review of psychological factors related to bullying victimization in schools. *Aggression and Violent Behavior, 17*, 383–387.

Hanson, R. K., & Morton-Bourgon, K. (2005). The characteristics of persistent sexual offenders: A meta-analysis of recidivism studies. *Journal of Consulting and Clinical Psychology, 73*, 1154–1163.

Hanson, R. K., & Thornton, D. (1999). *Static-99: Improving actuarial risk assessments for sex offenders*. User Report 99-02. Ottawa: Department of the Solicitor General of Canada.

Harbin, H. T., & Madden, D. J. (1979). Battered parents: New syndrome. *American Journal of Psychiatry, 136*, 1288–1291.

Hardaker, C. (2010). Trolling in asynchronous computer-mediated communication: From user discussions to academic definitions. *Journal of Politeness Research, 6*, 215–242.

Hare, R. D. (1980). A research scale for the assessment of psychopathy in criminal populations. *Personality and Individual Differences, 1*, 111–119.

Hare, R. D. (1991). *The Hare Psychopathy Checklist-Revised*. Toronto, Ontario: Multi-Health Systems.

Hare, R. D. (2003). *The Hare Psychopathy Checklist-Revised*, (2nd ed.). Toronto, Ontario: Multi-Health Systems.

Harkins, L., & Dixon, L. (2010). Sexual offending in groups: An evaluation. *Aggression and Violent Behavior, 15*, 87–99.

Harries, K. D., Stadler, S. J., & Zdorkowski, R. T. (1984). Seasonality and assault: Explorations in inter-neighborhood variation, Dallas 1980. *Annals of the Association of American Geographers, 74*, 590–604.

Harris, P. B., & Houston, J. M. (2010). Recklessness in context: Individual and situational correlates to aggressive driving. *Environment and Behavior, 42*, 44–60.

Harris, S. T., Oakley, C., & Picchioni, M. M. (2014). A systematic review of the association between attributional bias/interpersonal style, and violence in schizophrenia/psychosis. *Aggression and Violent Behavior, 19*, 235–241.

Hartman, C. R., Burgess, A. W., & Lanning, K. V. (1984). Typology of collectors. In A. W. Burgess, & M. L. Clark (Eds.), *Child pornography and sex rings* (pp. 93–109). Toronto: Lexington Books.

Harvey, M. G., Heames, J. T., Richey, R. G., & Leonard, N. (2006). Bullying: From the playground to the boardroom. *Journal of Leadership & Organizational Studies, 12*, 1–11.

Hata, N., Kominato, Y., Shimada, I., Takizawa, H., Fujikura, T., ... & Sato, Y. (2001). Regional differences in homicide patterns in five areas of Japan. *Legal Medicine, 3*, 44–55.

Heath, K., Kobus, H., & Byard, R. W. (2011). Potential dangers of accelerant use in arson. *Journal of Forensic and Legal Medicine, 18*, 49–51.

Heaton, P. (2011). *Sunday liquor laws and crime*. Santa Monica, CA: RAND Corporation.

Heide, K. M., Beauregard, E., & Myers, W. C. (2009). Sexually motivated child abduction murders: Synthesis of the literature and case illustration. *Victims and Offenders, 4*, 58–75.

Heil, P., Ahlmeyer, S., & Simons, D. (2003). Crossover sexual offenses. *Sexual Abuse: A Journal of Research and Treatment, 15*, 221–236.

Heim, C., Shugart, M., Craighead, W. E., & Nemeroff, C. B. (2010). Neurobiological and psychiatric consequences of child abuse and neglect. *Developmental Psychobiology, 52*, 671–690.

Helfritz-Sinville, L. E., & Stanford, M. S. (2014). Hostile attribution bias in impulsive and premeditated aggression. *Personality and Individual Differences, 56*, 45–50.

Hellman, D. S., & Blackman, H. (1966). Enuresis, firesetting and cruelty to animals. *American Journal of Psychiatry, 122*, 1431–1435.

Helmus, L., Hanson, R. K., Babchishin, K. M., & Mann, R. E. (2013). Attitudes supportive of sexual offending predict recidivism: A meta-analysis. *Trauma, Violence, & Abuse, 14*, 34–53.

Henry, B. C. (2004). The relationship between animal cruelty, delinquency, and attitudes toward the treatment of animals. *Society & Animals, 12,* 185–207.

Henry, O., Mandeville-Norden, R., Hayes, E., & Egan, V. (2010). Do internet-based sexual offenders reduce to normal, inadequate and deviant groups? *Journal of Sexual Aggression, 16,* 33–46.

Hensley, C., & Tallichet, S. E. (2005a). Animal cruelty motivations: Assessing demographic and situational influences. *Journal of Interpersonal Violence, 20,* 1429–1443.

Hensley, C., & Tallichet, S. E. (2005b). Learning to be cruel? Exploring the onset and frequency of animal cruelty. *International Journal of Offender Therapy and Comparative Criminology, 49,* 37–47.

Hensley, C., Tallichet, S. E., & Dutkiewicz, E. L. (2012). Exploring the age of onset and recurrence of childhood animal cruelty: Can animal cruelty be learned from witnessing others commit it? *International Journal of Offender Therapy and Comparative Criminology, 56,* 614–626.

Hepburn, L. M., & Hemenway, D. (2004). Firearm availability and homicide: A review of the literature. *Aggression and Violent Behavior, 9,* 417–440.

Herzog, H. A. (2007). Gender differences in human-animal interactions: A review. *Anthrozoos: A Multidisciplinary Journal of The Interactions of People & Animals, 20,* 7–21.

Hickle, K. E., & Roe-Sepowitz, D. E. (2010). Female juvenile arsonists: An exploratory look at characteristics and solo and group arson offences. *Legal and Criminological Psychology, 15,* 385–399.

Hillberg, T., Hamilton-Giachritsis, C., & Dixon, L. (2011). Review of meta-analyses on the association between child sexual abuse and adult mental health difficulties: A systematic approach. *Trauma, Violence, & Abuse, 12,* 38–49.

Hills, D., & Joyce, C. (2013). A review of research on the prevalence, antecedents, consequences and prevention of workplace aggression in clinical medical practice. *Aggression and Violent Behavior, 18,* 554–569.

Hilton, N. Z., Harris, G. T., Popham, S., & Lang, C. (2010). Risk assessment among incarcerated male domestic violence offenders. *Criminal Justice and Behavior, 37,* 815–832.

Hilton, N. Z., Harris, G. T., Rice, M. E., Houghton, R. E., & Eke, A. W. (2008). An indepth actuarial assessment for wife assault recidivism: The Domestic Violence Risk Appraisal Guide. *Law and Human Behavior, 32,* 150–163.

Hinduja, S., & Patchin, J. (2008). Cyberbullying: An exploratory analysis of factors related to offending and victimization. *Deviant Behavior, 29,* 1–29.

Hipp, J. R., Bauer, D. J., Curran, P. J., & Bollen, K. A. (2004). Crimes of opportunity or crimes of emotion? Testing two explanations of seasonal change in crime. *Social Forces, 82,* 1333–1372.

Hoare, J., & Jansson, K. (2007). Extent of intimate violence, nature of partner abuse and serious sexual assault, 2004/05, 2005/06, 2006/07 BCS. In D. Povey, K. Coleman, P. Kaiza, J. Hoare, & K. Jansson (Eds.), *Homicides, firearm offences and intimate violence 2006/07* (3rd ed.). Home Office Statistical Bulletin 03/08. London: Home Office.

Hodges, M., Godbout, A., Briere, J., Lanktree, C., Gilbert, A., & Kletzka, N. T. (2013). Cumulative trauma and symptom complexity in children: A path analysis. *Child Abuse & Neglect, 37,* 891–898.

Hodgins, S. (2008). Violent behaviour among people with schizophrenia: A framework for investigations of causes, and effective treatment, and prevention. *Philosophical Transactions of the Royal Society B, 363,* 2505–2518.

Holden, G. W. (2003). Children exposed to domestic violence and child abuse: Terminology and taxonomy. *Clinical Child & Family Psychology Review, 6,* 151–160.

Hollin, C. R., Davies, S., Duggan, C., Huband, N., McCarthy, L., & Clarke, M. (2013). Patients with a history of arson admitted to medium security: Characteristics on admission and follow-up postdischarge. *Medicine, Science and the Law, 53,* 154–160.

Hollin, C. R., Epps, K., & Swaffer, T. (2002). Adolescent firesetters: Findings from an analysis of 47 cases. *Pakistan Journal of Psychological Research, 17,* 1–16.

Hollin, C. R., & Palmer, E. J. (2006). Criminogenic need and women offenders: A critique of the literature. *Legal and Criminological Psychology, 11,* 179–195.

Holt, M. K., & Espelage, D. L. (2005). Social support as a moderator between dating violence victimization and depression/anxiety among African American and Caucasian adolescents. *School Psychology Review, 34,* 309–328.

Holt, S., Buckley, H., & Whelan, S. (2008). The impact of exposure to domestic violence on children and young people: A review of the literature. *Child Abuse & Neglect, 32,* 797–810.

Home Office. (2012). *Hate crimes, England and Wales 2011 to 2012.* London: Author.

Hong, J. S., Hyunkag, C., Allen-Meares, P., Espelage, D. L. (2011). The social ecology of the Columbine High School shootings. *Children and Youth Services Review, 33,* 861–868.

Hong, J. S., Lee, N. Y., Park H. J., & Faller, K. C. (2011). Child maltreatment in South Korea: An ecological systems analysis. *Children and Youth Services Review, 33,* 1058–1066.

Hopkins, L., Taylor, L., Bowen, E., & Wood, C. (2013). A qualitative study investigating adolescents' understanding of aggression, bullying and violence. *Children and Youth Services Review, 35,* 685–693.

Horvath, M. A. H., Davidson, J. C., Grove-Hills, J., Gekoski, A., & Choak, C. (2014). *"It's a lonely journey": A rapid evidence assessment on intrafamilial child sexual abuse.* London: Office of the Children's Commissioner.

Houston, J. M., Harris, P. B., & Norman, M. (2003). The Aggressive Driving Behavior Scale: Developing a self-report measure of unsafe driving practices. *North American Journal of Psychology, 5,* 269–278.

Houtepen, J. A. B. M., Sijtsema, J. J., & Bogaerts, S. (2014). From child pornography offending to child sexual abuse: A review of child pornography offender characteristics and risks for cross-over. *Aggression and Violent Behavior, 19,* 466–473.

Hovland, C. I., & Sears, R. R. (1940). Minor studies in aggression: VI. Correlation of lynching with economic indices. *Journal of Psychology, 9,* 301–310.

Howard, C. J. (2012). Neurobiological correlates of partner abusive men: Equifinality in perpetrators of intimate partner violence. *Psychological Trauma: Theory, Research, Practice, and Policy, 4,* 330–337.

Howell, K. H. (2011). Resilience and psychopathology in children exposed to family violence. *Aggression and Violent Behavior, 16,* 562–569.

Hudson, S. M., & Ward, T. (2001). Adolescent sexual offenders: Assessment and treatment. In C. R. Hollin (Ed.), *Handbook of offender assessment and treatment* (pp. 363–377). Chichester, Sussex: John Wiley and Sons.

Huesmann, L. R., Dubow, E. F., & Boxer, P. (2009). Continuity of aggression from childhood to early adulthood as a predictor of life outcomes: Implications for the adolescent-limited and life-course-persistent models. *Aggressive Behavior, 35,* 136–149.

Hunter, J. A., Hazelwood, R. R., & Slesinger, D. (2000). Juvenile-perpetrated sex crimes: Patterns of offending and predictors of violence. *Journal of Family Violence, 15,* 81–93.

Hyde-Nolan, M. E., & Julio, T. (2012). Theoretical basis for family violence. In R. S. Fife & S. Schrager (Eds.), *Family violence: What health care providers need to know* (pp. 5–16). Sudbury, MA: Jones & Bartlett Learning.

Idsoe, T., Dyregrov, A., & Idsoe, E. C. (2012). Bullying and PTSD symptoms. *Journal of Abnormal Child Psychology, 40,* 901–911.

Institute of Alcohol Studies. (2010). *Alcohol & crime.* IAS Factsheet retrieved from http://www.ias.org.uk

Irish, L., Kobayashi, I., & Delahanty, D. L. (2010). Long-term physical health consequences of childhood sexual abuse: A meta-analytic review. *Journal of Pediatric Psychology, 35,* 450–461.

Ishida, K., Stupp, P., Melian, M., Serbanescu, F., & Goodwin, F. (2010). Exploring the associations between intimate partner violence and women's mental health: Evidence from a population-based study in Paraguay. *Social Science & Medicine, 71,* 1653–1661.

Iwaniec, D. (2006). *The emotionally abused and neglected child: Identification, assessment and intervention: A practice handbook* (2nd ed.). Chichester, Sussex: John Wiley & Sons.

Jackson, H., Glass, C., & Hope, S. (1987). A functional analysis of recidivistic arson. *British Journal of Clinical Psychology, 26,* 175–185.

Jackson, S. L., & Hafemeister, T. L. (2011). Risk factors associated with elder abuse: The importance of differentiating by type of elder maltreatment. *Violence and Victims, 26,* 738–757.

James, J., & Proulx, J. (2014). A psychological and developmental profile of sexual murderers: A systematic review. *Aggression and Violent Behavior, 19,* 592–607.

Jamieson, E., Butwell, M., Taylor, P., & Leese, M. (2000). Trends in special (high-security) hospitals: 1: Referrals and admissions. *British Journal of Psychiatry, 176,* 253–259.

Jay, T. (2009). Do offensive words harm people? *Psychology, Public Policy, and Law, 15,* 81–101.

Jenkins, M. F., Zapf, D., Winefield, H., & Sarris, A. (2012). Bullying allegations from the accused bully's perspective. *British Journal of Management, 23,* 489–501.

Jenkins, P. (1988). Serial murder in England 1940–1985. *Journal of Criminal Justice, 16,* 1–15.

Jennings, W. G., Piquero, A. R., & Reingle, J. M. (2012). On the overlap between victimization and offending: A review of the literature. *Aggression and Violent Behavior, 17,* 16–26.

Jespersen, A. F., Lalumière, M. L., & Seto, M. C. (2009). Sexual abuse history among adult sex offenders and non-sex offenders: A meta-analysis. *Child Abuse & Neglect, 33,* 179–192.

Ji, K., Finkelhor, D., & Dunne, M. (2013). Child sexual abuse in China: A meta-analysis of 27 studies. *Child Abuse & Neglect, 37,* 613–622.

Johannesen, M., & LoGiudice, D. (2013). Elder abuse: A systematic review of risk factors in community-dwelling elders. *Age and Ageing, 42,* 292–298.

Jonas, S., Bebbington, P., McManus, S., Meltzer, H., Jenkins, R., Kuipers, C., … & Brugha, T. (2011). Sexual abuse and psychiatric disorder in England: Results from the 2007 Adult Psychiatric Morbidity Survey. *Psychological Medicine, 41,* 709–719.

Jordan, C. E., Campbell, R., & Follingstad, D. (2010). Violence and women's mental health: The impact of physical, sexual, and psychological aggression. *Annual Review of Clinical Psychology, 6,* 1.1–1.22.

Jordan, C. E., Pritchard, A. J., Duckett, D., Wilcox, P., Corey, T., & Combest, M. (2010). Relationship and injury trends in the homicide of women across the life span: A research note. *Homicide Studies, 14,* 181–192.

Jouriles, E. N., Mueller, V., Rosenfield, D., McDonald, R., & Dodson, M. C. (2012). Teens' experiences of harsh parenting and exposure to severe intimate partner violence: Adding insult to injury in predicting teen dating violence. *Psychology of Violence, 2,* 125–138.

Jouriles, E. N., Rosenfield, D., McDonald, R., & Mueller, V. (2013). Child involvement in interparental conflict and child adjustment problems: A longitudinal study of violent families. *Journal of Abnormal Child Psychology, 45,* 693–704.

Kalof, L., & Fitzgerald, A. (2003). Reading the trophy: Exploring the display of dead animals in hunting magazines. *Visual Studies, 18,* 112–122.

Kalof, L., Fitzgerald, A., & Baralt, L. (2004). Animals, women, and weapons: Blurred sexual boundaries in the discourse of sport hunting. *Society & Animals, 12,* 237–251.

Katz, C. (2014). The dead end of domestic violence: Spotlight on children's narratives during forensic investigations following domestic homicide. *Child Abuse & Neglect, 38,* 1976–1984.

Kazemian, L., Widom, C. S., & Farrington, D. P. (2011). A prospective examination of the relationship between childhood neglect and juvenile delinquency in the Cambridge Study in Delinquent Development. *International Journal of Child, Youth and Family Studies, 1&2,* 65–82.

Kellert, S. R., & Felthous, A. R. (1985). Childhood cruelty to animals among criminals and noncriminals. *Human Relations, 38,* 1113–1129.

Kelley, H. H. (1967). Attribution theory in social psychology. *Nebraska Symposium on Motivation, 15,* 192–238.

Kelley, H. H., & Michela, J. L. (1980). Attribution theory and research. *Annual Review of Psychology, 31,* 457–501.

Kelly, L., Lovett, J., & Regan, L. (2005). *A gap or a chasm? Attrition in reported rape cases.* Research Study 293. London: Home Office.

Kelty, S. F., Hall, G., & O'Brien-Malone, A. (2012). You have to hit some people! Endorsing violent sentiments and the experience of grievance escalation in Australia. *Psychiatry, Psychology and Law, 19,* 299–313.

Kempe, C. H., Silverman, F. N., Steele, B. B., Droegemuller, W., & Silver, H. K. (1962). The battered child syndrome. *Journal of the American Medical Association, 181,* 17–24.

Kennedy, P. J., Vale, E. L. E., Khan, S. J., & McAnaney, A. (2006). Factors predicting recidivism in child and adolescent fire-setters: A systematic review of the literature. *Journal of Forensic Psychiatry and Psychology, 17,* 151–164.

Kerr, J. H. (2005). *Rethinking aggression and violence in sport.* London: Routledge.

Kerr, J. H. (2006). Examining the Bertuzzi–Moore NHL ice hockey incident: Crossing the line between sanctioned and unsanctioned violence in sport. *Aggression and Violent Behavior, 11,* 313–322.

Kerr, J. H. (2009). Analysis of recent incidents of on-field violence in sport: Legal decisions and additional considerations from Psychology. *Aggressive Behavior, 35,* 41–48.

Kerr, K. J., Beech, A. R., & Murphy, D. (2013). Sexual homicide: Definition, motivation and comparison with other forms of sexual offending. *Aggression and Violent Behavior, 18,* 1–10.

Kim, K., Trickett, P. K., Putnam, F. W. (2010). Childhood experiences of sexual abuse and later parenting practices among non-offending mothers of sexually abused and comparison girls. *Child Abuse & Neglect, 34,* 610–622.

Kimble, N. B., Russo, S. A., Bergman, B. G., & Galindo, V. H. (2010). Revealing an empirical understanding of aggression and violent behavior in athletics. *Aggression and Violent Behavior, 15,* 446–462.

Kitzmann, K. M., Gaylord, N. K., Holt, A. R., & Kenny, E. D. (2003). Child witnesses to domestic violence: A meta-analytic review. *Journal of Consulting and Clinical Psychology*, *71*, 339–352.

Klein, A. R., & Tobin, T. (2008). A longitudinal study of arrested batterers, 1995–2005 career criminals. *Violence Against Women*, *14*, 136–157.

Kloess, J. A., Beech, A. R., & Harkins, L. (2014). Online child sexual exploitation: Prevalence, process, and offender characteristics. *Trauma Violence and Abuse*, *15*, 126–139.

Knoll, J. L., & Hazelwood, R. R. (2009). Becoming the victim: Beyond sadism in serial sexual murderers. *Aggression and Violent Behavior*, *14*, 106–114.

Knox, M. (2010). On hitting children: A review of corporal punishment in the United States. *Journal of Pediatric Health Care*, *24*, 103–107.

Kokko, K., Pulkkinen, L., Huesmann, L. R., Dubow, E. F., & Boxer, P. (2009). Intensity of aggression in childhood as a predictor of different forms of adult aggression: A two-country (Finland and United States) analysis. *Journal of Research in Adolescence*, *19*, 9–34.

Kordi, R., Maffulli, N., Wroble, R. R., & Wallace, W. A. (Eds.). (2009). *Combat sports medicine*. London: Springer-Verlag.

Kowalski, R. M., & Limber, S. P. (2007). Electronic bullying among middle school students. *Journal of Adolescent Health*, *41*, S22–S30.

Kowalski, R. M., Limber, S. P., & Agatston, P. W. (2008). *Cyberbullying: Bullying in the digital age*. Oxford: Wiley-Blackwell.

Knox, M. (2010). On hitting children: A review of corporal punishment in the United States. *Journal of Pediatric Health Care*, *24*, 103–107.

Kraanen, F. L., Vedel, E., Scholing, A., & Emmelkamp, P. M. G. (2014). Prediction of intimate partner violence by type of substance use disorder. *Journal of Substance Abuse Treatment*, *46*, 532–539.

Krahé, B., Tomaszewska, P., Kuyper, L., & Vanwesenbeeck, I. (2014). Prevalence of sexual aggression among young people in Europe: A review of the evidence from 27 EU countries. *Aggression and Violent Behavior*, *19*, 545–558.

Krienert, J. L., & Walsh, J. A. (2010). Eldercide: A gendered examination of elderly homicide in the United States, 2000–2005. *Homicide Studies*, *14*, 52–71.

Krug, E. G., Dahlberg, L. L., Mercy, J. A., Zwi, A. B., & Lozano, R. (Eds.). (2002). *World report on violence and health*. Geneva: World Health Organization.

Krug, E. G., Mercy, J. A., Dahlberg, L. L., & Zwi, A. B. (2002). The world report on violence and health. *Lancet*, *360*, 1083–1088.

Kubzansky, L. D., Cole, S. R., Kawachi, I., Vokonas, P., & Sparrow, D. (2006). Shared and unique contributions of anger, anxiety, and depression to coronary heart disease: A prospective study in the normative aging study. *Annals of Behavioral Medicine*, *31*, 21–29.

Kulig, J., Valentine, J., Griffith, J., & Ruthazer, R. (1998). Predictive model of weapon carrying mong urban high school students: Results and validation. *Journal of Adolescent Health*, *22*, 312–319.

Kurrle, S., & Naughtin, G. (2008). An overview of elder abuse and neglect in Australia. *Journal of Elder Abuse & Neglect*, *20*, 108–125.

Kurtz, P. D., Gaudin, J. M., Howing, P. T., & Wodarski, J. S. (1993). The consequences of physical abuse and neglect on the school age child: Mediating factors. *Children and Youth Services Review*, *15*, 85–104.

Kurzweil, R. (2005). *The singularity is near: When humans transcend biology*. New York: Penguin.

Labree, W., Nijman, H., van Marle, H., & Rassin, E. (2010). Backgrounds and characteristics of arsonists. *International Journal of Law and Psychiatry, 33*, 149–153.

Lachs, M. S., & Pillemer, K. (2004). Elder abuse. *Lancet, 364*, 1263–1272.

Lajunen, T., Parker, D., & Stradling, S. G. (1998). Dimensions of driver anger, aggressive and highway code violations and their mediation by safety orientation in UK drivers. *Transportation Research Part F: Traffic Psychology and Behaviour, 1*, 107–121.

Lambie, I., & Randell, I. (2011). Creating a firestorm: A review of children who deliberately light fires. *Clinical Psychology Review, 31*, 307–327.

Lansford, J. E. (2010). The special problem of cultural differences in effects of corporal punishment. *Law and Contemporary Problems, 73*, 89–106.

Lansford, J. E., Miller-Johnson, S., Berlin, L. J., Dodge, K. A., Bates, J. E., & Pettit, G. S. (2007). Early physical abuse and later violent delinquency: A prospective longitudinal study. *Child Maltreatment, 12*, 233–245.

Lansford, J. E., Wager, L. B., Bates, J. E., Pettit, G. S., & Dodge, K. A. (2012). Forms of spanking and children's externalizing behaviors. *Family Relations, 61*, 224–236.

Large, M. M., Smith, G., & Nielssen, O. (2009). The relationship between the rate of homicide by those with schizophrenia and the overall homicide rate: A systematic review and meta-analysis. *Schizophrenia Research, 112*, 123–129.

Larrick, R. P., Timmerman, T. A., Carton, A. M., & Abrevaya, J. (2011). Temper, temperature, and temptation: Heat-related retaliation in baseball. *Psychological Science, 22*, 423–428.

Larzelere, R. E., & Baumrind, D. (2010). Are spanking injunctions scientifically supported? *Law and Contemporary Problems, 73*, 57–87.

LeBlanc, S. A., & Register, K. E. (2003). *Constant battles: Why we fight.* New York: St Martin's Griffin.

Lee, S. J., Grogan-Kaylor, A., & Berger, L. M. (2014). Parental spanking of 1-year-old children and subsequent child protective services involvement. *Child Abuse & Neglect, 38*, 875–883.

Lee, S. J., Taylor, C. A., Altschu, I., & Rice, J. C. (2013). Parental spanking and subsequent risk for child aggression in father-involved families of young children. *Children and Youth Services Review, 35*, 1476–1485.

Lemerise, E. A., & Dodge, K. A. (2008). The development of anger and hostile interactions. In M. Lewis, J. M. Haviland-Jones & L. F. Barrett (Eds.), *Handbook of emotions* (3rd ed.) (pp. 730–741). New York: Guildford Press.

Lennon, A., & Watson, B. (2011). "Teaching them a lesson?": A qualitative exploration of underlying motivations for driver aggression. *Accident Analysis and Prevention, 43*, 2200–2208.

Lennon, A. J., Watson, B. C., Arlidge, C., & Fraine, G. (2011). "You're a bad driver but I just made a mistake": Attribution differences between the "victims" and "perpetrators" of scenario-based aggressive driving incidents. *Transportation Research Part F: Traffic Psychology and Behaviour, 14*, 209–211.

Lereya, S. T., Samara, M., & Wolke, D. (2013). Parenting behavior and the risk of becoming a victim and a bully/victim: A meta-analysis study. *Child Abuse & Neglect, 37*, 1091–1108.

Lereya, S. T., Winsper, C., Heron, J., Lewis, G., Gunnell, D., Fisher, H. L., & Wolke, D. (2013). Being bullied during childhood and the prospective pathways to self-harm in late adolescence. *Journal of the American Academy of Child & Adolescent Psychiatry, 52*, 608–618.

LeRoy, M., Mahoney, A., Boxer, P., Gullan, R. L., & Fang, Q. (2014). Parents who hit and scream: Interactive effects of verbal and severe physical aggression on clinic-referred adolescents' adjustment. *Child Abuse & Neglect, 38*, 893–901.

Lestico, A. R., Salekin, R. S., DeCoster, J., & Rogers, R. (2008). A large scale meta-analysis relating Hare measures of psychopathy to antisocial conduct. *Law and Human Behavior, 32*, 28–45.

Levine, M., Taylor, P. J., & Best, R. (2011). Third parties, violence, and conflict resolution: The role of group size and collective action in the microregulation of violence. *Psychological Science, 22*, 406–412.

Lewin, K. (1952). *Field theory in social science: Selected theoretical papers by Kurt Lewin.* London: Tavistock.

Lewis, D., & Gunn, R. (2007). Workplace bullying in the public sector: Understanding the racial dimension. *Public Administration, 85*, 641–665.

Li, Q. (2006). Cyberbullying in schools: A research of gender differences. *School Psychology International, 27*, 157–170.

Li, Q. (2007). New bottle but old wine: A research of cyberbullying in schools. *Computers in Human Behavior, 23*, 1777–1791.

Liem, M. (2010). Homicide followed by suicide: A review. *Aggression and Violent Behavior, 15*, 153–161.

Liem, M. (2013). Homicide offender recidivism: A review of the literature. *Aggression and Violent Behavior, 18*, 19–25.

Liem, M., Zahn, M. A., & Tichavsky, L. (2014). Criminal recidivism among homicide offenders. *Journal of Interpersonal Violence, 29*, 2630–2651.

Lim, L., Day, A., & Casey, S. (2011). Social cognitive processing in violent male offenders. *Psychiatry, Psychology and Law, 18*, 177–189.

Lindberg, N., Holi, M. M., Tani, P., & Virkkunen, M. (2005). Looking for pyromania: Characteristics of a consecutive sample of Finnish male criminals with histories of recidivist fire-setting between 1973 and 1993. *BMC Psychiatry, 5/47*. (Available at http://www.biomedcentral.com/1471–244X/5/47)

Lindert, J., de Luna, J., Torres-Gonzales, F., Barros, H., Ioannidi-Kopolou, E., Melchiorre, M. G., … & Soares, J. F. (2013). Abuse and neglect of older persons in seven cities in seven countries in Europe: A cross-sectional community study. *International Journal of Public Health, 58*, 121–132.

Linton, D. K., & Power, J. L. (2013). The personality traits of workplace bullies are often shared by their victims: Is there a dark side to victims? *Personality and Individual Differences, 54*, 738–743.

Litzow, J. M., & Silverstein, M. (2008). Corporal punishment: A discussion of the debate. *Paediatrics and Child Health, 18*, 542–544.

Long, C. G., Banyard, E., Fulton, B., & Hollin, C. R. (2013). Developing an assessment of fire setting to guide treatment in secure settings: The St Andrew's Fire and Arson Risk Instrument (SAFARI). *Behavioural and Cognitive Psychotherapy, 19*, 1–12.

Lorenz, K. (1966). *On aggression.* New York: Harcourt, Brace & World.

Lösel, F., & Bender, D. (2011). Emotional and antisocial outcomes of bullying and victimization at school: A follow-up from childhood to adolescence. *Journal of Aggression, Conflict and Peace Research, 3*, 89–96.

Lowenstein, A., Eisikovits, Z., Band-Winterstein, T., & Enosh, G. (2009). Is elder abuse and neglect a social phenomenon? Data from the First National Prevalence Survey in Israel. *Journal of Elder Abuse & Neglect, 21*, 253–277.

Lucia, S., & Killias, M. (2011). Is animal cruelty a marker of interpersonal violence and delinquency? Results of a Swiss national self-report study. *Psychology of Violence, 1*, 93–105.

Luckenbill, D. F. (1977). Criminal homicide as a situated transaction. *Social Problems, 25*, 176–186.

Luckenbill, D. F., & Doyle, D. P. (1989). Structural position and violence. *Criminology, 27*, 419–436.

Lundberg, G. D. (1983). Boxing should be banned in civilized countries. *Journal of the American Medical Association, 249*, 250.

Lundberg, G. D. (1984). Boxing should be banned in civilized countries: Round 2. *Journal of the American Medical Association, 25*, 2696–2698.

Lundberg, G. D. (1985). Brain injury in boxing. *American Journal of Forensic Medicine and Pathology, 6*, 192–198.

Lundberg G. D. (1986). Boxing should be banned in civilised countries: Round 3. *Journal of the American Medical Association, 255*, 2482.

Lussier, P., Bouchard, M., & Beauregard, E. (2011). Patterns of criminal achievement in sexual offending: Unravelling the "successful" sex offender. *Journal of Criminal Justice, 39*, 433–444.

Lutgen-Sandvik, P., & Tracy, S. J. (2012). Answering five key questions about workplace bullying: How communication scholarship provides thought leadership for transforming abuse at work. *Management Communication Quarterly, 26*, 3–47.

Ma, J. Han, Y., Grogan-Kaylorb, A., Delvab, J., & Castillo, M. (2012). Corporal punishment and youth externalizing behavior in Santiago, Chile. *Child Abuse & Neglect, 36*, 481–490.

MacAskill, S., Parkes, T., Brooks, O., Graham, L., McAuley, A., & Brown, A. (2011). Assessment of alcohol problems using AUDIT in a prison setting: More than an "aye or no" question. *BMC Public Health, 11*, 865–877.

MacKenzie, M. J., Nicklas, E., Brooks-Gunn., J., & Waldfogel, J. (2011). Who spanks infants and toddlers? Evidence from the Fragile Families and Child Well-Being Study. *Child Youth Services Review, 33*, 1364–1373.

MacKenzie, M. J., Nicklas, E., Waldfogel, J., & Brooks-Gunn, J. (2012). Corporal punishment and child behavioural and cognitive outcomes through 5 years of age: Evidence from a contemporary urban birth cohort study. *Infant and Child Development, 21*, 3–33.

MacMillan, H. L., Wathen, C. N., & Varcoed, C. M. (2013). Intimate partner violence in the family: Considerations for children's safety. *Child Abuse & Neglect, 37*, 1186–1191.

Maikovich-Fong, A. K., & Jaffee, S. R. (2010). Sex differences in childhood sexual abuse characteristics and victims' emotional and behavioral problems: Findings from a national sample of youth. *Child Abuse & Neglect, 34*, 429–437.

Makhlouf, F., & Rambaud, C. (2014). Child homicide and neglect in France: 1991–2008. *Child Abuse & Neglect, 38*, 37–41.

Maldonado, M. (2004). Cultural issues in the corporal punishment of children. *Hispanic Journal of Behavioural Sciences, 17*, 275–304.

Malmquist, C. P. (2010). Adolescent parricide as a clinical and legal problem. *Journal of the American Academy of Psychiatry and the Law, 38*, 73–79.

Malta, L. S., Blanchard, E. B., & Freidenberg, B. M. (2005). Psychiatric and behavioural problems in aggressive drivers. *Behaviour Research and Therapy, 43*, 1467–1484.

Manchak, S. M., Skeem, J. L., Douglas, K. S., & Siranosian, M. (2009). Does gender moderate the predictive utility of the Level of Service Inventory-Revised (LSI-R) for serious violent offenders? *Criminal Justice and Behavior, 36*, 425–442.

Maniglio, R. (2010). The role of deviant sexual fantasy in the etiopathogenesis of sexual homicide: A systematic review. *Aggression and Violent Behavior, 15,* 294–302.

Mann, R. E., & Hollin, C. R. (2007). Sexual offenders' explanations for their offending. *Journal of Sexual Aggression, 13,* 3–9.

Mann, R., & Hollin, C. R. (2010). Self-reported schemas in sexual offenders. *Journal of Forensic Psychiatry & Psychology, 21,* 834–851.

Mann, R. E., Smart, R. G., Stoduto, G., Adlaf, E. M., & Ialomiteanu, A. (2004). Alcohol consumption and problems among road rage victims and perpetrators. *Journal of Studies on Alcohol, 65,* 161–168.

Mann, R. E., Zhao, J., Stoduto, G., Adlaf, E. M., Smart, R. G., & Donovan, J. E. (2007). Road rage and collision involvement. *American Journal of Health Behavior, 31,* 384–391.

Marcum, C. D., Higgins, G. E., Freiburger, T. L., & Ricketts, M. L. (2012). Battle of the sexes: An examination of male and female cyber bullying. *International Journal of Cyber Criminology, 6,* 904–911.

Marsh, L., McGee, R., Nada-Raja, S., & Williams, S. (2010). Brief report: Text bullying and traditional bullying among New Zealand secondary school students. *Journal of Adolescence, 33,* 237–240.

Marshall, A. D., & Holtzworth-Munroe, A. (2010). Recognition of wives' emotional expressions: A mechanism in the relationship between psychopathology and intimate partner violence perpetration. *Journal of Family Psychology, 24,* 21–30.

Marshall, W. L., Anderson, D., & Fernandez, Y. (1999). *Cognitive behavioural treatment of sexual offenders.* Chichester, Sussex: John Wiley & Sons.

Marshall, W. L., & Barbaree, H. E. (1990). An integrated theory of the etiology of sexual offending. In W. L. Marshall, D. R. Laws & H. E. Barbaree (Eds.), *Handbook of sexual assault: Issues, theories, and treatment of the offender* (pp. 257–275). New York: Plenum Press.

Marshall, W. L., & Eccles, A. (1991). Issues in clinical practice with sex offenders. *Journal of Interpersonal Violence, 6,* 68–93.

Marshall, W. L., & Marshall, L. E. (2000). The origins of sexual offending. *Trauma, Violence, and Abuse, 1,* 250–263.

Martin, G., Bergen, H. A., Richardson, A. S., Roeger, L., & Allison, S. (2004). Correlates of firesetting in a community sample of young adolescents. *Australian and New Zealand Journal of Psychiatry, 38,* 148–154.

Martin, S. E. (2001). The links between alcohol, crime and the criminal justice system: Explanations, evidence and interventions. *American Journal on Addictions, 10,* 136–158.

Martin-Storey, A. (2015). Prevalence of dating violence among sexual minority youth: Variation across gender, sexual minority identity and gender of sexual partners. *Journal of Youth and Adolescence, 44,* 211–224.

Mason, G. (2011). Naming the "R" word in racial victimization: Violence against Indian students in Australia. *International Review of Victimology, 18,* 39–56.

Mathesius, J., & Lussier, P. (2014). The successful onset of sex offending: Determining the correlates of actual and official onset of sex offending. *Journal of Criminal Justice, 42,* 134–144.

Maxfield, M. G., & Widom, C. S. (1996). The cycle of violence revisited 6 years later. *Archives of Paediatric and Adolescent Medicine, 150,* 390–395.

May-Chahal, C., & Cawson, P. (2005). Measuring child maltreatment in the United Kingdom: A study of the prevalence of child abuse and neglect. *Child Abuse & Neglect, 29,* 969–984.

McAuliffe, M. D., Hubbard, J. A., Rubin, R. M., Morrow, M. T., & Dearing, K. F. (2006). Reactive and proactive aggression: Stability of constructs and relations to correlates. *Journal of Genetic Psychology, 167,* 365–382.

McCall, P. L., Parker, K. F., & MacDonald, J. M. (2008). The dynamic relationship between homicide rates and social, economic, and political factors from 1970 to 2000. *Social Science Research, 37,* 721–735.

McCarty, C. A., & McMahon, R. (2005). Domains of risk in the developmental continuity of fire setting. *Behavior Therapy, 36,* 185–195.

McClusky, C. P., McClusky, J. D., & Bynum, T. S. (2006). Early onset offending and later violent and gun outcomes in a contemporary youth cohort. *Journal of Criminal Justice, 34,* 531–541.

McCord, J. (1983). A forty year perspective on effects of child abuse and neglect. *Child Abuse & Neglect, 7,* 265–270.

McEwen, F. S., Moffitt, T. E., & Arseneault, A. (2014). Is childhood cruelty to animals a marker for physical maltreatment in a prospective cohort study of children? *Child Abuse & Neglect, 38,* 533–543.

McIntyre, J. K., & Widom, C. S. (2011). Childhood victimization and crime victimization. *Journal of Interpersonal Violence, 26,* 640–663.

McKee, A., & Egan, V. (2013). A case series of twenty one maternal filicides in the UK. *Child Abuse & Neglect, 37,* 753–761.

McKibbin, W. F., Shackelford, T. K., Goetz, A. T., & Starratt, V. G. (2008). Why do men rape? An evolutionary psychological perspective. *Review of General Psychology, 12,* 86–97.

McLaughlin, H., Uggena, C., & Blackstone, A. (2012). Sexual harassment, workplace authority, and the paradox of power. *American Sociological Review, 77,* 625–647.

McLaughlin, K. A., Koenen, K. C., Hill, E. D., Petukhova, M., Sampson, N. A., Zaslavsky, A. M., & Kessler, R. C. (2013). Trauma exposure and posttraumatic stress disorder in a national sample of adolescents. *Journal of the American Academy of Child & Adolescent Psychiatry, 52,* 815–830.

McLean, M. (2005). Domestic violence and repeat victimization. *International Review of Victimology, 12,* 51–74.

McMahon, S., Huang, C-C., Boxer, P., & Postmus, J. L. (2011). The impact of emotional and physical violence during pregnancy on maternal and child health at one year post-partum. *Children and Youth Services Review, 33,* 2103–2111.

McMurran, M. (2007). The relationships between alcohol-aggression proneness, general alcohol expectancies, hazardous drinking, and alcohol-related violence in adult male prisoners. *Psychology, Crime, & Law, 13,* 275–284.

McMurran, M. (Ed.). (2013). *Alcohol-related violence: Prevention and treatment.* Oxford: Wiley-Blackwell.

McMurran, M., Hoyte, H., & Jinks, M. (2012). Triggers for alcohol-related violence in young male offenders. *Legal and Criminological Psychology, 17,* 307–321.

McMurran, M., Jinks, M., Howells, K., & Howard, R. (2011). Investigation of a typology of alcohol-related violence defined by ultimate goals. *Legal and Criminological Psychology, 16,* 75–89.

McMurran, M., & McGuire, J. (Eds.). (2005). *Social problem solving and offending: Evidence, evaluation and evolution.* Chichester, Sussex: John Wiley & Sons.

McNally, M. R., & Fremouw, W. J. (2014). Examining risk of escalation: A critical review of the exhibitionistic behavior literature. *Aggression and Violent Behavior, 19,* 474–485.

McPhedran, S. (2009). A review of the evidence for associations between empathy, violence, and animal cruelty. *Aggression and Violent Behavior, 14*, 1–4.

Mears, D. P., Cochran, J. C., & Bales, W. D. (2012). Gender differences in the effects of prison on recidivism. *Journal of Criminal Justice, 40*, 370–378.

Meehan, J., Flynn, S., Hunt, I. M., Robinson, J., Bickley, H., Parsons, R., … . Shaw, J. (2006). Perpetrators of homicide with schizophrenia: A national clinical survey in England and Wales. *Psychiatric Services, 57*, 1648–1651.

Meloy, J. R. (2000). The nature and dynamics of sexual homicide: An integrative review. *Aggression and Violent Behavior, 5*, 1–22.

Meloy, J. R., Davis, B., & Lovett, J. (2001). Risk factors for violence among stalkers. *Journal of Threat Assessment, 1*, 3–16.

Menard, S., Weiss, A. J., Franzese, R. J., & Covey, H. C. (2014). Types of adolescent exposure to violence as predictors of adult intimate partner violence. *Child Abuse & Neglect, 38*, 627–639.

Merskey, H. (1995). Post-traumatic stress disorder and shell shock - clinical section. In G. E. Berrios & R. Porter (Eds.), *A history of clinical psychiatry* (pp. 490–500). London: Athlone Press.

Merz-Perez, L., & Heide, K. M. (2004). *Animal cruelty: Pathway to violence against people.* Lanham, MD: Rowman & Littlefield.

Messman-Moore, T. L., & Brown, A. L. (2004). Child maltreatment and perceived family environment as risk factors for adult rape: Is child sexual abuse the most salient experience? *Child Abuse & Neglect, 28*, 1019–1034.

Mider, D. (2013). The anatomy of violence: A study of the literature. *Aggression and Violent Behavior, 18*, 702–708.

Miles, C. (2012). Intoxication and homicide: A context-specific approach. *British Journal of Criminology, 52*, 870–888.

Miller, B. A., & Welte, J. W. (1986). Comparisons of incarcerated offenders according to use of alcohol and/or drugs prior to offence. *Criminal Justice and Behavior, 13*, 366–392.

Miller, C. (2001). Childhood animal cruelty and interpersonal violence. *Clinical Psychology Review, 21*, 735–749.

Miller, L. (2012a). Stalking: Patterns, motives, and intervention strategies. *Aggression and Violent Behavior, 17*, 495–506.

Miller, L. (2012b). Posttraumatic stress disorder and criminal violence: Basic concepts and clinical-forensic applications. *Aggression and Violent Behavior, 17*, 354–364.

Miller, L. (2013). Sexual offenses against children: Patterns and motives. *Aggression and Violent Behavior, 18*, 506–519.

Miller, T. Q., Smith, T. W., Turner, C. W., Guijarro, M. L., & Hallet, A. J. (1996). A meta-analytic review of research on hostility and physical health. *Psychological Bulletin, 119*, 322–348.

Miller-Perrin, C. L., Perrin, R. D., & Kocur, J. L. (2009). Parental physical and psychological aggression: Psychological symptoms in young adults. *Child Abuse & Neglect, 33*, 1–11.

Milliken, C. S., Auchterlonie, J. L., & Hoge, C. W. (2007). Longitudinal assessment of mental health problems among active and reserve component soldiers returning from the Iraq war. *JAMA: The Journal of the American Medical Association, 298*, 2141–2148.

Mills, R., Scott, J., Alati, R., O'Callaghan, M., Najman, J. M., & Strathearn, L. (2013). Child maltreatment and adolescent mental health problems in a large birth cohort. *Child Abuse & Neglect, 37*, 292–302.

Ministry of Justice. (2009). *Offender Management Caseload Statistics 2008*. London: Author.

Ministry of Justice. (2010a). *Statistics on women and the criminal justice system. A Ministry of Justice publication under Section 95 of the Criminal Justice Act 1991*. London: Author.

Ministry of Justice. (2010b). *Safety in Custody Statistics 2008/2009*. London: Author.

Ministry of Justice. (2010c). *Statistics on women and the criminal justice system*. London: Author.

Ministry of Justice. (2013). *Prison population projections 2013–2019 England and Wales. Ministry of Justice Statistics Bulletin*. London: Author.

Ministry of Justice. (2014). *Statistics on women and the criminal justice system 2013. A Ministry of Justice publication under Section 95 of the Criminal Justice Act 1991*. London: Author.

Ministry of Justice, Home Office & the Office for National Statistics. (2013). *An Overview of sexual offending in England and Wales. Statistics Bulletin*. London: Author.

Mlisa, L. N., Ward, C. L., Flisher, A. J., & Lombard, C. J. (2008). Bullying at rural high schools in the Eastern Cape Province, South Africa: Prevalence, and risk, and protective factors at school and in the family. *Journal of Psychology in Africa, 18*, 261–268.

Moeller, S. J., Crocker, J., & Bushman, B. J. (2009). Creating hostility and conflict: Effects of entitlement and self-image goals. *Journal of Experimental Social Psychology, 45*, 448–452.

Moffitt, E. T. (1993). Adolescence-limited and life-course-persistent antisocial behavior: A developmental taxonomy. *Psychological Review, 100*, 674–701.

Möller, I., & Krahé, B. (2009). Exposure to violent video games and aggression in German adolescents: A longitudinal analysis. *Aggressive Behavior, 35*, 75–89.

Monahan, J. (1992). Mental disorder and violent behaviour: Perceptions and evidence. *American Psychologist, 47*, 511–521.

Monk, L., & Jones, A. (2014). Alcohol consumption as a risk factor for sexual assault: A retrospective analysis. *Journal of Forensic and Legal Medicine, 23*, 55–6.

Moody, S. R., & Clark, I. (2004). Dealing with racist victimisation: Racially aggravated offences in Scotland. *International Review of Victimology, 10*, 261–280.

Moore, E., Gaskin, C., & Indig, D. (2013). Childhood maltreatment and post-traumatic stress disorder among incarcerated young offenders. *Child Abuse & Neglect, 37*, 861–870.

Moore, T. M., & Stuart, G. L. (2004). Illicit substance use and intimate partner violence among men in batterers' intervention. *Psychology of Addictive Behaviors, 18*, 385–389.

Moore, T. M., Stuart, G. L., Meehan, J. C., Rhatigan, D. L., Hellmuth, J. C., & Keen, S. M. (2008). Drug abuse and aggression between intimate partners: A meta-analytic review. *Clinical Psychology Review, 28*, 247–274.

Moreno, A. S. (2013). Age differences among victims of sexual assault: A comparison between children, adolescents and adults. *Journal of Forensic and Legal Medicine, 20*, 465–470.

Muftić L. R., & Hunt, D. E. (2013). Victim precipitation: Further understanding the linkage between victimization and offending in homicide. *Homicide Studies, 17*, 239–254.

Murphy C. M. (2013). Social information processing and the perpetration of intimate partner violence: It is (and isn't) what you think. *Psychology of Violence, 3*, 212–217.

Mustaine, E. E., Tewksbury, R., Huff-Corzine, L., Corzine, J., & Marshall, H. (2014). Community characteristics and child sexual assault: Social disorganization and age. *Journal of Criminal Justice, 42*, 173–183.

Myhill, A., & Allen, J. (2002). *Rape and sexual assault of women: The extent and nature of the problem. Findings from the British Crime Survey*. Home Office Research Study 237. London: Home Office.

Neal, T. M. S., & Clements, C. B. (2010). Prison rape and psychological sequelae: A call for research. *Psychology, Public Policy, and Law, 16*, 284–299.

Negriff, S., Schneiderman, J. U., Smith, C., Schreyer, J. K., & Trickett, P. K. (2014). Characterizing the sexual abuse experiences of young adolescents. *Child Abuse & Neglect, 38*, 261–270.

Neutze, J., Grundmann, D., Scherner, G., & Beier, K. M. (2012). Undetected and detected child sexual abuse and child pornography offenders. *International Journal of Law and Psychiatry, 35*, 168–175.

Newiss, G., & Fairbrother, L. (2004). Child abduction: Understanding police recorded crime statistics. *Findings 225*. London: Home Office.

Ng, B., Kumar, S., Ranclaud, M., & Robinson, E. (2001). Ward crowding and incidents of violence on an acute psychiatric inpatient unit. *Psychiatric Services, 52*, 521–525.

Nietzel, M. T., Hasemann, D. M., & Lynam, D. R. (1999). Behavioral perspective on violent behavior. In V. B. Van Hasselt & M. Hersen (Eds.), *Handbook of psychological approaches with violent offenders: Contemporary strategies and issues* (pp. 39–66). New York: Kluwer Academic/Plenum.

Niv, S., Tuvblad, C., Raine, A., & Baker, L. A. (2013). Aggression and rule-breaking: Heritability and stability of antisocial behavior problems in childhood and adolescence. *Journal of Criminal Justice, 41*, 285–291.

Niveau, G. (2010). Cyber-pedocriminality: Characteristics of a sample of internet child pornography offenders. *Child Abuse & Neglect, 34*, 570–575.

Nock, M. K., & Kazdin, A. E. (2002). Parent-directed physical aggression by clinic-referred youths. *Journal of Clinical Child and Adolescent Psychology, 31*, 193–205.

Noll, J. G., Shenk, C. E., & Putnam, K. T. (2009). Childhood sexual abuse and adolescent pregnancy: A meta-analytic update. *Journal of Pediatric Psychology, 34*, 366–378.

Noonan, J. H., & Vavra, M. C. (2007). *Crime in schools and colleges: A study of offenders and arrestees reported via national incident-based reporting system data*. Washington, DC: US Department of Justice, Federal Bureau of Investigation.

Norman, R,E., Byambaa, M., Rumna, D., Butchart, A., Scott J., & Vos, J. (2012). The long-term health consequences of child physical abuse, emotional abuse, and neglect: A systematic review and meta-analysis. *PLoS Medicine, 9*(11): e1001349.

Novaco, R. W. (1975). *Anger control: The development and evaluation of an experimental treatment*. Lexington, MA: D. C. Heath.

Novaco, R. W. (1994). Anger as a risk factor for violence among the mentally disordered. In J. Monahan & H. J. Steadman (Eds), *Violence and mental disorder: Developments in risk assessment* (pp. 21–59). Chicago, IL: University of Chicago Press.

Novaco, R. W. (2007). Anger dysregulation: Its assessment and treatment. In T. A. Cavell & K. T. Malcolm (Eds.), *Anger, aggression and interventions for interpersonal violence* (pp. 3–54). Mahwah, NJ: Erlbaum.

Novaco, R. W., & Welsh, W. N. (1989). Anger disturbances: Cognitive mediation and clinical prescriptions. In K. Howells & C. R. Hollin (Eds.), *Clinical approaches to violence* (pp. 39–60). Chichester, Sussex: John Wiley & Sons.

Nurse, A. (Ed.). (2013). *Animal harm: Perspective on why people harm and kill animals*. Abingdon, Oxfordshire: Ashgate.

Office of the Deputy Prime Minister. (2003). *Arson Control Forum Annual Report*. London: Office of the Deputy Prime Minster.

Office for National Statistics. (2014a). *Crime Statistics, focus on violent crime and sexual offences, 2012/13*. London: Author.

Office for National Statistics. (2014b). *Crime in England and Wales, year ending December 2013*. London: Author.

O'Leary, K. D., & Slep, A. S. (2003). A dyadic longitudinal model of adolescent dating aggression. *Journal of Clinical Child and Adolescent Psychology, 32*, 314 –327.

O'Leary, K. D., Tintle, N., & Bromet, E. (2014). Risk factors for physical violence against partners in the U.S. *Psychology of Violence, 4*, 65–77.

Olivier, B., & van Oorschot, R. (2005). 5–HT1B receptors and aggression: A review. *European Journal of Pharmacology, 526*, 207–217.

Olweus, D. (2011). Bullying at school and later criminality: Findings from three Swedish community samples of males. *Criminal Behavior and Mental Health, 21*, 151–156.

Olweus, D. (2012). Cyberbullying: An overrated phenomenon? *European Journal of Developmental Psychology, 9*, 520–538.

Olweus, D. (2013). School bullying: Development and some important challenges. *Annual Review of Clinical Psychology, 9*, 751–80.

Oravec, J. A. (2012). Bullying and mobbing in academe: challenges for distance education and social media applications. *Journal of Academic Administration in Higher Education, 8*, 49–58.

Örmon, K., Torstensson-Levander, M., Sunnqvist, C., & Bahtsevani, C. (2014). Vulnerable and without protection: Lifetime experiences of abuse and its influence on mental ill health. An interview study among Swedish women within general psychiatric care. *Open Journal of Nursing, 4*, 34–41.

Orobio de Castro, B. (2004). The development of social information processing and aggressive behaviour: Current issues. *European Journal of Developmental Psychology, 1*, 87–102.

Orobio de Castro, B., Veerman, J. W., Koops, J. D., & Monshouwer, H. J. (2002). Hostile attribution of intent and aggressive behavior: A meta-analysis. *Child Development, 73*, 916–934.

Ostrowsky, M. K. (2014). The social psychology of alcohol use and violent behavior among sports spectators. *Aggression and Violent Behavior, 19*, 303–310.

Owens, D. J., & Straus, M. A. (1975). The social structure of violence in childhood and approval of violence as an adult. *Aggressive Behavior, 1*, 193–211.

Oxenstierna, G., Elofsson, S., Gjerde, M., Hanson, L. M., & Theorell, T. (2012). Workplace bullying, working environment and health. *Industrial Health, 50*, 180–188.

Oyamot, C. M., Fisher, E. L., Deason, G., & Borgida, E. (2012). Attitudes toward immigrants: The interactive role of the authoritarian predisposition, social norms, and humanitarian values. *Journal of Experimental Social Psychology, 48*, 97–105.

Ozdemir, B., Celbis, O., & Kaya, A. (2013). Cut throat injuries and honor killings: Review of 15 cases in eastern Turkey. *Journal of Forensic and Legal Medicine, 20*, 198–203.

Palasinski, M., & Riggs, D. W. (2012). Young white British men and knife-carrying in public: Discourses of masculinity, protection and vulnerability. *Critical Criminology, 20*, 463–476.

Paolucci, E. O., Genuis, M. L., & Violato, C. (2001). A meta-analysis of the published research on the effects of child sexual abuse. *The Journal of Psychology, 135*, 17–36.

Pantucci, R. (2011). What have we learned about lone wolves from Anders Behring Breivik? *Perspectives on Terrorism 5*, 27–42.

Papachristos, A. V., Wildeman, C., & Roberto, E. (2015). Tragic, but not random: The social contagion of nonfatal gunshot injuries. *Social Science & Medicine, 125*, 139–150.

Parkhill, M. R., Abbey, A., & Jacques-Tiura, A. J. (2009). How do sexual assault characteristics vary as a function of perpetrators' level of intoxication? *Addictive Behaviors, 34*, 331–333.

Patchin, J., & Hinduja, S. (2006). Bullies move beyond the schoolyard: A preliminary look at cyber bullying. *Youth Violence and Juvenile Justice, 4*, 148–169.

Patterson-Kane, E. G., & Piper, H. (2009). Animal abuse as a sentinel for human violence: A critique. *Journal of Social Issues, 65*, 589–614.

Payne, D. L., Lonsway, K. A., & Fitzgerald, L. F. (1999). Rape myth acceptance: Exploration of its structure and its measurement using the Illinois Rape Myth Acceptance Scale. *Journal of Research in Personality, 33*, 27–68.

Peluola, A., Mela, M., & Adelugba, O. O. (2013). A review of violent incidents in a multilevel secure forensic psychiatric hospital: Is there a seasonal variation? *Medicine, Science and the Law, 53*, 72–79.

Peng, C., Xueming, S., Hongyong, Y., & Dengsheng, L. (2011). Assessing temporal and weather influences on property crime in Beijing, China. *Crime, Law and Social Change, 55*, 1–13.

Penhale, B. (2003). Older women, domestic violence, and elder abuse: A review of commonalities, differences, and shared approaches. *Journal of Elder Abuse & Neglect, 15*, 163–183.

Penny, H., Walker, J., & Gudjonsson, G. H. (2011). Development and preliminary validation of the Penny Beliefs Scale–Weapons (PBS–W). *Personality and Individual Differences, 51*, 102–106.

Pepler, D., Craig, W., Yuile, A., & Connolly, J. (2004). Girls who bully: A developmental and relational perspective. In M. Putallaz & K. L. Bierman (Eds.), *Aggression, antisocial behavior, and violence among girls: A developmental perspective* (pp. 90–109). New York: Guilford Press.

Pérez-Fuentes, G., Olfson, M., Villegas, L., Morcillo, C., Wang, S., & Blanco, C. (2013). Prevalence and correlates of child sexual abuse: A national study. *Comprehensive Psychiatry, 54*, 16–27.

Perilloux, C., Duntley, J. D., & Buss, D. M. (2014). Blame attribution in sexual victimization. *Personality and Individual Differences, 63*, 81–86.

Peterson, B. E., & Zurbriggen, E. L. (2010). Gender, sexuality, and the authoritarian personality. *Journal of Personality, 78*, 1801–1826.

Peterson, M. L., & Farrington, D. P. (2007). Cruelty to animals and violence to people. *Victims and Offenders, 2*, 21–43.

Peterson, Z., Voller, E. K., Polusny, M. A., & Murdoch, M. (2011). Prevalence and consequences of adult sexual assault of men: Review of empirical findings and state of the literature. *Clinical Psychology Review, 31*, 1–24.

Phillips, J., & Land, K. C. (2012). The link between unemployment and crime rate fluctuations: An analysis at the county, state, and national levels. *Social Science Research, 41*, 681–694.

Phillips, R. T. M. (2007). Celebrity and presidential candidates. In D. A. Pinals (Ed.), *Stalking: Psychiatric perspectives and practical approaches* (pp. 227–250). New York: Oxford University Press.

Pina, A., Gannon, T. A., & Saunders, B. (2009). An overview of the literature on sexual harassment: Perpetrator, theory, and treatment issues. *Aggression and Violent Behavior, 14*, 126–138.

Pinto, L. A., Sullivan, E. L., Rosenbaum, A., Wyngarden, N., Umhau, J. C., Miller, M. W., & Taft, C. T. (2010). Biological correlates of intimate partner violence perpetration. *Aggression and Violent Behavior, 15*, 387–398.

Piotrowski, C. C., Tailor, K., & Cormier, D. C. (2014). Siblings exposed to intimate partner violence: Linking sibling relationship quality & child adjustment problems. *Child Abuse & Neglect, 38*, 123–134.

Piquero, A. R., Carriaga, M. L., Diamond, B., Kazemian, L., & Farrington, D. P. (2012). Stability in aggression revisited. *Aggression and Violent Behavior, 17*, 365–372.

Piquero, A. R., Connell, N. M., Piquero, N. L., Farrington, D. P., & Jennings, W. G. (2013). Does adolescent bullying distinguish between male offending trajectories in late middle age? *Journal of Youth and Adolescence, 42*, 444–453.

Piquero, A. R., Farrington, D. P., Jennings, W. G., Diamond, B., & Craig, J. (2012). Sex offenders and sex offending in the Cambridge study in delinquent development: Prevalence, frequency, specialization, recidivism, and (dis)continuity over the life-course. *Journal of Crime and Justice, 35*, 412–426.

Piquero, A. R., Jennings, W. G., & Farrington, D. P. (2015). The life-course offending trajectories of football hooligans. *European Journal of Criminology, 12*, 113–125.

Piquero, A. R., Theobald, D., & Farrington, D. P. (2014). The overlap between offending trajectories, criminal violence, and intimate partner violence. *International Journal of Offender Therapy and Comparative Criminology, 58*, 286–302.

Piquero, N. L., Piquero, A. R., Craig, J. M., & Clipper, S. J. (2013). Assessing research on workplace violence, 2000–2012. *Aggression and Violent Behavior, 18*, 383–394.

Ploughman, P., & Stensrud, J. (1986). The ecology of rape victimization: A case study of Buffalo, New York. *Genetic, Social, and General Psychology Monographs, 112*, 303–325.

Podnieks, E. (2008). Elder abuse: The Canadian experience. *Journal of Elder Abuse & Neglect, 20*, 126–150.

Podnieks, E., Anetzberger, G. J., Wilson, S. J., Teaster, P. B., & Wangmo, T. (2010). Worldview environmental scan on elder abuse. *Journal of Elder Abuse & Neglect, 22*, 164–179.

Polaschek, D. L. L., & Gannon, T. A. (2004). The implicit theories of rapists: What convicted offenders tell us. *Sexual Abuse: A Journal of Research and Treatment, 16*, 299–314.

Polaschek, D. L. L., & Ward, T. (2002). The implicit theories of potential rapists: What our questionnaires tell us. *Aggression and Violent Behavior, 7*, 385–406.

Polcari, A., Rabi, K., Bolger, E., & Teicher, M. H. (2014). Parental verbal affection and verbal aggression in childhood differentially influence psychiatric symptoms and wellbeing in young adulthood. *Child Abuse & Neglect, 38*, 91–102.

Pollinger, J., Samuels, L., & Stadolnik, R. (2005). A comparative study of the behavioral, personality, and fire history characteristics of residential and outpatient adolescents (ages 12–17) with firesetting behaviors. *Adolescence, 40*, 345–353.

Polman, H., Orobio de Castro, B., Koops, W., van Boxtel, H. W., & Merk, W. W. (2007). A meta-analysis of the distinction between reactive and proactive aggression in children and adolescents. *Journal of Abnormal Child Psychology, 35*, 552–535.

Polusny, M., Rosenthal, M. Z., Aban, I., & Follette, V. (2004). Experiential avoidance as a mediator of the effects of adolescent sexual victimization on negative adult outcomes. *Violence and Victims, 19*, 109–120.

Popovici, I., Homer, J. F., Fang, H., & French, M. T. (2012). Alcohol use and crime: Findings from a longitudinal sample of U.S. adolescents and young adults. *Alcoholism: Clinical and Experimental Research, 36*, 532–543.

Pournaghash-Tehrani, S. (2011). Domestic violence in Iran: A literature review. *Aggression and Violent Behavior, 16*, 1–5.

Pratt, H. D., & Greydanus, D. E. (2003). Violence: Concepts of its impact on children and youth. *Pediatric Clinics of North America, 50*, 963–1003.

Pratto, F., Sidanius, J., Stallworth, L. M., & Malle, B. F. (1994). Social dominance orientation: A personality variable predicting social and political attitudes. *Journal of Personality and Social Psychology, 72,* 741–763.

Prentky, R. A., Lee, A. F. S., Knight, R. A., & Cerce, D. (1997). Recidivism rates among child molesters and rapists: A methodological analysis. *Law and Human Behavior, 21,* 635–658.

Priks, M. (2010). Does frustration lead to violence? Evidence from the Swedish hooligan scene. *Kyklos, 63,* 450–460.

Pritchard, C., Davey, J., & Williams, R. (2013). Who kills children? Re-examining the evidence. *British Journal of Social Work, 43,* 1–36.

Proulx, J., Beauregard, É., Cusson, M., & Nicole, A. (Eds.). (2005). *Sexual murderers: A comparative analysis and new perspective.* (Translated by Steven Sacks.) Chichester: John Wiley & Sons.

Pruitt, J. N., Demes, K. W., & Dittrich-Reed, D. R. (2011). Temperature mediates shifts in individual aggressiveness, activity level, and social behavior in a spider. *Ethology, 117,* 318–325.

Purcell, R., Baksheev, G. N., & Mullen, P. E. (2014). A descriptive study of juvenile family violence: Data from intervention order applications in a Childrens Court. *International Journal of Law and Psychiatry, 37,* 558–563.

Purcell, R., Pathé, M., & Mullen, P. E. (2001). A study of women who stalk. *American Journal of Psychiatry, 158,* 2056–2060.

Purcell, R., Pathé, M., & Mullen, P. E. (2002). The prevalence and nature of stalking in the Australian community. *Australian and New Zealand Journal of Psychiatry, 36,* 114–120.

Putallaz, M., & Bierman, K. L. (Eds.). (2004). *Aggression, antisocial behavior, and violence among girls: A developmental perspective.* New York: Guildford Press.

Putkonen, A., Ryynänen, O-P., Eronen, M., & Tiihonen, J. (2007). Transmission of violent offending and crime across three generations. *Social Psychiatry and Psychiatric Epidemiology, 42,* 94–99.

Putkonen, H., Amon, S., Eronen, M., Klier, C. M., Almirone, M. P., Yourstone, J. C., & Weizmann-Henelius, G. (2011). Gender differences in filicide offense characteristics: A comprehensive register-based study of child murder in two European countries. *Child Abuse & Neglect, 35,* 319–328.

Quinsey, V. L., Chaplin, T. C., & Upfold, D. (1989). Arsonists and sexual arousal to firesetting: Correlation unsupported. *Journal of Behavior Therapy and Experimental Psychology, 20,* 203–209.

Radford, L., Corral, S., Bradley, C., & Fisher, H. L. (2013). The prevalence and impact of child maltreatment and other types of victimization in the UK: Findings from a population survey of caregivers, children and young people and young adults. *Child Abuse & Neglect, 37,* 801–813.

Randle, A. A., & Graham, C. A. (2011). A review of the evidence on the effects of intimate partner violence on men. *Psychology of Men & Masculinity, 12,* 97–111.

Ratcliffe, J. H. (2012). The spatial extent of criminogenic places: A changepoint regression of violence around bars. *Geographical Analysis, 44,* 302–320.

Ravensberg, V., & Miller, C. (2003). Stalking among young adults: A review of the preliminary research. *Aggression and Violent Behavior, 8,* 455–469.

Reagu, S., Jones, R., Kumari, V., & Taylor, P. J. (2013). Angry affect and violence in the context of a psychotic illness: A systematic review and meta-analysis of the literature. *Schizophrenia Research, 146,* 46–52.

Reese-Weber, M., & Smith, D. M. (2011). Outcomes of child sexual abuse as predictors of later sexual victimization. *Journal of Interpersonal Violence, 26,* 1884–1905.

Reijnders, U. J. L., & Ceelen, M. (2014). 7208 victims of domestic and public violence: An exploratory study based on the reports of assaulted individuals reporting to the police. *Journal of Forensic and Legal Medicine, 24,* 18–23.

Renner, L. M., & Slack, K. S. (2006). Intimate partner violence and child maltreatment: Understanding intra- and intergenerational connections. *Child Abuse & Neglect, 30,* 599–617.

Repo, E., Virkkunen, M., Rawlings, M., & Linnoila, M. (1997). Criminal and psychiatric histories of Finnish arsonists. *Acta Psychiatrica Scandinavica, 95,* 318–323.

Ressler, R. K., Burgess, A. W., Hartman, C. R., Douglas, J. E., & McCormack, A. (1998). Murderers who rape and mutilate. In R. Lockwood & F. A. Ascione (Eds.), *Cruelty to animals and interpersonal violence* (pp. 179–193). West Lafayette, IN: Purdue University Press.

Rice, M. E., & Harris, G. T. (1991). Firesetters admitted to a maximum security psychiatric institution: Offenders and offenses. *Journal of Interpersonal Violence, 6,* 641–675.

Rice, M. E., & Harris, G. T. (1996). Predicting the recidivism of mentally disordered offenders. *Journal of Interpersonal Violence, 11,* 364–375.

Rice, M. E., Quinsey, V. L., & Harris, G. T. (1991). Sexual recidivism among child molesters released from a maximum security psychiatric institution. *Journal of Consulting and Clinical Psychology, 59,* 381–386.

Ristock, J. (2005). *Relationship violence in Lesbian/Gay/Bisexual/Transgender/Queer LGBTQ] Communities: Moving beyond a gender-based framework.* Violence Against Women Online Resource. Retrieved from http://www.mincava.umn.edu/documents/lgbtqviolence/lgbtqviolence.pdf

Rivers, I. (2001). The bullying of sexual minorities at school: Its nature and long-term correlates. *Educational and Child Psychology, 18,* 32–46.

Rivers, I., & Noret, N. (2010). "I h 8 u": Findings from a five-year study of text and email bullying. *British Educational Research Journal, 36,* 643–671.

Roberts, A. D. L., & Coid, J. W. (2010). Personality disorder and offending behaviour: Findings from the national survey of male prisoners in England and Wales. *Journal of Forensic Psychiatry and Psychology, 21,* 221–237.

Roberts, A. L., Gilman, S. E., Fitzmaurice, G., Deckerf, M. R., & Koenen, K. C. (2010). Witness of intimate partner violence in childhood and perpetration of intimate partner violence in adulthood. *Epidemiology, 21,* 809–818.

Roberts, A. R., Zgoba, K. M., & Shahidullah, S. M. (2007). Recidivism among four types of homicide offenders: An exploratory analysis of 336 homicide offenders in New Jersey. *Aggression and Violent Behavior, 12,* 493–507.

Roberts, L., & Indermaur, D. (2005). Boys and road rage: Driving–related violence in Western Australia. *Australian and New Zealand Journal of Criminology, 38,* 361–380.

Robertson, K., & Murachver, R. (2007). Correlates of partner violence for incarcerated women and men. *Journal of Interpersonal Violence, 22,* 639–655.

Robin, M., & ten Bensel, R. (1985). Pets and the socialization of children. *Marriage and Family Review, 8,* 63–78.

Robins, S., & Novaco, R. W. (1999). A systems conceptualization and treatment of anger. *Journal of Clinical Psychology, 55,* 325–337.

Robinson, A. (2010). Domestic violence. In F. Brookman, M. Maguire, H. Pierpoint, & T. Bennett (Eds.), *Handbook on crime* (pp. 245–269). Cullompton, Devon: Willan Publishing.

Rodway, C., Norrington-Moore V., While, D., Hunt, I. M., Flynn, S., Swinson, N., … & Shaw, J. (2011). A population-based study of juvenile perpetrators of homicide in England and Wales. *Journal of Adolescence, 34*, 19–28.

Roe, S. (2010). Intimate violence: 2008/09 BCS. In K. Smith, J. Flatley, K. Coleman, S. Osborne, P. Kaiza, & S. Roe (Eds.), Homicides, firearm offences and intimate violence 2008/09. Supplementary Volume 2 to Crime in England and Wales 2008/09. *Home Office Statistical Bulletin 01/10.* London: Home Office.

Romitoa, P., & Gerin, D. (2002). Asking patients about violence: A survey of 510 women attending social and health services in Trieste, Italy. *Social Science & Medicine, 54*, 1813–1824.

Rosen, T., Lachs, M. S., & Pillemer, K. (2010). Sexual aggression between residents in nursing homes: Literature synthesis of an underrecognized problem. *Journal of the American Geriatrics Society, 58*, 1970–1979.

Rossow, I. (1996). Alcohol and homicide: A cross-cultural comparison of the relationship in 14 European countries. *Addiction, 96*, 77–92.

RSPCA (Royal Society for the Prevention of Cruelty to Animals). (2012). *Step inside our worlds: RSPCA Prosecutions Department Annual Report 2012.* Horsham, West Sussex: RSPCA.

Russell, G. W., & Arms, R. L. (1995). False consensus effect, physical aggression, anger, and a willingness to escalate a disturbance. *Aggressive Behavior, 21*, 381–386.

Ruvio, A. A., & Shoham, A. (2011). Aggressive driving: A consumption experience. *Psychology & Marketing, 28*, 1089–1114.

Ruzich, D., Reichert, J., & Lurigioc, A. J. (2014). Probable posttraumatic stress disorder in a sample of urban jail detainees. *International Journal of Law and Psychiatry, 37*, 455–463.

Ryan, K. M. (2004). Further evidence for a cognitive component of rape. *Aggression and Violent Behavior, 9*, 579–604.

Sabo, S., Shaw, S., Ingram, M., Teufel-Shone, N., Carvajal, S., de Zapien, J. G., … Rubio-Goldsmith, R. (2014). Everyday violence, structural racism and mistreatment at the US–Mexico border. *Social Science & Medicine, 109*, 66–74.

Salin, D. (2003). Ways of explaining workplace bullying: A review of enabling, motivating and precipitating structures and processes in the work environment. *Human Relations, 56*, 1213–1232.

Salmivalli, C. (2010). Bullying and the peer group: A review. *Aggression and Violent Behavior, 15*, 112–120.

Samnani, A-K., & Singh, P. (2012). 20 Years of workplace bullying research: A review of the antecedents and consequences of bullying in the workplace. *Aggression and Violent Behavior, 17*, 581–589.

Sandler, J. C., & Freeman, N. J. (2007). Typology of female sex offenders: A test of Vandiver and Kercher. *Sexual Abuse: A Journal of Research and Treatment, 19*, 73–89.

Sandler, J. C., & Freeman, N. J. (2009). Female sex offender recidivism: A large-scale empirical analysis. *Sexual Abuse: A Journal of Research and Treatment, 21*, 455–473.

Sanner-Stiehr, E., & Ward-Smith, P. (2013). Psychological distress among targets for lateral violence: A conceptual framework. *Journal of Nursing Education and Practice, 3*, 84–90.

Sansone, R. A., Lam, C., & Wiederman, M. W. (2010). Road rage: Relationships with borderline personality and driving citations. *International Journal of Psychiatry in Medicine, 40*, 21–29.

Sansone, R. A., & Sansone, L. A. (2010). Road rage: What's driving it? *Psychiatry*, *7*, 14–18.

Sapouna, M., & Wolke, D. (2013). Resilience to bullying victimization: The role of individual, family and peer characteristics. *Child Abuse & Neglect*, *37*, 997–1006.

Săucan, D-S., Micle, M-I., Popa, C., & Oancea, G. (2012). Violence and aggressiveness in traffic. *Procedia – Social and Behavioral Sciences*, *33*, 343–347.

Saudino, K., & Hines, D. (2007). Etiological similarities between psychological and physical aggression in intimate relationships: A behavioral genetic exploration. *Journal of Family Violence*, *22*, 121–129.

Savage, J., & Yancey C. (2008). The effects of media violence exposure on criminal aggression: A meta-analysis. *Criminal Justice and Behavior*, *35*, 772–791.

Savitz, L. D., Kumar, K. S., & Zahn M. A. (1991). Quantifying Luckenbill. *Deviant Behavior*, *12*, 19–29.

Scarce, M. (1997). *Male on male rape: The hidden toll of stigma and shame*. New York: Perseus Books.

Scheffran, J., Brzoska, M., Kominek, J., Link, P. M., & Schilling, J. (2012). Climate change and violent conflict. *Science*, *336*, 869–871.

Schenk, A. M., & Fremouw, W. J. (2012). Individual characteristics related to prison violence: A critical review of the literature. *Aggression and Violent Behavior*, *17*, 430–442.

Schenk, A. M., Fremouw, W. J., & Keelan, C. M. (2013). Characteristics of college cyberbullies. *Computers in Human Behavior*, *29*, 2320–2327.

Scherr, T. G., & Lawson, J. (2010). Bullying dynamics associated with race, ethnicity, and immigration status. In S. R. Jimerson, S. M. Swearer & D. L. Espelage (Eds.), *Handbook of bullying in schools: An international perspective* (pp. 223–235). New York: Routledge.

Schiamberg, L. B., & Gans, D. (1999). An ecological framework for contextual risk factors in elder abuse by adult children. *Journal of Elder Abuse & Neglect*, *11*, 79–103.

Schiamberg, L. B., Oehmke, J., Zhang, Z., Barboza, G. E., Griffore, R. J., Von Heydrich, L., … Mastin, T. (2012). Physical abuse of older adults in nursing homes: A random sample survey of adults with an elderly family member in a nursing home. *Journal of Elder Abuse & Neglect*, *24*, 65–83.

Schlack, R., Rüdel, J., Karger, A., & Hölling, H. (2013). Physical and psychological violence perpetration and violent victimisation in the German adult population. Results of the German Health Interview and Examination Survey for Adults (DEGS1). [English version of "Körperliche und psychische Gewalterfahrungen in der deutschen Erwachsenenbevölkerung.] Ergebnisse der Studie zur Gesundheit Erwachsener in Deutschland (DEGS1). *Bundesgesundheitsbl*, *56*, 755–764.

Scully, D., & Marolla, J. (1985). "Riding the bull at Gilley's": Convicted rapists describe the rewards of rape. *Social Problems*, *32*, 251–263.

Seidel, E-M., Pfabigan, D. M., Melitta, D., Keckeis, K., Wucherer, A. M., Jahn, T., Lamm, C., & Derntl, B. (2013). Empathic competencies in violent offenders. *Psychiatry Research*, *210*, 1168–1175.

Sekot, A. (2009). Violence in sports. *European Journal for Sport and Society*, *6*, 37–49.

Sentenac, M., Arnaud, C., Gavin, A., Molcho, M., Gabhainn, S. N., & Godeau, E. (2012). Peer victimization among school-aged children with chronic conditions. *Epidemiologic Reviews*, *34*, 120–128.

Sentencing Guidelines Secretariat. (2007). *Sexual Offences Act 2003: Definitive guideline*. London: Author.

Seto, M. C., Hanson, R. K., & Babchishin, K. M. (2011). Contact sexual offending by men with online sexual offenses. *Sexual Abuse: A Journal of Research and Treatment*, *23*, 124–145.

Seto, M., & Lalumière, M. L. (2010). What is so special about male adolescent sexual offending? A review and test of explanations through meta-analysis. *Psychological Bulletin, 136,* 526–575.

Seto, M. C., Reeves, L., & Jung, S. (2010). Explanations given by child pornography offenders for their crimes. *Journal of Sexual Aggression, 16,* 169–180.

Shaikh, M. A., Shaikh, I. A., & Siddiqui, Z. (2012). Road rage and road traffic accidents among commercial vehicle drivers in Lahore, Pakistan. *Eastern Mediterranean Health Journal, 18,* 402–405.

Shallcross, L., Sheehan, M., & Ramsay, S. (2008). Workplace mobbing: Experiences in the public sector. *International Journal of Organizational Behaviour, 13,* 56–70.

Shamoa-Nir, L., & Koslowsky, M. (2010). Aggression on the road as a function of stress, coping strategies and driver style. *Psychology, 1,* 35–44.

Shapiro, D. N., Kaplow, J. B., Amaya-Jackson, L., & Dodge, K. A. (2012). Behavioral markers of coping and psychiatric symptoms among sexually abused children. *Journal of Traumatic Stress, 25,* 157–163.

Shaw, J., Hunt, I. M., Flynn, S., Amos, T., Meehan, J., Robinson, J., … Appleby, L. (2006). The role of alcohol and drugs in homicides in England and Wales. *Addiction, 101,* 1117–1124.

Sheehan, V., & Sullivan, J. (2010). A qualitative analysis of child sex offenders involved in the manufacture of indecent images of children. *Journal of Sexual Aggression, 16,* 143–167.

Sheikh, A., Ali, S. A., Saleem, A., Ali, S., & Salman, S. (2013). Health consequences of cricket: View from South Asia. *International Archives of Medicine, 6:30,* http://www.intarchmed.com/content/6/1/30.

Sheldon, K., & Howitt, D. (2007). *Sex offenders and the internet.* Chichester, Sussex: John Wiley & Sons.

Sheridan L., & Lyndon, A. E. (2012). The influence of prior relationship, gender, and fear on the consequences of stalking victimization. *Sex Roles, 66,* 340–350.

Shinar, D., & Compton, R. (2004). Aggressive driving: An observational study of driver, vehicle and situational variables. *Accident Analysis & Prevention, 36,* 429–437.

Shurley, J. P., & Todd, J. S. (2012). Boxing lessons: An historical review of chronic head trauma in boxing and football. *Kinesiology Review, 1,* 170–184.

Siann, G. (1985). *Accounting for aggression: Perspectives on aggression and violence.* London: Allen & Unwin.

Sim, D. J., & Proeve, M. (2010). Crossover and stability of victim type in child molesters. *Legal and Criminological Psychology, 15,* 401–413.

Simmons, C. A., Lehmann, P., & Cobb, N. (2008). Women arrested for partner violence and substance use: An exploration of discrepancies in the literature. *Journal of Interpersonal Violence, 23,* 707–727.

Simons, D. A., & Wurtele, S. K. (2010). Relationships between parents' use of corporal punishment and their children's endorsement of spanking and hitting other children. *Child Abuse & Neglect, 34,* 639–646.

Simons, D. A., Wurtele, S. K., & Durham, R. L. (2008). Developmental experiences of child sexual abusers and rapists. *Child Abuse & Neglect, 32,* 549–560.

Slabbert, A. D., & Ukpere, W. I. (2010). A preliminary comparative study of rugby and football spectators' attitudes towards violence. *African Journal of Business Management, 4,* 459–466.

Smith, C., & Thornberry, T. P. (1995). The relationship between child maltreatment and adolescent involvement in delinquency. *Criminology, 33,* 451–481.

Smith, K., Flatley, J., Coleman, K., Osborne, S., Kaiza, P., & Roe, S. (2010). *Homicides, firearm offences and intimate violence 2008/09*. Supplementary Volume 2 to *Crime in England and Wales 2008/09*. Home Office Statistical Bulletin, 01/10. London: Home Office.

Smith, K., Lader, D., Hoare, J., & Lau, I. (2012). *Hate crime, cyber security and the experience of crime among children: Findings from the 2010/11 British Crime Survey*. London: Home Office.

Smith, P. K., & Jones, A. P. (2012). The importance of developmental science for studies in bullying and victimization. *International Journal of Developmental Science, 6*, 71–74.

Somander, L. K. H., & Rammer, L. M. (1991). Intra and extrafamilial child homicide in Sweden 1971–1980. *Child Abuse & Neglect, 15*, 45–55.

Song, E. T., & Taylor, R. B. (2011). Community-level impacts of temperature on urban street robbery. *Journal of Criminal Justice, 39*, 463–470.

Soothill, K. L., Ackerley, E., & Francis, B. (2004). The criminal careers of arsonists. *Medicine, Science, and Law, 44*, 27–40.

Soothill, K., Francis, B., & Ackerley, E. (2007). Kidnapping: A criminal profile of persons convicted 1979–2001. *Behavioral Sciences and the Law, 25*, 69–84.

Soothill, K. L., & Gibbens, T. N. C. (1978). Recidivism of sexual offenders: A re-appraisal. *British Journal of Criminology, 18*, 267–276.

Soothill, K. L., & Pope, P. J. (1973). Arson: A twenty-year cohort study. *Medicine, Science, and Law, 18*, 247–254.

Sorenson, J. R., Cunningham, M. D., Vigen, M. P., & Woods, S. O. (2011). Serious assaults on prison staff: A descriptive analysis. *Journal of Criminal Justice, 39*, 143–150.

Sourander, A., Klomek, A. B., Ikonen, M., Lindroos, J., Luntamo, T., Koskelainen, M., Ristkari, T., & Helenius, H. (2010). Psychosocial risk factors associated with cyberbullying among adolescents: A population-based study. *Archives of General Psychiatry, 67*, 720–728.

Soyka, M., Graz, C., Bottlender, R., Dirschedl, P., & Schoech, H. (2007). Clinical correlates of later violence and criminal offences in schizophrenia. *Schizophrenia Research, 94*, 89–98.

Soylu, N., & Alpaslan, A. H. (2013). Suicidal behavior and associated factors in sexually abused adolescents. *Children and Youth Services Review, 35*, 253–257.

Spaaij, R. (2014). Sports crowd violence: An interdisciplinary synthesis. *Aggression and Violent Behavior, 19*, 46–155.

Sparks, K., Faragher, B., & Cooper, C. L. (2001). Well-being and occupational health in the 21st century workplace. *Journal of Occupational and Organizational Psychology, 74*, 489–509.

Spitzberg, B. H. (2002). The tactical topography of stalking victimization and management. *Trauma, Violence, & Abuse, 3*, 261–288.

Spitzberg, B. H., & Cupach, W. R. (2007). The state of the art of stalking: Taking stock of the emerging literature. *Aggression and Violent Behavior, 12*, 64–86.

Steadman, H., Mulvey, E., Monahan, J., Robbins. P., Applebaum, P., Grisso, T., … Silver, E. (1998). Violence by people discharged from acute psychiatric inpatient facilities and by others in the same neighborhoods. *Archives of General Psychiatry, 55*, 393–401.

Steele, C., & Josephs, R. (1990). Alcohol myopia: Its prized and dangerous effects. *American Psychologist, 45*, 921–933.

Steffgen, G., Recchia, S., & Viechtbauer, W. (2013). The link between school climate and violence in school: A meta-analytic review. *Aggression and Violent Behavior, 18*, 300–309.

Steinert, T., & Whittington, R. (2013). A bio-psycho-social model of violence related to mental health problems. *International Journal of Law and Psychiatry, 36*, 168–175.

Steinfeldt, J. A., Vaughan, E. L., LaFollette, J. R., & Steinfeldt, M. C. (2012). Bullying among adolescent football players: Role of masculinity and moral atmosphere. *Psychology of Men & Masculinity, 13*, 340–353.

Stevenson, K., Davies, A., & Gunn, M. (2003). *Blackstone's Guide to the Sexual Offences Act 2003*. Oxford: Oxford University Press.

Stewart, E. A. (2003). School social bonds, school climate, and school misbehavior: A multi-level analysis. *Justice Quarterly, 20*, 575–604.

Stieger, S., Burger, C., & Schild, A. (2008). Lifetime prevalence and impact of stalking: Epidemiological data from Eastern Austria. *European Journal of Psychiatry, 22*, 235–241.

Stith, S. M., Green, N. M., Smith, D. B., & Ward, D. B. (2008). Marital satisfaction and marital discord as risk markers for intimate partner violence: A meta-analytic review. *Journal of Family Violence, 23*, 149–160.

Stith, S. M., Liu, T. L., Davies, C., Boykin, E. L., Alder, M. C., Harris, J. M., … & Dees, J. E. M. E. G. (2009). Risk factors in child maltreatment: A meta-analytic review of the literature. *Aggression and Violent Behavior, 14*, 13–29.

Stockdale, K. C., Olver, M. E., & Wong, S. C. P. (2010). The Psychopathy Checklist: Youth Version and adolescent and adult recidivism: Considerations with respect to gender, ethnicity, and age. *Psychological Assessment, 22*, 768–781.

Stoltenborgh, M., van IJzendoorn, M. J., Euser, E. M., & Bakermans-Kranenburg, M. J. (2011). A global perspective on child sexual abuse: Meta-analysis of prevalence around the world. *Child Maltreatment, 16*, 79–101.

Strand, S., & McEwan, T. E. (2011). Same-gender stalking in Sweden and Australia. *Behavioral Sciences & the Law, 29*, 202–219.

Straus, M. A. (2000). Corporal punishment and primary prevention of physical abuse. *Child Abuse & Neglect, 24*, 1009–1104.

Straus, M. A., & Michel-Smith, Y. (2014). Mutuality, severity, and chronicity of violence by father-only, mother-only, and mutually violent parents as reported by university students in 15 nations. *Child Abuse & Neglect, 38*, 664–676.

Stroebe, W. (2013). Firearm possession and violent death: A critical review. *Aggression and Violent Behavior, 18*, 709–721.

Suarez, E., & Gadalla, T. M. (2010). Stop blaming the victim: A meta-analysis on rape myths. *Journal of Interpersonal Violence, 25*, 2010–2035.

Sugarman, P., & Dickens, G. (2009). Dangerousness in firesetters: A survey of psychiatrists' views. *Psychiatric Bulletin, 33*, 99–101.

Sullivan, J., & Beech, A. (2004). Assessing internet sex offenders. In M. C. Calder (Ed.), *Child sexual abuse and the internet: Tackling the new frontier* (pp. 69–83). Lyme Regis, Dorset: Russell House.

Swaffer, T., & Hollin, C. (2000). Anger and impulse control. In R. Newell & K. Gournay (Eds.), *Mental health nursing: An evidence-based approach* (pp. 265–289). Edinburgh: Churchill Livingstone.

Swearer, S. M., Turner, R. K., Givens, J. E., & Pollock, W. S. (2008). "You're so gay!" Do different forms of bullying matter for adolescent males? *School Psychology Review, 37*, 160–173.

Swogger, M. T., You, S., Cashman-Brown, S., & Conner, K. R. (2011). Childhood physical abuse, aggression, and suicide attempts among criminal offenders. *Psychiatry Research, 185*, 363–367.

Taillieu, T. L., & Brownridge, D. A. (2010). Violence against pregnant women: Prevalence, patterns, risk factors, theories, and directions for future research. *Aggression and Violent Behavior, 15*, 14–35.

Tallichet, S. E., & Hensley, C. (2009). The social and emotional context of childhood and adolescent animal cruelty. *International Journal of Offender Therapy and Comparative Criminology, 53*, 596–606.

Tartaro, C., & Levy, M. P. (2007). Density, inmate assaults, and direct supervision jails. *Criminal Justice Policy Review, 18*, 395–417.

Taylor, M., Holland, G., & Quayle, M. (2001). Typology of paedophile picture collections. *The Police Journal, 74*, 97–107.

Taylor, M., & Quayle, E. (2006). *Child pornography: An internet crime.* Hove, Sussex: Brunner-Routledge.

Temcheff, C. E., Serbin, L. A., Martin-Storey, A., Stack, D. M., Hodgins, S., Ledingham, J., & Schwartzman, A. E. (2008). Continuity and pathways from aggression in childhood to family violence in adulthood: A 30–year longitudinal study. *Journal of Family Violence, 23*, 231–242.

Temple, J. R., Shorey, R. C., Tortolero, S. R., Wolfe, D. A., & Stuart, G. L. (2013). Importance of gender and attitudes about violence in the relationship between exposure to interparental violence and the perpetration of teen dating violence. *Child Abuse & Neglect, 37*, 343–352.

Thabet, A. A., Tawahina, A. A., Eyad, E. L., Vostanis, P. (2008). Exposure to war trauma and PTSD among parents and children in the Gaza strip. *European Child & Adolescent Psychiatry, 17*, 191–199.

Theobald, D., & Farrington, D. P. (2012). Child and adolescent predictors of male intimate partner violence. *Journal of Child Psychology and Psychiatry, 53*, 1242–1249.

Thomas, D. E., Bierman K. L., & The Conduct Problems Prevention Research Group (2006). The impact of classroom aggression on the development of aggressive behavior problems in children. *Development and Psychopathology, 18*, 471–487.

Thompson, A., Nelson, B., McNab, C., Simmons, M., Leicester, S., McGorry, P. D., ... & Yung, A. R. (2010). Psychotic symptoms with sexual content in the "ultra-high risk" for psychosis population: Frequency and association with sexual trauma. *Psychiatry Research, 177*, 84–91.

Thompson, A. D., Nelson, B., Yuen, H. P., Lin A, Amminger, G. P., McGorry P. D., et al. (2014). Sexual trauma increases the risk of developing psychosis in an ultra high-risk "prodromal" population. *Schizophrenia Bulletin, 40*, 697–706.

Thornberry, T. P., Freeman-Gallant, A., & Lovegrove, P. J. (2009). Intergenerational linkages in antisocial behaviour. *Criminal Behaviour and Mental Health, 19*, 80–93.

Thornberry, T. P., Matsuda, M., Greenman, S. J., Augustyn, M. B., Henry, K. L., Smith, C. A., & Ireland, T. O. (2014). Adolescent risk factors for child maltreatment. *Child Abuse & Neglect, 38*, 706–722.

Tiihonen, J., Rossi, R., Laakso, M. P., Hodgins, S., Testa, C., Perez, J., ... Frisoni, G. B. (2010). Brain anatomy of persistent violent offenders: More rather than less. *Psychiatry Research: Neuroimaging, 163*, 201–212.

Tillyer, M. S., Wilcox, P., & Gialopsos, B. M. (2010). Adolescent school-based sexual victimization: Exploring the role of opportunity in a gender-specific multilevel analysis. *Journal of Criminal Justice, 38*, 1071–1081.

Tinbergen, N. (1948). Social releasers and the experimental method required for their study. *Wilson Bulletin, 60*, 6–51.

Toffler, A. (1970). *Future shock.* New York: Bantam Books.

Tolan, P., Gorman-Smith, D., & Henry, D. (2006). Family violence. *Annual Review of Psychology, 57*, 557–583.

Traclet, A., Rascle, O., Souchon, N., Coulomb-Cabagno, G., Petrucci, C., & Ohbuchi, K-I. (2009). Aggression in soccer: An exploratory study of accounts preference. *Research Quarterly for Exercise and Sport, 80,* 398–402.

Trickett, P. K., & McBride-Chang, C. (1995). The developmental impact of different forms of child abuse and neglect. *Developmental Review, 15,* 311–337.

Trocmé, N., Fallon, B., MacLaurin, B., Daciuk, J., Felstiner, C., Black, T., … Holroyd, J. (2005). *Canadian incidence study of reported child abuse and neglect—2003: Major findings.* Minister of Public Works and Government Services, Canada.

Tsopelas, C., Spyridoula, T., & Athanasios, D. (2011). Review on female sexual offenders: Findings about profile and personality. *International Journal of Law and Psychiatry, 34,* 122–126.

Ttofi, M. M., Bowes, L., Farrington, D. P., & Lösel, F. (2014). Protective factors interrupting the continuity from school bullying to later internalizing and externalizing problems: A systematic review of prospective longitudinal studies. *Journal of School Violence, 13,* 5–38.

Ttofi, M. M., & Farrington, D. P. (2008). Bullying: Short-term and long-term effects, and the importance of defiance theory in explanation and prevention. *Victims & Offenders, 3,* 289–312.

Ttofi, M. M., Farrington, D. P., & Lösel, F. (2012). School bullying as a predictor of violence later in life: A systematic review and meta-analysis of prospective longitudinal studies. *Aggression and Violent Behavior, 17,* 405–418.

Turchik, J. A., & Edwards, K. M. (2012). Myths about male rape: A literature review. *Psychology of Men & Masculinity, 13,* 211–226.

Turner, H. A., Finkelhor, D., & Ormrod, R. (2006). The effect of lifetime victimization on the mental health of children and adolescents. *Social Science & Medicine, 62,* 13–27.

Turner, H. A., Finkelhor, D., & Ormrod, R. (2010). Poly-victimization in a national sample of children and youth. *American Journal of Preventive Medicine, 38,* 323–330.

Turner, M. G., Exum, M. L., Brame, R., & Holt, T. J. (2013). Bullying victimization and adolescent mental health: General and typological effects across sex. *Journal of Criminal Justice, 41,* 53–59.

Twardosz, S., & Lutzker, J. R. (2010). Child maltreatment and the developing brain: A review of neuroscience perspectives. *Aggression and Violent Behavior, 15,* 59–68.

Tzoumakis, S., Lussier, P., & Corrado, R. R. (2014). The persistence of early childhood physical aggression: Examining maternal delinquency and offending, mental health, and cultural differences. *Journal of Criminal Justice, 42,* 408–420.

Umukoro, S., Aladeokin, A. C., & Eduviere, A. T. (2013). Aggressive behaviour: A comprehensive review of its neurochemical mechanisms and management. *Aggression and Violent Behavior, 18,* 195–203.

United Nations. (2007). *World population prospects: The 2006 revision. Highlights.* New York: United Nations.

Valdez-Santiago, R., Híjar, M., Martínez, R. R., Burgos, L. A., & Arenas Monreal, M.d.l.L. (2013). Prevalence and severity of intimate partner violence in women living in eight indigenous regions of Mexico. *Social Science & Medicine, 82,* 51–57.

Van Bruggen, L. K., Runtz, M. G., & Kadlec, H. (2006). Sexual revictimization: The role of sexual self-esteem and dysfunctional sexual behaviors. *Child Maltreatment, 11,* 131–145.

Van Horn, P., & Lieberman, A. F. (2011). Psychological impact on and treatment of children who witness domestic violence. In C. Jenny (Ed.), *Child abuse and neglect: Diagnosis, treatment, and evidence* (pp. 501–515). St Louis, MO: Elsevier Saunders.

Van Vugt, E., Lanctôt, N., Paquette, G., Collin-Vézina, D., & Lemieux, A. (2014). Girls in residential care: From child maltreatment to trauma-related symptoms in emerging adulthood. *Child Abuse & Neglect, 38,* 114–122.

Vandello, J. A., Ransom, S., Hettinger, V., & Askew, K. (2009). Men's misperceptions about the acceptability and attractiveness of aggression. *Journal of Experimental Social Psychology, 45,* 1209–1219.

Varano, S. P., McCluskey, J. D., Patchin, J. W., & Bynum, T. S. (2004). Exploring the drugs-homicide connection. *Journal of Contemporary Criminal Justice, 20,* 369–392.

Vaughn, M. G., Fub, Q., DeLisic, M., Beaver, K. M., Perrone B. E., Terrell, K., & Howard, M. O. (2009). Correlates of cruelty to animals in the United States: Results from the National Epidemiologic Survey on Alcohol and Related Conditions. *Journal of Psychiatric Research, 43,* 1213–1218.

Verhulst, B., Eaves, L. J., & Hatemi, P. K. (2012). Correlation not causation: The relationship between personality traits and political ideologies. *American Journal of Political Science, 56,* 34–51.

Verhulst, B., Hatemi, P. K., & Martin, N. G. (2010). The nature of the relationship between personality traits and political attitudes. *Personality and Individual Differences, 49,* 306–316.

Virtanen, M., Vahtera, J., G. David Batty, Tuisku, K., Pentti, J., Oksanen, T, … & Kivimäki, M. (2011). Overcrowding in psychiatric wards and physical assaults on staff: Data-linked longitudinal study. *British Journal of Psychiatry, 198,* 149–155.

Vitacco, M. J., Rogers, R., Neumann, C. S., Harrison, K. S., & Vincent, G. (2005). A comparison of factor models on the PCL-R with mentally disordered offenders: The development of a four-factor model. *Criminal Justice and Behavior, 32,* 526–545.

Vittrup, B., & Holden, G. W. (2010). Children's assessments of corporal punishment and other disciplinary practices: The role of age, race, SES, and exposure to spanking. *Journal of Applied Developmental Psychology, 31,* 211–220.

Volkow, N. D. (2009). Substance use disorders in schizophrenia—clinical implications of comorbidity. *Schizophrenia Bulletin, 35,* 469–472.

Vries, A. M., & Liem, M. (2011). Recidivism of juvenile homicide offenders. *Behavioral Sciences and the Law, 29,* 483–498.

Wade, W. C. (1987). *The fiery cross: The Ku Klux Klan in America.* New York: Simon and Schuster.

Wall, L., & Quadara, A. (2014). *Acknowledging complexity in the impacts of sexual victimisation trauma.* Melbourne, Victoria: Australian Institute of Family Studies.

Wallace, C., Mullen, P. E., & Burgess, P. (2004). Criminal offending in schizophrenia over a 25–year period marked by deinstitutionalization and increasing prevalence of comorbid substance use disorders. *American Journal of Psychiatry, 161,* 716–727.

Walsh, K., Fortier, M. A., & DiLillo, D. (2010). Adult coping with childhood sexual abuse: A theoretical and empirical review. *Aggression and Violent Behavior, 15,* 1–13.

Walsh, K., Latzman, N. E., & Latzman, R. D. (2014). Pathway from child sexual and physical abuse to risky sex among emerging adults: The role of trauma-related intrusions and alcohol problems. *Journal of Adolescent Health, 54,* 442–448.

Walter, M., Wiesbeck, G. A., Dittmann, V., & Graf, M. (2010). Criminal recidivism in offenders with personality disorders and substance use disorders over 8 years of time at risk. *Psychiatry Research, 186,* 443–445.

Walters, G. D. (2013). Testing the specificity postulate of the violence graduation hypothesis: Meta-analyses of the animal cruelty-offending relationship. *Aggression and Violent Behavior, 18,* 797–802.

Wang, J., Iannotti, R. J., Tonja, R., & Nansel, T. R. (2009). School bullying among US adolescents: Physical, verbal, relational and cyber. *Journal of Adolescent Health, 45*, 368–375.

Ward, T. (2000). Sexual offenders' cognitive distortions as implicit theories. *Aggression and Violent Behavior, 5*, 491–507.

Ward, T., Polaschek, D. L. L., & Beech, A. R. (2006). *Theories of sexual offending*. Chichester, Sussex: John Wiley & Sons.

Weizmann-Henelius, G., Grönroos, L. M., Putkonen, H., Eronen, M., Lindberg, N., & Häkkänen-Nyholm, H. (2012). Gender-specific risk factors for intimate partner homicide: A nationwide register-based study. *Journal of Interpersonal Violence, 27*, 1519–1539.

Weizmann-Henelius, G., Putkonen, H., Grönroos, M., Lindberg, N., Eronen, M., & Häkkänen-Nyholm, H. (2010). Examination of psychopathy in female homicide offenders—Confirmatory factor analysis of the PCL-R. *International Journal of Law and Psychiatry, 33*, 177–183.

Welfare, H., & Hollin, C. R. (2012). Involvement in extreme violence and violence-related trauma: A review with relevance to young people in custody. *Legal and Criminological Psychology, 12*, 89–104.

Welfare, H., & Hollin, C. R.(in press). Childhood and offence-related trauma in young people imprisoned in England and Wales for murder and other acts of serious violence. *Journal of Aggression, Maltreatment & Trauma*.

Welsh, E., Bader, S., Evans, S. E. (2013). Situational variables related to aggression in institutional settings. *Aggression and Violent Behavior, 18*, 792–796.

West, R. (2005). Time for a change: Putting the Transtheoretical (Stages of Change) Model to rest. *Addiction, 100*, 1036–1039.

Westhues, K. (2006). *Remedy and prevention of mobbing in higher education*. Lewiston, NY: Mellen Press.

Whittle, H., Hamilton-Giachritsis, C., Beech, A., & Collings, G. (2013). A review of online grooming: Characteristics and concerns. *Aggression and Violent Behavior, 18*, 62–70.

Widom, C. S. (1989a). The cycle of violence. *Science, 244*, 160–166.

Widom, C. S. (1989b). Does violence beget violence? A critical examination of the literature. *Psychological Bulletin, 106*, 3–28.

Widom, C. S. (1999). Posttraumatic stress disorder in abused and neglected children grown up. *American Journal of Psychiatry, 156*, 1223–1229.

Widom, C. S. (2014). Varieties of violent behavior. *Criminology, 52*, 313–344.

Widom, C. S., Czaja, S., & Dutton, M. A. (2014). Child abuse and neglect and intimate partner violence victimization and perpetration: A prospective investigation. *Child Abuse & Neglect, 38*, 650–663.

Wiebe, D. J. (2003). Homicide and suicide risks associated with firearms in the home: A national case-control study. *Annals of Emergency Medicine, 41*, 771–782.

Williams, B. A., Sudore, R. L., Greifinger, R., & Morrison, R. S. (2011). Balancing punishment and compassion for seriously ill prisoners. *Annals of Internal Medicine, 55*, 122–126.

Williams, C., Richardson, D. S., Hammock, G. S., & Janit, A. S. (2012). Perceptions of physical and psychological aggression in close relationships: A review. *Aggression and Violent Behavior, 17*, 489–494.

Willoughby, T., Adachi, P. C., & Good, M. (2012). A longitudinal study of the association between violent video game play and aggression among adolescents. *Developmental Psychology, 48*, 1044–1057.

Wilton, C., & Campbell, M. A. (2011). An exploration of the reasons why adolescents engage in traditional and cyber bullying. *Journal of Educational Sciences & Psychology, 1,* 101–109.

Winder, B., & Gough, B. (2010). "I never touched anybody—that's my defence": A qualitative analysis of internet sex offender accounts. *Journal of Sexual Aggression, 16,* 125–141.

Winstok, Z., & Straus, M. A. (2014). Gender differences in the link between intimate partner physical violence and depression. *Aggression and Violent Behavior, 19,* 91–101.

Wolfgang, M. E. (1958). *Patterns in criminal homicide.* Philadelphia, PA: University of Pennsylvania Press.

Wolke, D., Woods, S., Bloomfield, L., & Karstadt, L. (2000). The association between direct and relational bullying and behaviour: Problems among primary school children. *Journal of Child Psychology and Psychiatry, 41,* 989–1002.

Wooldredge, J., & Steiner, B. (2009). Comparing methods for examining relationships between prison crowding and inmate violence. *Justice Quarterly, 26,* 795–826.

World Health Organization. (2002). *The Toronto declaration on the global prevention of elder abuse.* Geneva: WHO.

World Health Organization. (2007). *The cycles of violence: The relationship between childhood maltreatment and the risk of becoming a victim or perpetrator of violence: Key facts.* Rome: Author.

World Health Organization. (2008). *Interpersonal violence and alcohol policy briefing.* Geneva: WHO.

World Health Organization. (2013). *Global and regional estimates of violence against women: Prevalence and health effects of intimate partner violence and non-partner sexual violence.* Geneva: Author.

Yagil, D. (2008). When the customer is wrong: A review of research on aggression and sexual harassment in service encounters. *Aggression and Violent Behavior, 13,* 141–152.

Yancey, C. T., & Hansen, D. J. (2010). Relationship of personal, familial, and abuse-specific factors with outcome following childhood sexual abuse. *Aggression and Violent Behavior, 15,* 410–421.

Ybarra, G. J., Wilkens, S. L., & Lieberman, A. F. (2007). The influence of domestic violence on preschooler behavior and functioning. *Journal of Family Violence, 22,* 33–42.

Yildirim, A., Ozer, E., Bozkurt, H., Ozsoy, S., Enginyurt, O., Evcuman, D., Yilmaz, R., & Kuyucu, Y. E. (2014). Evaluation of social and demographic characteristics of incest cases in a university hospital in Turkey. *Medical Science Monitor, 20,* 693–697.

Yoo, J. A., & Huang, C.-C. (2102). The effects of domestic violence on children's behavior problems: Assessing the moderating roles of poverty and marital status. *Children and Youth Services Review, 34,* 2464–2473.

Yount, K. M., DiGirolamo, A. M., & Ramakrishnan, U. (2011). Impacts of domestic violence on child growth and nutrition: A conceptual review of the pathways of influence. *Social Science & Medicine, 72,* 1534–1554.

Yourstone, J., Lindhome, T., & Kristiansson, M. (2008). Women who kill: A comparison of the psychosocial background of female and male perpetrators. *International Journal of Law and Psychiatry, 31,* 374–383.

Zapf, D., Einarsen, S., Hoel, H., & Vartia, M. (2003). Empirical findings on bullying in the workplace. In S. Einarsen, H. Hoel, D. Zapf & C. Cooper (Eds.), *Bullying and emotional abuse in the workplace: International perspectives in research and practice* (pp. 103–126). London: Taylor & Francis.

Zaykowski, H., & Gunter, W. (2012). Youth victimization: School climate or deviant life-styles? *Journal of Interpersonal Violence, 27*, 431–452. [*Erratum* Journal of Interpersonal Violence, *27*, 1625–1627.]

Zheng, Y., & Cleveland, H. H. (2013). Identifying gender-specific developmental trajectories of nonviolent and violent delinquency from adolescence to young adulthood. *Journal of Adolescence, 36*, 371–381.

Zolotor, A. J., Theodore, A. D., Chang, J. J., Berkoff, M. C., & Runyan, D. K. (2008). Speak softly—and forget the stick: Corporal punishment and child physical abuse. *American Journal of Preventative Medicine, 35*, 364–369.

Zorza J. (2005). Are aging sex offenders still predators? *Victimization of the Elderly and Disabled, 8*, 33–35.

Zou, Z., Meng, H., Ma, Z., Deng, W., Du, L., Wang, H., Chen, P., & Hu, H. (2013). Executive functioning deficits and childhood trauma in juvenile violent offenders in China. *Psychiatry Research, 207*, 218–224.

Index

The Psychology of Interpersonal Violence, First Edition. Clive R. Hollin.
© 2016 John Wiley & Sons, Ltd. Published 2016 by John Wiley & Sons, Ltd.